ACHIEVING SUCCESS

Without Failing Your

FAMILY

ACHIEVING SUCCESS
Without Failing Your
FAMILY

How 30 successful families
achieved family excellence

DR. PAUL FAULKNER

HOWARD
PUBLISHING CO.

3117 North 7th Street
West Monroe, LA 71291

Our purpose at Howard Publishing is:

- *Inspiring* holiness in the lives of believers
- *Instilling* hope in the hearts of struggling people everywhere
- *Instructing* believers toward a deeper faith in Jesus Christ

Because He's coming again

Achieving Success Without Failing Your Family
© 1994 by Howard Publishing Co., Inc.
All rights reserved

Published by Howard Publishing Co., Inc.
3117 North 7th Street, West Monroe, LA 71291-2227

Printed in the United States of America

Cover Design: Steve Diggs & Friends
 LinDee Loveland

ISBN 1-878990-28-4

Perhaps the greatest privilege and joy Gladys and I have had in the past four years was being invited into the homes of couples who have been identified as successful in child rearing *and* in careers. This book is dedicated to those families. They risked themselves to us; they invited us into their "holy ground"—their home—and allowed us to explore what went on. We are deeply grateful to every one of them, and we think you will be indebted to them also for the many helps they share with you.

All of them were wonderful hosts, cooperative, loving, and genuine—we felt none were trying to "put on an act" for us. They seemed to live a "what you see is what you get" lifestyle.

There must be hundreds, perhaps thousands, of other families we could have interviewed. We wish we had unlimited time and money to interview them all.

The stories they and others share will give your family a "jump start" to a more exciting family life. So thanks from our hearts to:

Ed and Barbara Bonneau
Founder, Bonneau Sunglasses • *Farmers Branch, TX*

Tom and Sheila Bost
Attorney • *Los Angeles, CA*

Bob and Sandy Brackett
Businessman, Entrepreneur • *Vero Beach, FL*

R. A. Jr. and Peggy Brown
Cattleman • *Throckmorton, TX*

Don and Martha Jo Buck
Executive, Flur Daniel, Incorporated • *Laguna Hills, CA*

Paul and June Carter
CFO, Wal-Mart • *Bentonville, AR*

Don and Carol Crisp
CEO, Rosewood Corporation • *Dallas, TX*

Jerry and Martha Ebker
Division President, IBM • *Potomac, MD*

Miles and Gerry Ezell
President, Purity Dairies • *Nashville, TN*

Jack and Ann Griggs
Dean, College of Business, ACU • *Abilene, TX*

Marlin and Nelma Ivey
President, Ivey National Corporation • *Kosciusko, MS*

Stew and Marianne Leonard
President, Stew Leonard's • *West Point, CN*

Richard and Dema Lunsford
Insurance and Investments • *Olney, TX*

Bill and Ann Martin
Executive, Texas Instruments • *Austin, TX*

Walt and Shirley McIndoo
Executive, Delco Electronics Corp., General Motors • *Kokomo, IN*

Tom and Nancy Muccio
Executive, Procter and Gamble • *Fayetteville, AR*

Elliot and Sandra Popham
Business Executive • *Pulaski, TN*

Joe and Nancy Powell
President, Old Hickory Clay Company • *Hickory, KY*

Don and Peggy Rogers
Vice President, DuPont Company • *Wilmington, DE*

Kyle and Bernita Sheets
Entrepreneur and Medical Student • *Galveston, TX*

Don and Susie Shultz
Executive, Ford Motor Company • *Atlanta, GA*

Gene and Ruth Ann Stallings
Football Coach, University of Alabama • *Tuscaloosa, AL*

Bill and Virda Stevens
President, Triad Systems Corporation • *Atherton, CA*

John and Ev Stites
Founder, J & S Construction • *Cookeville, TN*

David and Margie Vanderpool
Surgeon, Past President of the Texas Medical Association • *Dallas, TX*

Bill and Virginia Vaught
CPA • *Dallas, TX*

Lamar and Joyce Wigington
Businessman, Professor, Scientist • *Bastrop, TX*

Don and Judy Williams
CEO, Trammell Crow • *Dallas, TX*

Randall and Joan Yearwood
Designer, Architect • *Nashville, TN*

CONTENTS

5 FAMILY TRADITIONS THAT LAST

ACKNOWLEDGMENTS

I must acknowledge three amazing women.

The first, of course, is Gladys, my wife, the lady who most nearly "practices what I preach." She was present for almost every interview and worked unceasingly the last several months to make sure the contents of this book accurately represented the views of the families. Four ears and two pens have proven to be much more accurate and thorough than two and one.

The second is Jan Hailey, my research assistant, a woman of immense capability in intellect and writing/reading skills, including Greek. She, along with her husband Mel, are true servants of Christ in our community. She has spent many hours writing and rewriting the material from these families and in extensive related reading and research.

The third is Philis Boultinghouse, the editor Howard Publishing selected for this book. A better choice could not have been made. She has been insightful, thorough, opinionated (in the best sense of that word), open—just a marvel to work with.

I must also express my appreciation to Bill and Dede. These dear friends have stood by us and this project in ways only the four of us can know. We are deeply indebted to them for their encouragement.

INTRODUCTION

Von, a young entrepreneur, was working frantically to get a new business going. He was putting in long hours traveling between two different cities. In addition to his new business, he had undertaken several other responsibilites—he was president of the Association of General Contractors, he was involved in civic activities, he had board meetings to attend, and on and on. His schedule was hectic and demanding. On a visit home, he passed the bathroom door and heard his three-year-old daughter and her younger sister splashing and playing in the bathtub and his wife talking and laughing with the girls. When he pushed open the door to greet his two little girls, his three-year-old looked up from her playing and innocently asked, "Who are you?"

"I'm your daddy," he replied.

She looked him squarely in the eye and said, "I don't have a daddy."

He came to attention! He and his wife made a decision then and there to get family and business in balance. He dropped his board memberships, he resigned as president of the Association of General Contractors, he cut his schedule back in every possible way, and concentrated all his energy on his family and his business. When I talked with him later, he and his girls had just returned from a fabulous weekend. They'd gone to San Marcos to see Fred, the swimming pig, and then to San Antonio to see the killer whale, and then the whole family had gone to the rodeo. Not only did his *family* benefit from his refocus, but as he cut out all the extras, he was able to do a better job in his business as well. Soon after his reassessment, his business completed one of the largest projects in the industry. This man turned his life around, because he *listened* to his three-year-old.

As a man or woman looking to the future, you too want to achieve career success. That's one reason you were attracted to this book. However, you don't want this success at the expense of the most valuable treasure in your life—your family. That's the other reason you were drawn to this book.

You want to leave your mark on the world, to count for something and at the same time provide warmth, security, and all the best for your family. But therein lies the rub, the tension. Can you accomplish both of these honorable missions at the same time?

▼

She looked him squarely in the eye and said, "I don't have a daddy."

When Suzanne Allford, vice president of personnel at Wal-Mart, called me and asked, "Paul, do you have any material about getting ahead and taking your family with you?" I had to tell her that I didn't; and furthermore, I didn't know of any such material, anywhere. But I loved her question.

I have spent years observing what it takes to make a family work. I have been a professor of marriage and family therapy since 1970, I founded a nationally approved marriage and family therapy training program in 1978 and directed that program for eleven years, and I have professionally counseled thousands of marriages and families over the last twenty-six years. But I had never seen any material that would answer Suzanne's specific question. The topic sparked my interest, and I promised to do some research.

But when I began researching this topic, I was *not* encouraged. Much of what I found followed the thinking of Tom Peters, who is considered the guru of business success:

> We are frequently asked if it is possible to have it all: a full and satisfying personal life *and* a full and satisfying and hard-working professional one. Our answer is *no*. The price of excellence is time, energy, attention, and focus at the very same time that energy, attention, and focus could have gone toward enjoying your daughter's soccer game. We have found that the majority of those that are successful in business have given up family vacations, little league games, birthday dinners, evenings, weekends, and lunch hours, gardening, reading, movies, and most other pastimes. We have a number of friends whose marriages even crumbled under the weight of a devotion to a dream.[1]

Dr. Frank Pittman, one of the nation's leading psychiatrists, was no more encouraging. He wrote in *Family Process* that he is convinced that the ideal child-raising personality is not a super-achiever.

> People who get rich have a very special talent, and an obsessive dedication to marketing it that is usually associated with a single-mindedness that tends to leave out time-consuming relationships with husbands, wives, and children. More often, those who get rich are highly competitive and therefore intolerant people who experience situations less as adventures than opportunities and other people as either competitors or tools or obstacles.[2]

Ralph Minear—pediatrician, professor of pediatrics, and author of a book about "affluenza or wealthism"—agrees with Pittman. In *Kids Who Have Too Much,* Minear speaks about the cost to the family in frightening terms. He says the children of the successful often have a "sense of worthlessness and lack of self-esteem" and fail "to mature emotionally." Often they are greedy, proud, and spoiled, with a resistance to intimacy and an inability to work well with others.

However, my own experience told me that there was hope, that it could be done. I knew of families who had done it—who had achieved success without failing their family. And as I began to look outside my own experiences, I found dozens of people who had managed to raise strong, vibrant families while achieving great success in their careers. I narrowed my research to thirty families. If I could learn the secrets of their success, I would have some good news to pass on to my friend from Wal-Mart.

My own precious wife, Gladys, was my partner in this phase of the research. We interviewed these families together, usually in their own homes. Gladys and I spent anywhere from three hours to three days talking with Mom and Dad, the children, their spouses, and the grandchildren. We asked them what they had done and what they were doing and what ideas they would like to pass on to other people. We didn't go with a preconceived concept (although we had three pages of questions to make sure we covered the essentials); we just asked them to tell us what worked for them. It was truly a great experience being in their homes. It would have been the most helpful experience imaginable to have done this before we reared our family.

None of the families we interviewed sought to be seen as experts in "family." In fact, they all said something like, "Hey, if you are looking for a perfect family, then you don't need to interview us." They knew they weren't perfect, and you'll see this as we go along. These families didn't come looking for us. All of them were recommended to us by several others as examples of exceptionally good, strong families.

All of the families held to a faith in God. At the time of the interviews, there were no divorces in any of the families. Twenty-eight families had children old enough to be married and have children of their own. We are talking about multiple generations who have survived the test of time.

We talked to people from California to Connecticut, from Texas to Michigan. We interviewed top lawyers in California and Texas; the CEO of a large company in San Francisco; a rancher in West Texas who runs cattle on his 110,000 acre spread; the operator of the largest dairy in Tennessee; the owner of one of the top ten construction companies in the nation; a vice president of Ford; a division president of IBM; a vice president of DuPont; a nationally successful coach; vice president of Procter and Gamble; one of the nation's leading entrepreneurs, a grocery store owner who does over 100 million dollars in sales per year; physicians; a successful architect; and many others in various lines of work.

In addition to our interviews with financially successful individuals, I did extensive research on the characteristics of strong families in general. I turned to the research of Stinnett, Guarendi,

Curran, and others. (See Appendix Three.) Each researcher had compiled a list of priorities that were found in successful families. Interestingly, all the lists were similar.

Even *more* interesting was the fact that the thirty families we talked with had intuitively discovered on their own *all* of the priorities highlighted by the experts. They had not studied the research, but they seemed to know instinctively what would work and what wouldn't. They learned it from observing others, listening to their children, and reading. They seemed to *learn* better than most from the experiences of others. They looked to see what was (or wasn't) working in other families and then acted on what they saw.

I wasn't really surprised that these families could find their own solutions. I have always been impressed with the ability of the common man *who has an uncommon focus* to unravel his own problems. This is not to deny the place of the professional marriage therapist, psychologist, or psychiatrist, but it takes more than good training: it takes earnest, persistent application.

▼

These successful families had not studied the research, but they seemed to know instinctively what would work and what wouldn't.

The only problem that was unique to these financially successful families was that of "having money." Without exception, every family said that "money makes it tougher." They clearly understood the biblical principle: "Give me neither poverty nor riches, but give me only my daily bread. . . . Otherwise, I may have too much and disown you and say, 'Who is the Lord?' Or I may become poor and steal, and so dishonor the name of my God."[3]

These thirty families confirmed what I found in extended research and what I have found in other strong families of *all* income brackets that I have counseled with over the years. Most importantly, however, they confirmed what we found in the Word. The principles in the Bible are the foundation for any strong family. The timeless principles work in all kinds of families, regardless of their socioeconomic conditions, race, education, gender, morality problems, or physical handicaps.

As you read this book, you may find yourself thinking of opportunities lost and time gone by that cannot be retrieved. But the teachings in this book are certainly not meant to make you feel guilty—*please don't!*

You need to remember that this is a compendium of the best thoughts and ideas from *all* of the families we visited *and* from the extended research of others *and* from my own counseling files. There are no perfect families. Every family is made up of flawed individuals. This book tells about the ideal, the best of the best.

Start where you are *now* and move forward from there. Life is full of second chances and fresh starts. If you find yourself with rebellious children in spite of your best efforts, remember that Adam and Eve rejected God's teachings even in a perfect environment, with a perfect genetic code, and with the perfect parent.

No one feels greater pain than those earnest parents who, despite their best efforts, see their children reject their values. The last thing I want to do is add to your pain. You don't have to be a perfect parent. Just don't make the big mistake of not *loving* them!

What about those parents who were reared in a dysfunctional, unhappy home? Is there hope for them and for their families? You bet there is! The difference for those of you in this situation is that you must learn *from someone else* how to become effective parents. Please refuse to remain victims of your childhood. You must resolve to rise above your background and determine to use those painful memories to fuel your drive to become genuinely good parents. You *can* do it!

After five years of study and research, I offer this book as a *wellness* model. This book does not concentrate on cures for serious family problems (although it surely can help). Rather, this book offers guidelines and practical help for creating an atmosphere where things can go *right* with the family. I believe, along with psychiatrist William Glasser, author of *Reality Therapy,* and many researchers since, that if we work aggressively on the positive and right choices in our personal lives and in our families, the wrong choices will be crowded out.

This book will provide you with a hundred or so practical suggestions, along with timeless concepts that can substantially change your family. These strategies and concepts come from three sources: research, my personal counseling files, and these successful families. They have been proven to work, and work well, in homes all across America.

I am delighted to bring to you what I believe to be the basic characteristics, traits, strategies, techniques of motivation, and principles of discipline gleaned from great and effective families, most of whom have *maintained* these rare families for several generations.

Oh, yes . . . remember Von, the guy I told you about at the beginning of the introduction? Well, just so you'll know that you really can turn it around, let me give you an update on his story. Four years after his decision to make sure his little girl knew she had a daddy, he received the following unsolicited letter from his seven-year-old daughter, Michael.

My Dad is the greatest because he gives the best hugs and tickles. He reads me bedtime stories and scratches my back. He takes me to school in the morning and picks me up. He plays games with me. He married a good woman. He teaches me about God. He loves me. He is the best Daddy in the whole wide world.

Michael J

EIGHT MESSAGES
Loud and Clear

▼

"From the time they were born, we had goals for the children's lives."

What was it that made these thirty families successful? What did they do *right* that other families don't? As Gladys and I interviewed these families, we listened carefully for the spoken and unspoken messages that would answer our questions, and what we heard—loud and clear—was that there are definite characteristics that can be defined and imitated. Eight basic messages emerged as we compiled all the information from these interviews. And surprisingly, or perhaps not so surprisingly, these messages are reflected in various forms in the research compiled by family "experts." (See Appendix Three.)

Since we will be using these thirty families as role models throughout this book, it's important that you understand that these people in no way thought they had all the answers or that they had perfect families. In fact, these were gracious, humble people. Time and again, these folks would say that they were lucky. None claimed to have a secret, God-given talent for child rearing or magic words to anticipate and heal all the parenting issues. They acknowledged that others tried as hard as they did and still had problems with their children or their marriages. And they hurt for those others. And somehow, through all their successes and their difficulties, they were able to concentrate on

their blessings from God—not on what they had accomplished on their own. Instinctively they practiced the admonition, "Each counting the other better than himself."[1]
In their own words:

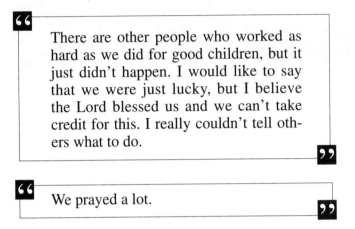

> There are other people who worked as hard as we did for good children, but it just didn't happen. I would like to say that we were just lucky, but I believe the Lord blessed us and we can't take credit for this. I really couldn't tell others what to do.

> We prayed a lot.

Although every family was different and although different families emphasized different messages, the eight messages in this section were the basic ingredients that kept coming to the surface.

1

PARENT ON PURPOSE—
Intentionally

One of the first messages we heard from these families was that they parented on *purpose*—they were *intentional*. Intentional is the opposite of *haphazard*. Intentionality means *knowing what you want and aiming precisely to get it with all diligence.*

We found this characteristic to be one of the most essential ingredients to raising strong families. This concept, if integrated into your parenting style, could change the future of your family. It is truly one of the most valuable secrets of success we came across and is a philosophy you will see woven throughout this book.

James Collins and Jerry Porras provide us with some intriguing information concerning intentionality in the business world. They did a study of six major corporations with the goal of identifying why some organizations are more successful than others.[2]

They paired competitors whom they considered "visionary" with those they considered "nonvisionary": IBM (visionary) and

Burroughs Corporation (nonvisionary); Motorola (visionary) and Zenith (nonvisionary); Disney (visionary) and Columbia (nonvisionary). Their findings were consistent: vision-driven companies performed *eight times* better than their nonvisionary competitors.

They uncovered two factors that made the difference: (1) visionary companies had a *focused mission,* and (2) visionary companies had clearly articulated *core values.*

The analogy is obvious: Intentionality—in terms of a *focused mission* and *core values*—is a key ingredient in both business and family success.

▼

Intentionality means knowing what you want and aiming precisely to get it with all diligence.

The parents we interviewed clearly demonstrated both of these ingredients. These families had an "uncommon focus" or goal directedness about them. As one of the fathers said, "you gotta get your life in focus, *like with a magnifying glass.*"

So many of us jump on our horses and ride off in five different directions. Not these folks. They had a clear mission for their lives and a vision for their children. William Bennett, former secretary of education, said, "I'd rather ride in a VW that knows where it is going than in a Lexus that is wandering around." One of the fathers we interviewed put it this way, "Winners focus; losers spray." These people had an aggressive parenting style characterized by thinking about what they wanted and actively pursuing that goal, no matter the obstacles.

Many of them told us that *before* they were married, they had developed plans and goals concerning what kind of a family they wanted to have. While dating, they had considered whether that date could be a partner in their goals for their families. Before they had children, they had given thought to the goals they had for those children's lives.

One wife recalled thinking while she was still in the hospital with her first baby, "This is serious business!" We heard comments like the following from almost all of the families:

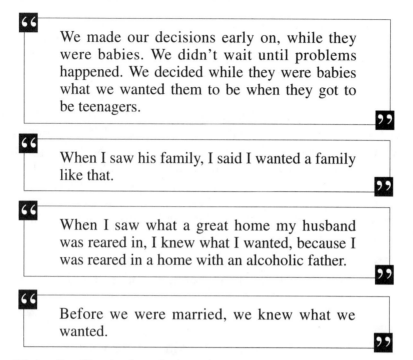

> We made our decisions early on, while they were babies. We didn't wait until problems happened. We decided while they were babies what we wanted them to be when they got to be teenagers.

> When I saw his family, I said I wanted a family like that.

> When I saw what a great home my husband was reared in, I knew what I wanted, because I was reared in a home with an alcoholic father.

> Before we were married, we knew what we wanted.

These families had a mission plan *early.* Jesus knew his mission at age twelve. He came *on* purpose *for* a purpose. Great things happen intentionally, not by accident or luck.

As a professor at a Christian university, I asked my students to define their mission in life. One of my older students provided an inspiring example of how intentionality can change a life.

Seven years ago, while I was president of the . . . Bank, I was told by an insurance man that, according to the actuarial tables, I had only 28 more years to live. This started me thinking about the rest of my life. I was tired of fighting bank examiners and a very poor banking environment. I wanted my life to count for something in the kingdom of God, not in the world of banking. This thinking started me on my way . . . to work on a Master of Divinity. I have never done a great thing, and I am not going to do a great thing. I doubt if I will even be remembered after I die except by my kids, but I want to be remembered by God on the day of resurrection. My mission is to have a heart read by Jesus. A heart that has been melted by my appreciation of him and God and the Holy Spirit. I cannot fathom in the least the nature of a God who will look into my life and read my heart and care even slightly for me. I must respond. I must arm my-self and respond. My mission in life is to spend the rest of my life with my sweet wife in the work of the Lord in whatever it is that is waiting for us to do. The only auditor that counts for anything is God.

When you establish a life mission, you get *focused*. And when you get focused, you receive *joy* because your life has meaning. Knowing this keeps me writing in my journal most mornings after I spend some time with the Lord. It keeps me honing my mission in life. When you have a mission, you are like a nail. The harder life pounds you, the deeper it drives you into your goal.

When the parents we interviewed spoke about intentionality, we heard these comments:

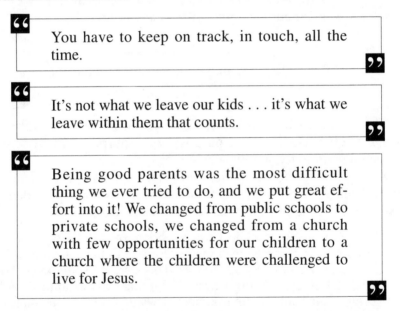

> " You have to keep on track, in touch, all the time. "

> " It's not what we leave our kids . . . it's what we leave within them that counts. "

> " Being good parents was the most difficult thing we ever tried to do, and we put great ef-fort into it! We changed from public schools to private schools, we changed from a church with few opportunities for our children to a church where the children were challenged to live for Jesus. "

When an architect builds an exceptional house, he puts much forethought into the plans and the foundation because he knows that all that comes later (plumbing, electricity, heating, and air conditioning) is made easier or more difficult depending on how thoroughly the plans and foundation were conceived. You can rest assured that problems *will* arise in your family. Taking the time to develop a master plan *now* can save you much grief later.

Tied to the concept of intentional parenting, we found three mind-sets that fueled their *intentionality*.

1. Set Your Sights on the Target

One father keeps his goals written on a paper in his billfold. He whipped them right out and showed them to us. Another father faithfully rededicates himself to the Lord and to his goals the first thing every morning. This executive said that the difference between dreams and goals is that "goals are something you *do something about.*"

One family spends time every New Year's Day looking at goals for the coming year. They categorize these into financial, educational, personal, and spiritual goals; and they talk about what they need to do to accomplish these goals. It's like a strategy planning session. Although the children did not always enjoy these sessions, they now feel they were excellent training. They have grown up understanding the difference between true resolve and New Year's "resolutions" that are made and then forgotten.

One of the sons said,

> **66**
> We were raised on setting goals.
> **99**

His mother made goal posters for all the children and hung them in their rooms. We talked with this boy about the goals he had set for himself in high school. He had thirty goals he wanted to accomplish by the time he graduated from high school. He accomplished twenty-eight of them. How many would he have accomplished had he not set any goals?

▼

"I can hit the target. It's the bull's eye that's tough."

One of his goals was to run the quarter mile in a specific time. When he crossed the finish line in his race, he asked the timekeeper what his time was. The reply was "59.3." The boy sat down and took a piece of paper out of his shoe with "59.3" written on it. Needless to say, his family has gotten across the power of goal setting.

I discovered this beautiful example of a family plan on the refrigerator of some loved ones.

Clinton Family Values

"Children are arrows intended to be aimed at a specific target."

Our Family Belief System

1. God is real and he loves us.
2. We show God we love him by obeying, giving, sharing, and praying.
3. The Bible is our guide to what is good and right.
4. People are more important than things.
5. Doing right is never wrong.

Targets for Hunter and Hailey

1. To love God and live life with a pure heart.
2. To be a contributor to family and community.
   To have a heart for giving and sharing.
3. To independently make good decisions and solve problems when faced with obstacles and peer pressure.
4. To be responsible and resourceful.
5. To have a perspective about life that is joyful . . . to seek out humor or the positive even when it gets tough.
6. To love themselves for who they are and to recognize their capabilities.

Our Family Plan

1. Read the Bible, pray together, and worship with our church.
2. Model and teach giving. Be involved in volunteer projects.
3. Provide "tools" to promote decision-making skills.
4. Teach responsible behavior and expect it consistently.
5. Model a sense of humor and positive attitude.
   Allow for mistakes.
6. Promote Hunter and Hailey's interests and strengths. Nurture their self-esteem.
7. Foster curiosity, creativity, and a love for learning.
8. Listen and always have time for our children.

Every family and business needs a mission statement. One of the most powerful statements I've heard on *focus* came not from a

professor or researcher, but from one of the fathers we interviewed, "Faulkner, I can hit the target. It's the bull's eye that's
tough." What a clincher! Jesus is all about hitting the bull's eye,
about focusing on the *heart* of the matter.

2. Commit to Hitting the Bull's Eye

Parents who have great children put their time and energy and
creativity "where their mouths are." When we asked if they would
consider moving if one of the children had a problem, the answer
was always, "Yes. We would do *anything.*" Some of them did
move for their children's sake. One father, when he was promoted
to a job in another city, lengthened his commuting time by two
hours a day rather than force his high-school-age children to relo-
cate. When these families were forced to move around, as many of
them were, Mom and Dad always placed the highest priority on
finding the right church and the right school for the children, not
on finding "the best deal."

These parents believed they could make a difference in the lives
of their children, and they were committed to investing their all in
them. When asked what advice they had for others, they said,

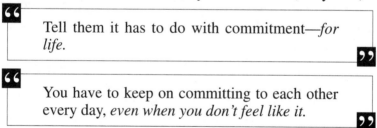

Tell them it has to do with commitment—*for
life.*

You have to keep on committing to each other
every day, *even when you don't feel like it.*

Without commitment there is no mechanism to get the family
mission accomplished. John DeFrain and Nick Stinnett, well-
known researchers of family strengths, state, "Commitment is the
foundation on which all other family strengths rest."[3]

The fact that *extraordinary outcome* requires *extraordinary effort* is not a new revelation. This principle is true with any endeavor. Take piano playing, for instance. No one can sit down and
rip off Beethoven's Fifth or a Chopin concerto without immense
effort. It takes high investment and years of study and practice.

It is not acceptable to Van Cliburn to miss every tenth note
when he performs, although that would be getting ninety percent

of the notes right. Would you buy a recording in which every tenth note was wrong? What about every hundredth note? My guess is that none of us would be satisfied with that on our stereo. The great musicians aim for the highest quality—the ultimate one hundred percent.

The Motorola Company is committed to quality—quality greater than 99 percent accuracy. They have printed this statement in *Industry Week* magazine.

> We believe our goal is 99.9999998 percent accuracy. Ninety-nine percent accuracy is not good enough. Using a medical model, with 99 percent accuracy, the hospital workers in obstetrics wards in American hospitals would drop 30,000 babies every year.

A lot of parents wouldn't think dropping only one percent of the babies they handled was good enough. If Motorola tries that hard to be accurate, shouldn't we try that hard too? We are talking about the souls of our children here. God's grace covers us when we make mistakes, even dumb mistakes, but there is no excuse for being continuously careless and sloppy. If we can do better, we should.

One couple summed it up best when they explained their philosophy of family to me.

> **❝**
>
> Parenting requires your best, your dedication, your attention. It involves self-discipline. Good families don't just happen. Sometimes you have to choose between what you *want* to do and what you *ought* to do. It is difficult to be good at both golf and tennis. You have to select and choose. You have to take time and do it right. We have our children for such a short time. If you don't do it now, it won't get done.
>
> Early in the marriage we decided we wanted children. We also decided we would make them a top priority in our lives. Parents need to be there not just to conceive them, but to nurture them. If the parents don't nurture their children, it won't get done.
>
> **❞**

In order to achieve success without failing your family, you must make conscious, deliberate choices about where to spend your time and energy. Choose hobbies and recreational activities that involve the whole family. Extra pursuits and hobbies that are for you alone may have to take a backseat if you are to keep your life focused and intentional.

3. Never, Never Give Up

These parents understood that no matter what their children got into or out of, they would never, *never* give up. When we commit ourselves to our children, we must realize that we are in it for the long haul. We must discipline ourselves to follow through—to the very end. One of the fathers told me, "Very few people make a decision and follow through with it."

▼

"Very few people make a decision and follow through with it."

As Charles Spurgeon, a well known Baptist preacher, said, "The snail would never have made it on the ark except through perseverance." The book of James states, "Consider it pure joy, my brothers, whenever you face trials of many kinds, because you know that the testing of your faith develops perseverance."[4]

The CEO of a multimillion-dollar business said, "Finish it— wrap it up." That means *perseverance*. Business cannot afford loose ends, and neither can families. A statement attributed to Grover Cleveland says a lot about the importance of perseverance.

> Press on; nothing in the world can take the place of persistence. Talent will not; nothing is more common than unsuccessful people with talent. Genius will not; unrewarded genius is almost a proverb. Education will not; the world is full of educated derelicts. Persistence and determination alone are omnipotent.

In our child rearing, do we just hunt and peck around or do we wrap it up? Do we persevere to the end? An apostle of Jesus speaks about persevering when he says, "I have finished the race. I have kept the faith,"[5] and he did this through all kinds of insults, injuries, and hardships. My favorite quote on persistence comes from Winston Churchill, who refused to be intimidated by his past mistakes. Someone said to him, "Sir Winston, what in your school experience best prepared you to lead Britain out of her darkest hour?"

Winston thought a minute and said, "It was the two years I spent at the same level in high school."

"Did you fail?"

"No, I had two opportunities to get it right. What Britain needed most in those dark days was not brilliance, but perseverance."

Perseverance is never more needed than when dealing with teenage and young adult children who reject their parents' value system or refuse to live according to the family standards.

▼

These parents understood that no matter what their children got into or out of, they would never, *never* give up.

It's true that sometimes we have to allow our children to suffer the consequences of their behavior, but we must always keep communication open and must work with our children on whatever common ground can be found.

When approval and support are not possible, we can still extend our unconditional love, and we can always leave the door open so they can come home. While there are no guarantees, many children do eventually find their way back home and return to the values they learned from their family. Learning from the parenting style of our heavenly Father, we can find the strength to persevere with our child and *never give up!*

One of the most beautiful stories coming out of our interviews concerns a family with four children of their own who adopted a teenage girl with a lot of problems. She was a very troubled girl—

street smart and strong for her age. She had been involved with drugs and alcohol and was really acting out, but this mother and father believed in their ability to make a difference with that girl. The parents had done everything they knew to love and control her, but nothing seemed to work. They even allowed her to remain in jail for a day or two to help her understand the seriousness of her behavior. Nevertheless, after her return, the father came in and found her literally destroying the house, pulling down pictures, breaking the TVs, smashing windows, etc. The father knew of only three options: to physically restrain her, to knock her out, or to let her destroy the house. He opted to restrain her. In the process, she broke one of his ribs. Still, they stuck with her, even though the people in the community, and even the folks in the church, tried to persuade them to give up on her. "Let her go," they said. "After all, she's not really your daughter." But to that the dad always replied, "Yes, I know. *But I told her she was.*"

Today, you would never know that this young woman had caused them that kind of grief. We met her and her precious husband and family at the interview, and she is a lovely Christian mother of four beautiful children. Those parents made all the difference. They *refused* to give up!

▼

"Worth is not determined by possessions. Our family concentrates on values, values that last."

2

VALUES—

The Foundation of the Family

The second message that came through loud and clear was that these families held to and lived out a clearly-defined value system. These values provided a framework, a measuring standard, for all they did and even for who they were. And when you think about it, such a system is absolutely essential for progress. If a foundation is flawed, no amount of architectural finesse will support the structure. The foundation is essential. To study the values of successful families is to study the very heart of their success.

The children of these men and women clearly understood what was valued by their parents:

> 66
> Mom and Dad would be the same people if they lost everything tomorrow. Their priority is not money.
> 99

> **"** Dealing with Dad is like dealing with a moral
> ledger. **"**

Dad's integrity was so high in his children's eyes that they all said they "never doubted that Dad would make the right decision. Ever." The daughters of a successful coach said,

> **"** Daddy is the most honest person you could
> ever come across. If something goes wrong,
> you just have to be ashamed because honesty
> and integrity are part of the family name. **"**

Our society as a whole is in desperate need of the kind of values exhibited by these families. Chuck Colson, who was an aide to President Nixon during the Watergate scandal and who is now a believer and head of an international prison ministry, noted a few years ago that our culture is not teaching the *wrong* values as much as it is teaching *no* values. How else can one account for the decision of an Illinois couple to take an extended vacation to Mexico at Christmas, leaving their two daughters, ages five and nine, at home by themselves?

Ted Koppel, news broadcaster for ABC, made the following observation while speaking at a graduation ceremony several years ago:

> Moses didn't give us ten suggestions. . . . In the place of truth we have substituted facts. In the place of moral absolutes we have substituted moral ambiguities. We now communicate with everyone and say absolutely nothing. We have reconstructed the Tower of Babel—the TV antenna.

The convictions we pass on to our children today will hold the world together (or let it fall apart) tomorrow. William Bennett put it succinctly:

> What determines a young person's behavior in academic, sexual, and social life are his deeply held convictions and beliefs. They determine behavior far more than race, class, economic background, or ethnicity. . . . If that soul is not filled with noble sentiments, with virtue, if we do not attend to the "better angels

of our nature," it will be filled by something else. . . . As the Roman scholar Pliny the Elder put it, "What we do to our children, they will do to society." [1]

Not long ago I had occasion to study at the Albert Einstein Medical School for a week with a number of psychologists. When I talked with them about morals and value systems, almost all of them expressed a *relative* value system, something like, "Well, everybody to his own thing," or "If religion means something to you, go with it." But in their minds *no* system of values gives any meaningful boundaries to life. They believed there were no sure guides to life. These highly skilled and professional people-helpers live in a state of moral flux.

Our present chaotic American value system reminds me of a cartoon where Charlie Brown, the comic strip character, is sitting on the deck of a cruise ship. Lucy says, "Charlie, some people unfold their deck chairs facing forward. They want to see where they are going. And some unfold their deck chairs facing the rear. They want to see where they have been. Charlie, how do you unfold your deck chair?" Charlie, like too many Americans, replies: "I don't know. I can't get the thing unfolded."

▼

To study the values of successful families is to study the very heart of their success.

Our children need structure and guidelines for ethics and morals, not just laws that tell them what is *legal*. Ralph Minear says we have been too busy with our own lives and too confused and vague about what we teach our children. "Children need to have clear, reliable road maps based on meaningful values and rules of morality."

An Effective Value System

How do we go about shaping an *effective value system* that will sustain us for all of life and provide guidelines to face life's tough issues? The fact is, there *are* principles that have worked for thousands of years and still are not outmoded—principles that answer the big questions of life.

There are at least five characteristics that are crucial in establishing an effective value system, or stable philosophy of life. Such a value system:

1. Blesses people

An effective value system ought to bless society in general—to uplift, to ennoble, to benefit. There are some value systems that do not bless folks. Communism did not bless people, rather it failed them. Furthermore, an adequate value system ought to bless *everybody, from all races*—rich or poor, educated or uneducated, beautiful or ugly, male or female—everybody!

▼

Whatever value system we hold, we must hold to one that has an antidote for sin.

2. Deals honestly with sin or wrongdoing

Most people refuse to call wrongdoing, *sin*. We call it mental dysfunction, bad choices, sickness, or poor decisions. But sin is real, and deep down we all know it. When we mess up, we need solutions that work. Without a way to make things right, hopelessness can pull us further into wrong. We yearn for real forgiveness, and we cry for the hope that only repentance can bring. Prisons are not the solution—lives are seldom changed for the better. Therapists can't forgive sins—forgiveness comes from above. We need to repent and gain forgiveness for our evil ways. "Somehow, someway, I need to have something that takes care of the worst fight I have every day—the fight within that causes the fight without."[2] Whatever value system we hold, we must hold to one that has an antidote for sin.

3. Lasts forever

A multitude of things may seem to be important, and they are—for the moment. But all of us are continually searching for life systems that last. We expect good houses, good cars, and, especially, good friendships to last. Fads are fads because they don't have within them lasting credentials. Stable value systems last because they have been proven through thousands of years. As Jesus said, "Do not store up for yourselves treasures on earth, where moth and rust destroy, and where thieves break in and steal. But store up for yourselves treasures in heaven, where moth and rust do not destroy, and where thieves do not break in and steal."[3] He says that earthly treasures *don't last.* We need a value system that is stable from birth through eternity.

4. Gives meaning and purpose to life

The zipper on my pants has a purpose, so does the button on my shirt. Some think that the coat, shirt, and button have a purpose, but the guy wearing them doesn't. That is craziness! It's sad that human beings continue to ask, "Why are we here?" Many don't know why they are here and where they are going, but they can put their finger on the purpose for a button or a zipper. To have a simple sanity, each person must believe there is meaning to his existence.

▼

To have a simple sanity, each person must believe there is meaning to his existence.

5. Answers the big questions

We all need a philosophy that answers the big questions of aging and death. Like cars and most of our "toys" that have built-in "obsolescence," our bodies are built to last only a little while, and then we are gone. Socrates said that the basic purpose of philosophy is to teach us how to die. How well do we deal with wrinkles, gray hair, and the slips in memory? Does life just go downhill after fifty until it flames out? Shouldn't we look for a philosophy that gives viable answers to death and dying—the really "big questions" that all of us face sooner or later?

The above five characteristics offer solid principles that address the core issues of life. When we talk about blessing everybody, we address *society*. When we talk about wrongdoing and sin, we address *ethics*. When we talk about what lasts, we address *time* and the *future*. Meaning addresses *the value of life*. And the big question addresses *death and dying*. These issues are matters of universal concern.

The value systems incorporated by our thirty families gave them balance and enabled them to deal with the real issues of life. Families without a trustworthy value system are unstable and drift with the whims of other unstable people.

A Strong Religious Faith

Another facet of the value system of these families was a strong religious faith, not simply a reliance on their own strategies and efforts. It was just a given in all the families. One child said,

> " It was just understood that religion was top priority in my parents' life. It formed the basis of our family. "

When these families talked about success, we noticed that they automatically connected success with faith. Before ever mentioning religion or money, I asked these families: "How would you define success?" Listen to some of their answers:

> " Success is glorifying God by fulfilling your potential. Success is not merely being a successful law partner. . . . I have seen so many of their families fall apart. "

> " Success is a Christian home, not money. "

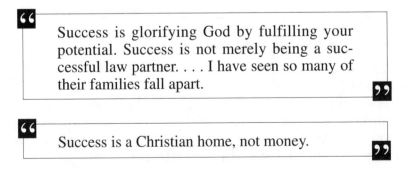

> " Our goal is a godly heritage, not money. "

> " Success is right relationships with those closest to you—your heavenly Father, your wife, and your family. "

> " Our goal is to live a Christian life. "

Money was not what these families valued. They valued their relationship with their creator. We noticed that their faith was real, verbally stated, and modeled. And while their demonstrations of faith were as individual as each family, faith was their driving force: "It is everything to us," said one wife, "all day long, at work, at school, it is our whole life."

▼

Secular authorities agree that one of the main components of all strong families is a solidly based religious faith.

Significantly, other researchers confirm the necessity for faith in developing effective families. Ray Guarendi, researcher and psychologist, conducted research in the public schools in all fifty states. Teachers helped him select families whom they considered strong and healthy. He then interviewed these families at length. Consider his assessment of the place of religion in great families:

> One theme to emerge most prominently [in my research] is spirituality, or the belief in a Creator and in living by his guidelines. Nearly ninety percent of the families pointed to spirituality as a significant, if not dominant, guiding force in their lives. . . . Spirituality is the umbrella which encompasses and fosters a more loving, close-knit family.[4]

Almost without exception, secular authorities who have studied family strengths agree that one of the main components of all strong families is belief in a solidly based, ethically responsible religious faith. (See Appendix Three.)

Furthermore, national polls attest to the fact that a vast majority of the American people believe in God, so much so that the professional counselors are beginning to give more attention to religion in the training of therapists. It is interesting to note that many leaders in the former Soviet state have determined that the communist ideology failed to give them a basis for moral values and integrity, so they have begun to seek out people from other cultures who can teach them religion in their schools and establish churches to fill the void in their national character.

Philip Yancy offers the following list of advantages of religious faith; and this list is just the beginning:[5]

Advantages of Religious Faith

1. Regular church attenders live longer.

2. Religion reduces the incidence of heart attacks, arteriosclerosis, high blood pressure, and hypertension.

3. Religious people are less likely to abuse alcohol, and far less likely to use illicit drugs.

4. Prison inmates who make a religious commitment are less likely than their counterparts to return to jail.

5. Marital satisfaction and overall well-being tend to increase with church attendance.

6. Depression rates decline.

7. Religious commitment offers one protection against the nation's greatest health problem—divorce.

8. A *Redbook* magazine survey said that married people who were religious had a whole lot more fun in bed than those who were not.

A High Esteem of Family

Before leaving the subject of values, let's consider one more concept: Something very interesting is happening in America . . . our perspective on what's really important is undergoing a change.

The eighties were marked by a spirit of selfishness. The purpose of the game was to get all you could, using whatever means were necessary. And after a decade of seeking fulfillment outside our families, many are finally returning to hearth and home, having learned the hard way that this is where true happiness lies.

From unexpected sources—Hollywood stars, powerful business executives, psychologists, and philosophers—we hear the same message over and over: "None of it is worth anything if you don't have people in your life to love and who love you."

▼

As you pursue your career, always keep a steady focus on what is even more important— your family.

Listen to what Emmitt Smith, the famous, all-pro, Dallas Cowboy running back said about family:

> There is nothing that I am today that I would be without family. I inherited my athletic skills, and I learned all about life—how to love, how to act, how to treat people, how to expect to be treated—from my family. It's family, not football, that has been the greatest gift of all. I could get hurt tomorrow, and football would be over. Family will always be there.[6]

Shortly before his death, Lee Atwater, Republican Party leader at the height of the Bush administration, graphically describes his reassessment of values.

> Long before I was struck with cancer, I felt something stirring in the American society. It was a sense among the people of the country—Republican and Democrat alike—that something was missing from their lives, *something crucial* . . . My

illness helped me to see that what was missing in society is
what was missing in me: *a little heart, a lot of brotherhood.*

The '80s were about acquiring—acquiring wealth, power,
prestige. I know. I acquired more wealth, power and prestige
than most. But you can acquire all you want and still feel
empty. What power wouldn't I trade for a little more time with
my family? What price wouldn't I pay for an evening with
friends? It took a deadly illness to put me eye to eye with that
truth, but it is a truth that the country, caught up in its ruthless
ambitions and moral decay, can learn on my dime. I don't
know who will lead us through the '90s, but they must be made
to speak to this spiritual vacuum at the heart of American society, this tumor of the soul.

Valuing the family plays a big part in filling the "spiritual vacuum at the heart of America." As you pursue your career, always
keep a steady focus on what is even more important—your family.
The thirty families we hold before you as models all understood
the value of the family. When you put first things first, all other
goals will be easier to accomplish.

▼

"The best friends I have
are in my family."

3

LOVE THEM—
Adore Them

A third message we heard from these families—and you knew we'd hear this one—was that they had an obvious, effervescent, overflowing love for each child, and they were extravagantly generous in their expressions of love. These children were loved and they knew it. One of the daughters said,

> Those who love me are so important. The best friends I have are my family. They are the ones who gave me self-confidence and courage.

But according to noted child psychiatrist and pediatrician Grace Ketterman, this love that was so evident in these families is *not* instinctual. Did you know that babies are born with only two basic emotions—fear and anger? They *learn* to love only by being

29

loved. One of the reasons, according to Ketterman, for so much delinquency is that "Teen mothers without adequate mothering themselves don't know how to mother." There is a tide of unloving families coming "down the pike," who are passing family dysfunction from generation to generation.

▼

Did you know that babies learn to love only by *being loved?*

Where do we start to turn this tide? What kind of *climate* does it take to teach and nurture love in a family? It starts at birth (even before birth) with a mom and dad who are deeply in love with their child. Then this "love affair" just keeps growing and developing within the family. Urie Bronfenbrenner concludes: "In sum, it can be said that human development occurs in the context of an escalating psychological ping-pong game between two people who are crazy about each other."[1]

Intimacy—Physical Expressions of Love

In the families we interviewed, there were lots of demonstrations of love—touching, holding hands, hugging, and kissing. Approximately eighty percent of the families were physically and emotionally demonstrative, and they weren't embarrassed about it. If anybody was a little reluctant, it was usually the father; yet not even the slightly reluctant ones were withdrawn. The phrases we kept hearing with reference to intimacy were "there is lots of touching and saying I love you," "I hug all the boys and girls," and "kissing on the cheek and on the lips." One family had a tradition that three squeezes of the hand meant "I love you." A family we admire has what they call a "hug-in" whenever a crisis strikes anyone in the family. They gather in a circle, put their arms around each other, and *hug*. They even include the family dog. Feelings of warmth and intimacy permeated the relationships in these families.

Biblical examples of intimacy abound. In the early church, the Christians washed each other's feet, laid hands on one another, and practiced the holy kiss. When the prodigal son returned home, "his father, filled with compassion, ran to meet him, threw his arms around him, and kissed him."[2] This is the kind of intimacy that all of us crave.

Our heavenly Father is most intimate with us. He knew us while we were still in our mothers' wombs. He knows our every thought.[3] He even knows the number of hairs on our heads.[4] He is thoroughly aware of us. He knows our secrets and still loves us. That is intimacy.

Secular research confirms biblical perspectives:

> The physical affection and warmth toward kids strongly predicts closer marriages, better mental health, more work success. Those who got these from both parents tended to be best adjusted of all. The result of a growing pool of evidence indicates that fathers play a more important part in shaping children than traditionally thought. Warmth and affection from parents really does increase the likeliness that children will grow into well adjusted adults with long, happy marriages and solid relationships with co-workers and friends.[5]

▼

Warm homes breed children who are less denying, defensive, and unsure of their worth.

Another sociologist said that children of warm homes are more sympathetic, more helpful, more caring, and more supporting. Warm homes also breed children who are less denying, defensive, and unsure of their worth. Since the time of Christ, Christians have confessed their sins to one another, loved one another, served one another, and ministered to one another. The many "one another" passages in the Bible suggest intimate concern.[6]

Virginia Satir, noted therapist, said:

> Hugging can be vital to your emotional well-being. Everybody feels skin hunger throughout their lives, and unless that hunger is satisfied by touching, there is a vital void in the emotional makeup that is going to cause deep unhappiness. . . . Adults are no different. When they are not patted on the hand, embraced

around the shoulder, or hugged, they withdraw into themselves. I prescribe four hugs a day to survive. Eight hugs a day are necessary for maintenance, and twelve hugs a day for growth.[7]

Many studies confirm that little babies need touching, stroking, and physical contact, or they will die.

When I was a young child, I suffered from painful earaches. In those days the cure was to put warm oil in the aching ear. My mother would put me in her lap, apply the oil, put my aching ear on her breast, and rock me until I could sleep. The memory of this brings warmth and comfort even today. And when my mother was ninety-two years old and near death, what she needed from me were hugs. She didn't need a car, a stereo set, or a big house. When we near death, the real issues of life surface. She and all her possessions barely took up one room. But she still needed assurance and hugging. When we come into this world as babies, we need hugging, and when we leave this world, we need hugging. It's also necessary in between coming and going. Great families never forget that.

Appreciation and Encouragement

One important way to express love is through *appreciation.* One of the great psychologists, William James, maintains that the *deepest,* the *most important* need for individuals is a craving for appreciation. I remember, working at camp in the summers, how the little boys would stop when they got to the end of the diving board and yell, "Look at me!" And they wouldn't jump off until somebody was looking. They wanted their dives to be appreciated by someone else.

▼

We *never* outgrow our need to be appreciated.

If you tell me that you like my tie, it gives me a boost. I don't care so much about the piece of cloth around my neck, but your compliment tells me that *I* made a good choice. We *never* outgrow our need to be appreciated. Adults need it, little children need it, kids in junior high with zits on their faces especially need it. If we don't receive appreciation and encouragement, our egos suffer.

Besides needing to receive positive affirmation, research now shows that negative comments carry tons more weight than positive ones. Some research I have read says it takes as many as forty-seven positives to counter just one negative. Other ratios I have read are fifteen to one and eight to one; the lowest I have ever seen is five to one. So at a *minimum,* it takes five positive comments to counter one negative one.[8]

Dr. Howard Markman says that fifteen to twenty acts of kindness are necessary to repair one criticism. I used to think that if I could be more positive than negative, I was doing good. Not so. The self-esteem and ego are so fragile that we must dish out *many* more positives than negatives just to break even.

John Gottman says that children are not the only ones affected by a negative environment. Pending divorce rates of newlyweds can be predicted with 87 percent accuracy based entirely on the negative attitudes picked up in their conversation. Negative interactions are ten to twenty times more powerful in predicting divorce than positive interactions.

> Amazing, we have found that it all comes down to a math formula . . . you must have at least five times as many positives as negative moments together if your marriage is to be stable.[9]

The opposite of being appreciative and encouraging is being negative and critical. The families we talked with understood the power of a positive environment and the failure that negativity can bring. All of these families had an obviously positive outlook on life. The children often talked about the uncritical nature of their parents. One daughter said,

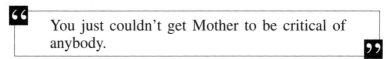

> You just couldn't get Mother to be critical of anybody.

This was also true in their marriages. Mom and Dad were not critical of each other. And these families extended this positive outlook to the people they worked with. There was no criticism of how "the company" or "the board" treated their dear ones. They seemed to predetermine that whatever company they worked for was *not* going to be trashed at home, even with its shortcomings. A negative spirit kills the positive atmosphere of the family. One entrepreneur told us,

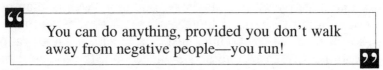

> You can do anything, provided you don't walk away from negative people—you run!

They had decided that a critical spirit was too high a price to pay, either at work or at home.

One of the families we interviewed understood this concept. Without even knowing what the experts found they said:

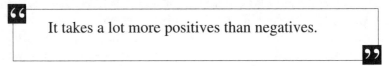

> It takes a lot more positives than negatives.

Forgiveness

I was told about a family in California who was trying to deal with a son who had really acted out—so much so that he was sent to prison. When the time for his release drew near, his father went to their minister to discuss how he and his wife should handle his return. The father told his preacher, "This time, I'm really going to lay down the law and tighten up the rules." But the preacher's response surprised him: "I know a guy in the Bible whose son messed up bad, and when he returned home, the father gave him a party," referring, of course, to the return of the prodigal son.[10] The parents began to rethink their response to their son's return. You guessed it. When the son came home, he saw lots of cars in front of his house. There was something big going on—a party! And come to find out, it was for *him*—complete with cake, candles, all his relatives, and a big banner that said, "Welcome home, son!"

When I told this story, there were some skeptics who asked, "Well, did it work?" So I checked with the preacher who told me the story to find out. He said, "Well, I haven't talked with the family lately, but I see them in church every Sunday. That boy sits with his folks, with his arm around his mom. Yes, I think it's working great."

I was brought up in a time when it was thought that this kind of extravagant forgiveness would encourage people to go out and sin more. Of course, different situations call for different actions; but sometimes the rules we make are more for the benefit of others than for our children: we don't want our friends to think we are slack. The moral is: let love be your guide in your dealings with your children, regardless of what they do.

The gospel is "good news." At the end of the story the message is "we win." Even though we still sin, He died for us. We can't be too ugly, too mean, too bad, for God not to love us and forgive us right where we are. And kids have to pick this up from Mom and Dad, or they may not pick it up at all.

▼

"The higher position you have, the more difficult it is to become a servant. Ego must be done away with."

4

BE A SERVANT—
Lead from the
Foot of the Table

If you don't know what an *oxymoron* is, the term "servant leadership" is a perfect example. An oxymoron is two seemingly contradictory terms that when combined create a whole new meaning, like "deafening silence" or "real simulated" (pearl).

When we picture a strong leader, we might picture him on his feet, standing before a crowd, giving an eloquent, stirring message. When we picture a servant, on the other hand, we conjure up the image of a poor, uneducated worker on hands and knees, cleaning up other people's messes.

But most of our world's greatest heroes are servants—like Gandhi, Martin Luther King Jr., and Mother Teresa. We respect most those who give themselves in service to others. Of course, Jesus is the greatest model of a servant leader. God himself, washed the disciples' feet, touched and healed lepers, relinquishing his heavenly role to show us how to serve "down in the trenches," doing the hard things—this is the kind of model that touches the hearts of our children and guides the direction of their lives.

Listen to the insightful observations of the bioethicist, Willard Gaylin:

> One of the most incredible things to me really is to see the typical middle class kid who's given everything he wants except the privilege of service, the privilege of self-sacrifice, and the joy of being a giver. We've become a passive society that sees everything in terms of our open mouth—fill it with something! The idea that we can actually do things for something broader—a community—is lost.
>
> I happen to know that service is empowering. It's great. It's terrific! Given that opportunity for training toward community and service, people love it and want it. I don't find I'm happy with the kind of narcissistic quick-fix that this society offers most people.[1]

As we visited with the thirty successful families, we found an attitude of service running throughout. And you'll find this theme throughout the book, because it permeated all they did. Creating a family success story constantly requires putting the needs of your children and your spouse above your own. A servant heart is essential. One of the mothers we interviewed made an interesting observation,

> 66
> The higher position you have, the more difficult it is to become a servant. Ego must be done away with.
> 99

While a few of the people we interviewed did involve themselves in community organizations, most of them served in ways that are seldom recognized. Their service was not the kind that was rewarded with a gold plaque or noted in the newspaper. Their service was real ministry; they toughed it out doing things others wouldn't.

One of the families we visited gave us three inspiring stories about their father. This man is a top-notch salesman, one of those usually on the million-dollar roundtable. While traveling with his whole family on vacation, he made a rest room stop in a public airport. But he stayed in the rest room for such a long time that the family was getting worried. When he finally came out, they wanted to know what in the world took so long.

"Daddy, what's wrong? Are you sick?"

"Aw, it wasn't anything. I'm not sick."

"Tell us what happened."

"Nah, it was nothing. Really."

They kept on insisting that he tell them until the truth finally came out. Somebody had written some racist remarks and trash language on the walls in the bathroom, and he had found some cleanser and cleaned it up—in a public airport. It wasn't his responsibility, but he did it anyway because of his servant mentality.

▼

It wasn't his responsibility, but he did it anyway because of his servant mentality.

This same father was with his family in a small, hot, overcrowded gym watching a basketball game. A mother with a small baby was sitting not far away. The child threw up all over the mother, child, and stands. The people around her quickly scooted away, leaving her alone in the center of space, like a bull's eye on a target. But this father rushed to the men's room, soaked some towels in the sink, and headed back to help the beleaguered mother. He even climbed under the littered stands and cleaned up the floor. This man *thinks* ministry. People like this really do exist in our world today.

This same family, after hearing how people in Russia stand in line for blocks just to receive Bibles, initiated a drive in their hometown to send Bibles to a "sister city" in Russia. Everybody joined in, whether or not they were believers. Photographs and inscriptions were included in each Bible to make the gift more personal. The idea was a big hit in Russia as well as their little hometown in the United States.

Another family, the father of which is an executive who oversees a one-billion-dollar account, was involved in an inner-city ministry for years. Every weekend they would leave their home and go down to an inner-city project to work. It was a part of the city where only one man in two city blocks had a regular job. This couple began working with the children, taking them places, teaching them how to work, and mainly just loving them. Then their ministry spread to the parents of the children. I believe this couple did more good for that area than the federal government.

One of the children from another family told us,

> My mother and dad are incredible servants, and people look to them for everything.

In my own family, I can remember Mother taking us with her when she took food and clothes to poor folks. Even when we had to put our car up on blocks because we couldn't afford to pay for the license, she would still feed the poor when they came to our back door.

Hospitality was another way these families served others.

> Our family took in children, strays, and unwed mothers. A missionary family lived with us a year.

The same family who worked in the inner city on weekends, frequently took those people into their home. Among those they took in were a teenage boy, who was a homosexual; his sister, who was a prostitute; and a ten-year-old mixed race child, the product of a rape. Another family, with five children of their own, took in six foster babies, an alcoholic woman trying to rebuild her life, several disabled children, a prostitute, and a missionary.

I was invited to a stockholders' meeting of Wal-Mart at Sam Walton's house, along with nine hundred others. He didn't invite just the upper echelon of the company to this meeting, he invited the plain ol' folks. It rained right before everyone arrived, and guess who was wiping the water out of the folding chairs in the front yard?—Helen Walton. And then I watched her greet those nine hundred people with a beautiful smile, even though they were tracking muddy footprints through her house. This takes a person with a servant heart. Her husband had the same mentality. While I was visiting Sam Walton in Bentonville, his hometown, he summed up his philosophy of servanthood in one sentence: "Paul, I see myself as the point of an *upside down* pyramid."

▼

Every weekend they would leave their home and go down to an inner-city project to work.

Somewhere along the line, men, we need to get off our high horses and our big egos and ask our wives and our children, "How can I be a better servant?" I guarantee they will tell us, because they know us. They know when we are proud and pompous. They know when we are not modeling what we say is important. I challenge you to ask them and let them help you see yourself as they do. The objective is to see who needs to be served and to serve them. That's what Jesus did.

▼

"On a scale of one to ten?
Humor is a fifteen!"

5

GIVE THE GIFT OF LAUGHTER

After all this talk about the effort and planning that goes into "making it work," you might get the idea that these families were all work and no play. Not at all! These people took their responsibilities seriously, but not themselves. They were *fun* to be around. One message that came through from all of the families was that they valued humor. They laughed easily and they laughed a lot.

These folks went out of their way to find humor in every situation. Some made a special effort to get out of themselves if their "natures" were quiet or serious, but they saw humor as one of the vital components of their family life. I asked each family this question, "What do you think about humor? Is it very important?" I'll never forget one mom's response,

> **"** On a scale of one to ten? Humor is a fifteen! **"**

Thumbing through a book of memories, we found this note:

Dear Mom and Dad—
It is such a great feeling to celebrate with you on your
40th anniversary. As I looked through the pictures, there
were so many great memories. It struck me that our family has always been a laughing family—what a great way
to grow up—laughing and loving even in "not so great"
times.

Love—Connie

I remember my own mother telling me, "Paul, I believe you are
going to make it."
"Make it? What do you mean, Mother?"
"I think you are going to make it because you have learned to
laugh at yourself."

▼

I looked over the door to see if there was any male plumbing on the wall.

Well, I've had a few chances in my life to practice what I
learned, and one of the funniest took place in the Dallas airport. I
know that airport like the back of my hand—I'm in and out so
much. But on this particular occasion when I went into the rest
room and got myself settled, I looked down and saw a woman's
shoe in the stall next to mine. I thought to myself, What on earth is
a woman doing in a men's rest room? And all of a sudden, a cold
sweat came all over me and I thought, My, do you suppose *I'm* in
a *women's* rest room? I stood up and looked over the door to see if
there was any male plumbing on the wall . . . and there wasn't.
And I knew I was in deep weeds. As I sat there with my feet off
the floor, I tried to figure out what I was going to do. My first
thought was, well, I'll just stay till everybody leaves, and then I'll
sneak out. But then I remembered that this was a twenty-four hour
airport, and if I followed that plan, I would *die* in the ladies rest
room. So after all other possibilities were discarded, I just stood up

and said out loud to everybody, "Ladies, you've got a man in a women's rest room. I'm embarrassed, and I'm comin' out."

And about that time one of the ladies piped up, "Well, just come on out." So, I ducked my head and headed for the door. I've never been so embarrassed in all my life. When I came out into the lobby of the airport, I had my head way down, but I noticed out of the corner of my eyes that folks were looking at me kinda funny. I headed off down the hallway just as quickly as I could, and I could almost feel some lady running after me with a policeman, shouting, "There's the weirdo, get him!" But luckily, it was just my imagination.

My first thought was that I must *never* tell this story to anyone. If I did, I would never live it down. But the more I thought about it, I knew that it was just too good a story not to tell. I've told this story in public a time or two and have collected more bathroom stories than you can imagine. But we haven't got time to tell 'em here.

The point is, can you laugh at yourself? If you can't, you inhibit your relationships with your children and others. This kind of transparency sets others at ease and is one of the best ways of teaching. All of us enjoy being around people who don't take themselves too seriously. Healthy minded people know that they can make mistakes and still recover and that one mistake is not the beginning of a slippery slide down into ridicule. Give the gift of laughter to your children, even if it is at your expense occasionally.

▼

One of them said he felt like it was his business to make sure the family had fun.

Remember the story of Norman Cousins? He was the man who laughed himself back to health. He is dead now, but he was supposed to have died long before he did—on two different occasions. They put him in the hospital with a grim prognosis, but he didn't die. He filled his days with laughter by watching funny movies of the Marx Brothers and other comedians, and it worked! He laughed himself back to health. The recovery of Norman Cousins is not unsubstantiated myth. Cousins taught in the medical school of the University of Southern California and carefully documented the physiological effects of humor and a positive attitude. It was a privilege to meet him personally a few years ago. He radiated a warm, gentle, likable spirit of good humor.

Even though one of the men we interviewed seemed to be a very thoughtful, quiet, stoic individual, his wife told us that around the family he was "always joking and kidding around." This seemed to be the pattern, even for the people I had a hard time imagining in that role. One staid businessman, a corporate vice president, would even dress up in crazy clothes and do slapstick-type stuff to entertain the children. These parents wanted home to be a fun place.

When we asked the question "What would you pass on to others?" many times the answer was,

Tell them to have fun.

A corporate executive in a high-stress position put it very well,

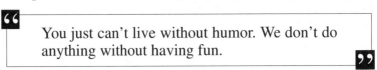

You just can't live without humor. We don't do anything without having fun.

When these fathers involved their young children in their business world, they worked hard to insure that fun went along with it. One of them said he felt like it was his business to make sure the family had fun.

These families cherished their funny stories and made them a part of the family "legends." One family laughed about the two youngest boys "borrowing" the fur stoles of visitors, chasing each other all through the house yelling, "It's an animal! It's an animal!" We heard about the practical joke played on a dear friend and guest who needed to wake up in time for a morning appointment. They "helped" him by hiding five different alarm clocks in his room, all set to go off at different times.

One of the kids told us what a big part humor played in their family.

> " Dad was always playing tricks on people, so we got Mom to play one on Dad. He was working out on construction sites, and she packed his lunch everyday. We got her to put a piece of rubber cheese on his sandwich. We couldn't wait for him to get home that day. When he came in, he acted sick as a dog and said he'd been sick ever since lunch. Mom got so worried because she thought he really had eaten that cheese—we all did. But of course, he hadn't; and as usual, he got the last laugh. "

The children in another family enjoyed recounting the time Dad was kind of pouting because he had to have Wheaties for breakfast, when what he really wanted was scrambled eggs, bacon, biscuits—the works! Mom said, "Oh, you want a hot breakfast?"

"Yeah!"

"Well, honey, you just set those Wheaties on fire." And the whole family went to the floor!

▼

It was wonderful to listen to them, because their humor was never caustic.

It was wonderful to listen to them, because their humor was never caustic. They never embarrassed or cut each other. The humor was never cruelty disguised as "Can't you take a joke?" It was always gentle. These people had a playful curiosity that enriched life and made it fun. It was a great bond that held them together even through not-so-fun times.

"Nothing was tabu or swept under the rug."

6

BE TRANSPARENT–

Communicate Openly and Honestly

These folks were so open, so willing to talk. The fact that they invited us into their "most holy places" to talk about their families was evidence of their transparency. Can you imagine a family allowing two strangers to come into their home to interview them about their family? All the interviews, except for one or two, took place in the presence of the children and the children's spouses and sometimes even the grandchildren. The important thing to note here is that there were no "family secrets." If there had been any skeletons in the closet, such an interview would have been too risky. I asked all the families if they had any family secrets. When I asked this question of one particular family, one of the adult kids leaned forward slowly and said in a near whisper, "Yes, we have lots of them." The room got quiet. Then he laughed and said, "And everybody knows them all."

So often, we have it exactly backwards. We think, "I can't let people see the real me because they won't like what they see. I must keep my sins hidden." That is just the opposite of what the Bible and good psychology teach. Each of us needs a prayer group or some special one to whom we are accountable—a place where the "real me" can be known. Otherwise, we will never know un-conditional love because we will always wonder, "Would they still love me if they knew the real me?" If transparency is not a charac-teristic of your family, your children, too, will be left wondering. Transparency, confession, and openness must begin with the par-ents, or it will rarely find its way to the children.

▼

There were no "family secrets."

One of the best things I heard was from one of the grown sons. As he talked about the difficulty of growing up in the shadow of his successful father, he said,

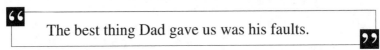

The best thing Dad gave us was his faults.

Ralph Minear writes,

> The best thing I can think of to describe good communication is openness: the child must be willing and able to express his deepest feelings and concerns to the parent; and the parent must be available and discerning in listening and responding to the child.[1]

Some of the comments we got from the parents about commu-nication and transparency were:

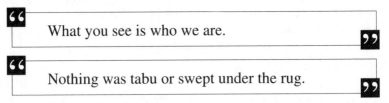

What you see is who we are.

Nothing was tabu or swept under the rug.

> We never let anything fester. We pick at it.

> We have always talked about everything, even if the timing wasn't the best.

It was obvious from what the kids said that they felt comfortable being open in their families:

> We were very frank about our failures. No one was afraid to stumble.

> About every two months we would just clear the air. Nothing was buried.

> When we got angry we didn't take it out by screaming or hollering—we talked it out verbally. We were blunt, straightforward.

> We could disagree with our parents all we wished. It was not so much differing, but *how* we differed that mattered.

While the children were still young, they taught them to stretch their wings.

7

HOLD THEM TIGHT, THEN TURN THEM LOOSE

Hodding Carter Sr. wrote,

> A wise woman once said to me that there are only two lasting
> bequests we can hope to give our children. One of these she
> said is roots, the other, wings. And they can only be grown,
> these roots and wings, *in the home.* [1]

Great families encourage both roots and wings.

The families we interviewed were made up of independent,
self-reliant people. They were both networked, recognizing that
they occasionally want and need others to help, *and* autonomous,
able to function self-sufficiently.

Mutual support was a high priority for these successful families.
Everyone supported everyone else. Mom and Dad functioned as a
team and supported each other's position. And even though it was a
struggle for a lot of these very busy, successful fathers, they made
time to support their kids' activities whenever possible. Almost

53

without exception, the children spoke about their fathers always being present at ball games, school activities, and special times. The fact that it took so much effort to arrange their schedules made it doubly precious. As one son said,

> **66**
> I knew he had a busy schedule, and it was really neat when he would take time to be just with me.
> **99**

Not only did Mom and Dad support the children, the children supported each other. In all of these families, the children call each other frequently if they live some distance away. They take pride in each other's accomplishments, and the whole family joins in celebrating any member's special occasions. One young man remembers with extra gratitude the fact that his sister came to his college graduation ceremony and sat on wooden bleachers for three hours just a week after having a baby.

As close and supportive as they were, they also encouraged *autonomy.* This surprised me a little. The very families who valued *closeness,* were the same ones who encouraged their children, at an earlier than usual age, to be independent. They kept their children close while they were young, and to the untrained eye, it might appear as if they were too close. But what made it work was that at the right time the children were launched—launched earlier than usual and made to be responsible. While the children were still young, they taught them to stretch their wings, and then released them to fly on their own as they grew older. (You'll see how they were able to do this in the chapters on "Motivation" and "Strategies of the Heart.")

As adults, the children remained connected to the family support system, but not so connected that they felt caught or entrapped. In fact, these families encouraged the children to become self-sufficient, so they could maintain the balance between being networked and self-governed. These people responded to the church in the same way—they were grateful and dependent on the church as a family, yet independent and free to study and think for themselves.

It might be helpful to take a moment to look at how failed families operate. They tend to produce one of two extremes: a family system that is *enmeshed* or a family system that is *disengaged.* The disengaged family member is frequently produced by absent, neglectful, or uncaring parents who allow their children to grow up with little or no supervision or control. This often happens with selfish, overworked parents or with single parents who are both overworked and underpaid.

▼

As adults, the children remained connected to the family support system, but not so connected that they felt caught or entrapped.

Enmeshed family members, on the other hand, are so entangled, so codependent on each other, that they can't think for themselves. Like dominoes stacked close to each other, when one falls, all the rest fall too. This type of family system usually includes a lot of family secrets.

On the other hand, Brenda Hunter warns against pushing for independence too quickly.

> Don't push your child into independence too early. Paradoxically, when he knows he has someone to rely on, he will become more self-reliant, better able to cope, and more motivated to be successful.[2]

Psychologist Robert Hampson gives a valuable mental picture of the right balance,

> Healthy families . . . provide a blend of the two styles. The satellite in orbit is a good analogy. They are not pulling too close or expelling too far. They are holding people in an orbit around the family, not too close, but not sending them to spin off and crash into the ocean either.[3]

The parents we interviewed grounded their children with "roots"—principles to live by and a strong loving environment, and then pushed them to try their "wings" when the time was right—wings made of high aspirations and dreams to carry them into the future.

▼

"It's not the losses that count, but how you deal with them."

8

LEARN TO COPE POSITIVELY
with Tragedy and Failure

A final message that came through loud and clear from these families was that they had learned how to cope with tragedy and failure in a positive way. These people were not victims, but *victors*.

It may seem as if successful families have everything going their way, that they lead a charmed life. Nothing could be further from the truth. The reason these families have been able to accomplish what they have is that they placed a high priority on overcoming problems and obstacles. They were not overwhelmed by difficulties or sorrows. They learned to cope positively with tragedy and failure. They persevered in spite of many negative, even desperate, circumstances. They *learned* to reframe, to make lemonade out of any lemons that were thrown at them.

Over half of those we surveyed had grown up poor, some extremely poor. One CEO was on his own when he was twelve years old. He had been in twelve different schools by the time he was in the sixth grade. Another grew up without electricity or indoor plumbing.

When one of the wives planned a "This Is Your Life" birthday party for her husband, she had to give it up when she discovered his earlier life. It was too sad to bring up. His father had died when he was three, and his mother had been institutionalized with a chronic illness when he was not much older. In high school, he worked forty-hour weeks and thirty-two hour weekends "just to survive." He stayed with many different relatives through his teen years.

▼

These people were not victims, but victors.

A number of these individuals grew up in dysfunctional homes with alcoholic parents. One mom grew up with only her mother and grandmother. She never knew her father. Several had lost parents at a young age, and a couple of them were reared in orphanages. Some came from families with multiple divorces.

Illness was a very real circumstance of life for many of these families. In one family, every one of the children had some kind of chronic health problem such as diabetes. Down's syndrome, dyslexia, detached retinas, seizures of unknown origin—all of these have affected children in the families we interviewed. Several of the families had lost children to accident, disease, or miscarriage. A close relative of one of the families was murdered, and her four children moved in with them. At the time of this writing, one of the mothers (about seventy years young) is undergoing treatment for recurring cancer and is now in her third series. But she doesn't let that keep her down. She just recently returned from scuba diving—one of her serious hobbies!

Many of the families had suffered from business difficulties and rejection as well. Some of the children didn't gain admission to the universities they had chosen. One CEO had been fired as president of a large high tech firm. A businessman had been defrauded by a fellow Christian, and he and his family had been forced to give up their lifestyle or declare bankruptcy. (They chose to give up their lifestyle, take several jobs, and pay off all of the creditors, even though they had been victims of a Christian brother's dishonesty.)

The church one family attended withdrew its fellowship (unjustly) from them. This couple believed some things and wanted to do some things that are widely accepted today, but that were not accepted in that congregation back then. The children remembered clearly how their father had stood up on their last Sunday in that church and prayed, with tears running down his face. It was the first time they had seen Mom or Dad cry in public. Even though the differences were worked out a year or so later, it was a very difficult year.

▼

Almost all of the families had dealt with normal adolescent rebellion.

They have all had their share of family problems, too. Almost all of the families had dealt with normal adolescent rebellion—kids wanting to date the wrong kind of person, having trouble with school work, being at odds with others in the family, having conflicts over rules. They have had to deal with differences in ability between the children and some religious differences. Through all of this, however, these families maintained the attitude of people who overcome, who learn from mistakes and problems, who can tolerate less than ideal. One father said,

> It's not the losses that count, but how you deal with them. 〞

There's a lot we can learn from these families about coping with tragedy, or "life's reverses." Even when life treated them "unfairly," they refused to give up. We can observe in them how victors handle "ill messages," not unlike Job in the Old Testament.

It's on the downside that we best learn to *reframe* and *reprioritize,* and to become *vulnerable, humble, adaptable,* and *empathetic.*

Reframe

First of all, we can learn not to develop a victim mind-set. As Dr. Howard Markman, professor at the University of Denver, would put it, survivors know how to "hunker down, instead of rolling over." Under pressure, survivors hunker down and prepare to launch themselves in a new and better direction. Dr. Markman points out that although 15 percent of adult children of alcoholics have a difficult time, we sometimes overlook the fact that 85 percent go on to lead happy, productive lives. How do they do it? Markman believes that the survivors have learned how to reframe their setting. They take their parents' drinking as a challenge instead of a defeat. They were emboldened by adversity. They elevated themselves through hardship.

▼

They were emboldened by adversity.

Ray Guarendi says,

> [good] parents refuse to remain victims of their own childhoods and resolve instead to rise above them. It is more than desire to avoid repeating their parents' mistakes. It is the determination to use painful memories to fuel the drive to become genuinely good parents despite a lack of childhood training.[1]

The inspired writer says,

> *In this you greatly rejoice, though now for a little while you may have had to suffer grief in all kinds of trials. These have come so that your faith—of greater worth than gold . . . may be proved genuine and may result in praise, glory and honor when Jesus Christ is revealed.*[2]

Writers often characterize these unusual people as *survivors.* I call them *overcomers* or *victors,* because they did more than survive, they overcame.

Reprioritize

When family and business tragedy struck Bob Buford, with God's help he learned to build on the ashes, and now he has blessed thousands of church leaders and business people in America through his seminars for entrepreneurs and church leaders.

When Ruth Ann Stallings, the wife of the nationally famous coach, Gene Stallings, gave birth to Johnny, who was disabled with Down's syndrome, it was no tragedy to dwell on. When I asked them, "Were there any turning points in your family?" the whole family, almost in unison, responded, "Oh yes! When Johnny was born!" The birth of Johnny allowed them to create a powerful "turning point" in the family. Because of Johnny's disabilities, the whole family was blessed to reprioritize their lives, to restate the question: "What is important and what is not?" It is no coincidence that Gene's favorite poem is Rudyard Kipling's "If," because it speaks of coping positively with life's trials.

> If you can keep your head when all about you
>   Are losing theirs and blaming it on you;
> If you can trust yourself when all men doubt you,
>   But make allowances for their doubting too;
> If you can wait and not be tired by waiting,
>   Or being lied about, don't deal in lies,
> Or being hated, don't give way to hating,
>   And yet don't look too good, nor talk too wise;
>
> If you can dream—and not make dreams your master;
>   If you can think—and not make thoughts your aim,
> If you can meet with Triumph and Disaster
>   And treat those two impostors just the same;
> If you can bear to hear the truth you've spoken
>   Twisted by knaves to make a trap for fools,
> Or watch the things you gave your life to, broken,
>   And stoop and build 'em up with worn-out tools;

If you can make one heap of all your winnings
    And risk it on one turn of pitch-and-toss,
And lose, and start again at your beginnings
    And never breathe a word about your loss;
If you can force your heart and nerve and sinew
    To serve your turn long after they are gone,
And so hold on when there is nothing in you
    Except the Will which says to them; "Hold on!"

If you can talk with crowds and keep your virtue,
    Or walk with Kings—not lose the common touch,
If neither foes nor loving friends can hurt you,
    If all men count with you, but none too much,
If you can fill the unforgiving minute
    With sixty seconds' worth of distance run,
Yours is the Earth and everything that's in it,
    And—which is more—you'll be a Man, my son!

On one summer vacation, Gene and Ruth set an expectation that all their children would memorize this poem, including Johnny (all four stanzas—thirty-two lines), and they did!

▼

When we become aware of how vulnerable we are, we are much more likely to be gracious and humble in spirit.

Become Vulnerable

When tragedy strikes, it hits the great and small. There are no exemptions. Tragedy, as nothing else, opens our eyes to our weakness, our frailness, how defenseless we really are. At times we all need this awareness, it helps us be more humble, more in touch, more sensitive.

Become Humble

When we become aware of how vulnerable we are, we are much more likely to be gracious and humble in spirit, "not thinking of ourselves more highly than we ought to think."[3] Compared to Christ, there is very little that separates the best of us from the worst of us.

▼

People who have been struck with tragedy develop an empathy that others don't have.

Become Adaptable

Tragedy brings to us the opportunity to change. My friend Mike LeFan, in his book *Patience My Foot,* tells about his tragedy of getting polio when just a child. The title of his book comes from the fact that the only thing, besides his head, that he can move is his *left foot.* But despite this tragedy, he has completed college, writes articles and books on his computer, runs his short wave radio and paints beautifully (I have one of his paintings)—and all this with his left foot! Indeed, he has adapted. He is not a victim of polio, he is a victor. As Gene Stallings said, "It is not what happens to you, it is how you look at what happens."

Become Empathetic

People who have been struck with tragedy develop an empathy that others don't have. Those who are in the midst of tragedy can tell instinctively when someone who has "been there" walks up. Somehow tragedy reveals itself to fellow sufferers—the empathy leaps the gap.

Yes, there is much we can learn from those who have learned how to cope with tragedy. One of the greatest victors in recent history is the great Soviet writer, Alexander Solzhenitsyn. Listen to his words:

What has happened, one wonders, to the older view that personal greatness is often forged into/by the flames of adversity? And do we no longer recognize a connection between the capacity for compassion and a person's own knowledge of suffering?[4]

In the Bible we read that the Son of Man must suffer and be rejected.[5] Who endured more stress in thirty-three years than Christ? Paul's prayer that the "thorn in the flesh" be removed was rejected.[6] First Peter is a whole book about how to respond under stress and suffering. With all of the misery, there are also real and lasting benefits to struggle and hardship. Malcolm Muggeridge said,

> I can say with complete truthfulness that everything I have learned in my 75 years in this world, everything that has truly enhanced and enlightened my experience, has been through affliction and not through happiness.

Solzhenitsyn, imprisoned with other dissidents, met prisoners like Dimitri Panin and Boris Kornfeld. The chapter in *The Gulag Archipelago* where Solzhenitsyn describes this visit and its impact on him may contain the most eloquent and moving words he has ever written. In his final words, Kornfeld spoke of transgression and suffering and of how suffering, more than anything else, develops one's soul. Prison, he discovered, had restored his soul. There in the camps, spiritual fires seared and, in the end, refined his soul. Forever after, he would look back with gratitude on his years in prison. "I nourished my soul there, and I say without hesitation: 'bless you, prison, for having been in my life.'" I think J. K. Gressett was correct when he said, "God prepares great men [and great families] for great tasks by great trials."

▼

"I say without hesitation: 'bless you, prison, for having been in my life.'"

Shortly after World War II, a horrible underground prison was uncovered in which the Germans had held captive a number of Jews. On one wall was an inscription which describes the indomitable spirit of survivors:

I believe in the sun, even if it doesn't shine.

I believe in love, even if it isn't shown.

I believe in God, even if He doesn't speak.[7]

Suffering makes us vulnerable, even as Christ was vulnerable. It puts us in the arena the highly successful lawyer termed "big league living." Struggle forces us to be adaptable, to refocus or prioritize our values. We have to reevaluate. A CEO and a father of five told us,

> 66 Our best work is when we are working against the wind. That is when we do our best work. 99

PARENTING THAT EMPOWERS

SECTION TWO

▼

"Everything is built around the parents."

> The role of father and mother . . . is the ab-
> solutely critical center of social force. Even when
> poverty and disorientation strike, as over the gen-
> erations they so often do, it is family strength that
> most defends individuals against alienation, lassi-
> tude, or despair. The world around the family is
> fundamentally unjust. The state and its agents,
> and the economic systems and its agencies, are
> never fully to be trusted. . . . One unforgettable
> law has been learned painfully through all the op-
> pressions, disasters, and injustices of the last
> thousand years: *if things go well with the family,
> life is worth living; when the family falters, life
> falls apart.*[1]

Even though our country sometimes loses sight of
this fact, the family is the crux of society. Parents *do*
have the power to make a difference. Molding, nur-
turing, and loving impressionable little lives is one of
the most noble ventures on earth. Don't ever underes-
timate the power of parenting.

9

THE POWER
OF PARENTING

The Power of the Parents

What sets really effective parents apart from the rest is their belief in the *power of parenting*. Effective parents recognize their power, and they don't give it up or delegate it to others—they assume it.

But too many parents have given up their power, and as a result, American families are in trouble. In fact, according to a poll taken in 1991 among the members of the American Psychological Association, the greatest threat to the mental health of Americans is the decline of the nuclear family.[2] Michael Novak, a well known writer and philosophy professor, states:

> The family is the original and most effective department of health, education and welfare. If it fails to teach honesty,

71

courage, the desire for excellence, and a host of basic skills, it is exceedingly difficult for any other agency to make up for its failures.

The family is a stronger agency of educational success than the school. The family is a stronger teacher of the religious imagination than the church. Political and social planning in a wise social order begin with the axiom: What strengthens the family strengthens society.[3]

The family is the bedrock institution in our society—in all societies. Its importance can't be overstated. As moms and dads, we must learn how to use the power of parenting; we cannot expect the government or any other institution to step in and rescue our families. It is up to us.

▼

What sets really effective parents apart from the rest is their belief in the power of parenting.

Armand Nicholi attests to the power of parenting:

> No human interaction has greater impact on our lives than our early family experience. If one factor influences the character development and emotional stability of a person, it is the quality of the relationship he experiences as a child with both of his parents. Conversely, if people suffering from severe non-organic emotional illness have one experience in common, it is the absence of a parent through death, divorce, a time-demanding job, or for some other reason. A parent's inaccessibility either physically, emotionally, or both, can exert a profound influence on the child's emotional health.[4]

In my travels, I hear from a number of parents who don't believe they have much influence on their kids. They say things like, "Their friends take them away from us; drugs take them away. Nothing I say counts. I'm just here to feed 'em and give 'em money." But nothing could be further from the truth. Studies in this area validate that *parents* are the most powerful influence in a child's life. Nothing else comes close!

A survey of teens and spirituality by Drs. David Lewis and Carley Dodd[5] found that of the three thousand plus teenagers surveyed, 69 percent said that the *strongest influence* on their spirituality was Mom and Dad. The next highest influence wasn't even close: youth ministers came in a distant second at 11 percent. That's quite a drop! The message is clear: Mom and Dad are at the top of the list.

An article in the *Journal of Marriage and Family* states,

> Some parents believe *they* have a major impact upon their child's values, self-concept, and life choices, while others maintain that factors largely outside of their control, such as personality, peer group, etc., are more important.

The following report from J. Allan Petersen should convince any remaining skeptics concerning the power of parenting.

> Max Jukes lived in New York. He did not believe in Christ or in Christian training. He refused to take his children to church, even when they asked to go. He has had 1,029 descendants; 300 were sent to prison for an average term of 13 years; 190 were public prostitutes; 680 were admitted alcoholics. His family, thus far, has cost the state in excess of $420,000. They made no contribution to society.
>
> Jonathon Edwards lived in the same state at the same time. He loved the Lord to the best of his ability. He has had 929 descendants, of whom 430 were ministers; 86 became university professors; 13 became university presidents; 75 authored good books; 5 were elected to the U.S. Congress and 2 to the Senate. One was Vice President of the U.S. His family never cost the state one cent but has contributed immeasurably to their nation.[6]

While at a convention, I was privileged to witness a "This Is Your Life" review of one of the division heads. When it came time for his son to speak, he said: "Many people see Joe Montana or Michael Jordan as their hero. I see my dad as a hero."

The parents we interviewed were among those who believed in their power to make a difference. One of the best testimonies came from one of the kids,

66 Everything is built around the parents. **99**

The Power of Modeling

The power of modeling lies in its *accuracy*. Words are difficult to understand and interpret: rules are often perceived as orders, and guidelines may be interpreted as hard and fast laws. But sacrificial models are seen accurately. The parents we interviewed modeled the people they wanted their children to be, showing them what it looked like to take the higher road.

▼

A child is a little video camera on legs.

This is the same method God used. God sent Jesus to show us what he meant. Jesus said, "If you have seen me, you have seen the Father." God knew that we needed a model with "skin on"— not just a list of rules and guidelines. God knows how we are: "Monkey see, monkey do!" It's crazy how we copy others without even thinking about it. One of my sons spreads peanut butter evenly to every corner of his bread, just like he saw me do while he was growing up. Now one of his daughters is doing the same thing. And how often have you heard children, when told not to do something, say, "But, Daddy does it. . . ."

A child is a little video camera on legs. Their *recorder* is going all the time, and the pictures of the parents that are recorded need to be consistent with the words, or there will be a trust problem. Your child's video needs to see quality in the home, because what is recorded plays for the rest of the child's life. You'll get to see a replay of that video when you are about forty and your children are grown—you'll see them imitating *you* in their lives.

One young man we interviewed said,

> ❝
> My mom's garage is the only garage in the world that is mopped. ❞

Mom probably wasn't aware that her son noticed her mopping the garage, but his little camera caught it all.

My own father never knew I was recording as he cut cardboard from the Post Toasties boxes to fit into his shoes during depression days, so he could put off half-soling them a little longer and still not wear out his socks. I remember going with my mother to take clothes to the poor and sharing what little we had, even though my dad brought home wilted, limp carrots and wrinkly potatoes for our table from the little grocery store he owned. My camera was running.

My mother was a great prayer model. When I was a teenager and acting out a bit, it was her prayers that kept me in line. Her legacy of prayer was passed on to my wife. When one of our own sons was acting out in high school—really giving us concern—I told him, "You're not going to get away with this!"

▼

The children we interviewed kept talking about how their parents lived.

"What do you mean," he retorted, "not get away with this?" (You need to know that this guy was big—6'5", and 200 or more pounds. He came complete with hair down his back, a pickup truck, a gun rack, a Saint Bernard dog, and a bigger beard than Grizzly Adams.)

"You're not going to get away from my mother's prayers. When I was your age, she wrapped me in a cobweb of prayer, and I didn't have a chance; and now she's praying for *you*. And not only are you wrapped in her prayers, you're covered with the prayers of your mother and me. You are so covered in a web of prayers, you'll never be able to get loose! You can forget it. You're caught." Those prayers got him through high school and college, and now he's wrapping his own two children in a network of prayers.

The children we interviewed kept talking about how their parents *lived*—their servant hearts were manifested in what they *did*, not only in what they *said*. A young lawyer, the son of a CEO, said, "We were always taking things to shut-ins as we were growing up." They regularly ministered to widows; and at Christmas time, the whole family was involved in delivering gifts to others.

Sure enough, it "caught," because several of those children are now doing the same kinds of deeds with their children that Dad and Mom did with them.

The son of a corporate vice president of an international firm said,

> Mother and Dad had a fantastic influence on our lives by living a Christian life, by talking about religion, and by teaching Sunday school classes.

Other kids also told us how their parents modeled service.

> They visited nursing homes, kept unwed mothers in our home, and took in foster children. They gave time, money, and effort to charities— not just to church work.

> Dad taught a Bible class on Sunday morning, and he was always working on his lesson. Mom and Dad were always helping and teaching others. This motivated us to serve.

A grown son commented,

> I try to live my Christianity in the business world, just like my dad did.

Christianity, unlike other religions, is most significant in that the Son of God came to this earth to model for us what the ideal life is like, how it is lived, and how one behaves under fire—it is all there in living color—rugged cross and all. Without the model, there is no Christianity.

First Samuel 2:21 speaks of how Samuel "grew up in the presence of the Lord." I think that implies how all children should grow up: by seeing God incarnate, as it were, in their own parents.

A beautiful model *draws* us to follow. A father may command, but he cannot draw his son to read the Bible if the father is not reading himself.

The words of the Old Testament still ring true: "To this day their children and grandchildren continue to do as their fathers did." [7] The key to parenting, then, is to "walk our talk," so that if the children follow in our steps, they really won't go far off the path. We have got to be that model, that straight stick that they can line up with. Dorothy Nolte was right when she wrote, "Children learn what they live."

The Power of Teamwork

When a team works right, there is a kind of synergism generated that makes the unit more effective than either part alone. The parents we interviewed had learned to function as a team. They blocked for each other and defended one another and worked with one another. As one dad told us, "We are *together.*" This couple worked so well as a team that they had even learned to wallpaper together and play tennis together. (I flunked the tennis test with Gladys, but I passed the wallpaper test.)

Another husband and wife told us how they had worked together to formulate a philosophy regarding religion, beliefs, child rearing—the whole nine yards. The best testimony to their success came out of the time when Mom had to leave the five children for a whole month with Dad while she helped out with a family illness. "I never heard one word of criticism from him," she said. One executive, a father of four, said,

> The greatest gift we ever gave our children was a great marriage.

Mom and Dad need time together

This kind of teamwork does not come without deliberate effort. In order to create the cohesiveness necessary for powerful teamwork, the moms and dads we interviewed made sure that they spent regular time *together*—we're not talking about sexual time —although that's important too—we're talking about a time when

Mom and Dad sat down together, looked each other in the eye, and *talked.* For some, this was a special weekly date or just having a cup of coffee together before the kids got up. It sounds simple, but it's so easy to put off.

▼

Mom and Dad sat down together, looked each other in the eye, and *talked.*

When parents are juggling the needs and demands of small children and the pressure of time-consuming careers, the important "together times" often get pushed aside or postponed. It is essential for parents to have a common philosophy, a singular way of looking at life, child rearing, and marriage. Two different people don't become one easily. It takes regular, consistent communication to smooth out the differences that naturally exist between two people. It takes time to make two into one—one in heart, thought, direction, aims, and purpose.

Focus and refocus on what is important—over and over again! Take time to plan, to think about your mission as Mom and Dad. If this is done, almost everything else in your life will be easier. When the two of you agree on a game plan, you can start the day with smiles on your faces, and you can handle the daily decisions and challenges of parenting.

Mom and Dad need time alone

As important as time together is, don't forget that a team is only as strong as the individuals who make it up. To be an effective team member, these parents knew that they must also make time for themselves individually. Everybody needs time to recalibrate and to rethink, especially about priorities and values—things that really count. God put a very high premium on the Sabbath rest. He understood that rest time to be very significant. Perhaps we are overlooking the biblical principle of having a quiet time in our day. There is healing in silence. We know that even in a therapeutic situation, distraught people are calmed when put in a quiet room with no distractions.

This strategy is as old as David, who wrote about sitting out in the fields observing the stars. It is as old as Solomon, who pondered the ways of the ants and the sloths. A number of the parents we interviewed spent time in nature observing God's creation. Some, like my own mother, made time for themselves by reading late at night or early in the morning. Music and devotional time functioned well for still others. If I don't spend some time early in the morning in meditation, Bible reading, and keeping a journal, I am convinced that my day doesn't go as well. My priorities and focus are greatly enhanced by a daily quiet time. Whatever method we use, all of us need some quiet time, time apart, time in prayer—some *think* and *rethink* time.

▼

Everybody needs time alone—to recalibrate and to rethink.

Parents have a power for good in the lives of their children that no one else has. During one interview, the children talked about their mother's devotional time and how much she prayed and studied the Word. The mother was a little surprised that they knew about her prayer time. She had never talked about it much, and she thought they had always been asleep when she had her quiet time.

"How did you know about the time I spent praying and studying?"

"We saw your knee prints in the carpet by the big chair in your bedroom. We saw your Bible open there on the table, and it was worn from use."

There *is* power in parenting! Don't let yours go to waste.

"Mothers are the first book read and the last book put aside in every child's library."

10

THE INTENTIONAL MOTHER

In order for Greg Louganis to win two gold medals in succeeding Olympics (and be the first person ever to do that in diving), he must do *this* dive perfectly. Greg is standing on the diving platform in the 1988 Olympics, ten meters above the water, ready to make his last dive. He is the last diver of the day, and he is following young Xiang Ni, the Chinese diver who currently has the leading score. Ni, just moments before, had beautifully executed the same dive that Greg must do. (Do you remember the tension of that moment?) Greg has a bruised wrist and a cut on the back of his head from an earlier dive, and his stomach is giving him trouble. Greg pauses a moment before he steps up. Then he rips the dive—powerfully, flawlessly, and he wins it!

A reporter asked him, "What were you thinking about, standing up there on that platform?"

"Well, I was thinking: If I don't win, my mother will still love me." The bond between a mother and her child is a powerful thing.

Judith Viorst tells of her visit to a children's hospital. She came upon a little boy with burns over 60 percent of his body. Someone had poured coal oil on his body and set him on fire. In his pain, he was crying out for his mother . . . even though it was his *mother* who had set him on fire. The bond between a mother and child is truly an amazing force.

With that bond comes the power for good or ill, and the influence of her power is passed on for generations to come.

▼

"If I don't win, my mother will still love me."

A nurse who had worked on the front lines during a war told me that mortally wounded young men always cry out for their mothers. "I never once heard them call for anyone else. It was always *mother.*" In those great victories when the football hero crosses the line, smashes the ball down on the goal line, and looks into the camera, what does he say? "Hi, Mom!" What power do mothers hold over 265 pound behemoths? The bond between a mother and her child is great. *Truly, the hand that rocks the cradle, rules the world.*

The Heart of the Home

While the bond between mother and child comes about almost *naturally*—unintentionally—the moms we interviewed were anything but unintentional. They *worked* at being great moms. They planned and set goals—they were *intentional.* These women were the very *heart* of the home.

Spirit

While fathers who are active in their Christianity have a tremendous influence on their adult children's church attendance, one study found that the number-one influence on faith for both men and women was their mothers.[1] The children in the families we interviewed knew where their mothers' hearts were.

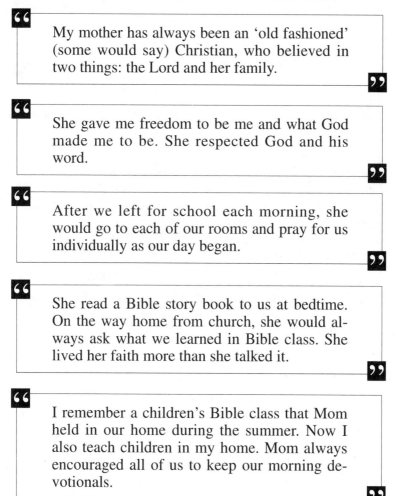

> My mother has always been an 'old fashioned' (some would say) Christian, who believed in two things: the Lord and her family.

> She gave me freedom to be me and what God made me to be. She respected God and his word.

> After we left for school each morning, she would go to each of our rooms and pray for us individually as our day began.

> She read a Bible story book to us at bedtime. On the way home from church, she would always ask what we learned in Bible class. She lived her faith more than she talked it.

> I remember a children's Bible class that Mom held in our home during the summer. Now I also teach children in my home. Mom always encouraged all of us to keep our morning devotionals.

When we asked these children, "What is the most important thing to your mom?" most all the responses concerned their mother's faith in God.

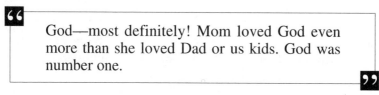

> God—most definitely! Mom loved God even more than she loved Dad or us kids. God was number one.

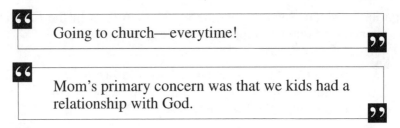

> " Going to church—everytime! "

> " Mom's primary concern was that we kids had a relationship with God. "

About a hundred years ago, the great religious historian William Ramsay wrote,

> We can indeed see with certainty, in comparing nation with nation and religion with religion, that one of the most important forces in the progress of society lies in the education which the mother conveys to her children. [A nation] cannot maintain itself on that [high moral] plane unless its women rise to it and kindle and foster similar ideas in the minds of succeeding generations when young.

I read an article the other day about a boy who stabbed a girl nineteen times and when asked, "How did you feel?" he replied, "I didn't feel anything." Mothers are desperately needed to transmit Christian values to children.

Emotion

Another thing we found throughout these families was that Mother was the emotional hub of the family. Emotions, even passion, are *so* essential to life. A marching band, a sentimental poem, a gospel hymn—all evoke emotion. Moms have a way of showing their own emotions and tapping into the emotions of others that is central to a warm, loving home.

The children in these homes felt loved and cared for. Listen to some of their comments.

> " I remember her sweet kisses every night at bedtime. "

> " Mom tucked us in bed every night—even up to the day before we got married. "

> Dad gave me the gift of wisdom and strength and the mechanics of life. Mom gave me the gift of feelings and warmth. She taught me how to have compassion on people. She taught me a side of God I would not have learned without her.

All of us remember times we burned our fingers on a hot stove or our hands were frost bitten or we had an earache, and the first thing we did was run to mother—because she provided the emotional balm we needed.

The unconditional, never-ending love of mother was a reliable constant in these families—no matter how hectic their lives.

> There was *never* a time when we doubted that we were loved.

> Even when she was upset with us, we always knew she would get over it. We knew she loved us unconditionally.

It was interesting to note the effect of Mother's *tears* on these children. One daughter said,

> Every single time I came home from a date or any activity, Mama was looking for me and waiting to hear about it. Once I was four (yes, *four*) minutes late. Mama was sitting on the sofa crying when I walked in the door. I wasn't late anymore. Daddy's belt put the fear into me, but Mama's tears were worse!

A son told about the time he came home from a week-long ski trip. When his mom asked him how his trip was, he gave the typical, teenage boy answer—"Fine." He didn't know it at the time, but this really bothered his mother. After picking him up from school one day, she drove him to the back of the farm and parked the car so they could talk. She opened her heart to him and told him how important he was to her and that she wanted to know more about his life than just "fine." Of course, during the conversation, tears mingled with words. Now he hadn't seen Mom cry a lot—she didn't use tears as a weapon to manipulate her family—so this son knew that she was really baring her heart. The boy said that this was a special eye-opening time for him. (By the way, he also said he's a lot more thoughtful now and tries to be more open with his mom.)

▼

Do you get the idea that these moms made their kids feel special?

Presence

We heard over and over from these children: "Mother was always there for me." This was not confined to her physical presence, but encompassed the moral support and encouragement she provided. Mom was a constant in their lives—no matter what!

One son wrote us a letter about his mother. Listen to what he said,

> **66**
> My mother was always there. Whether it was for school or for church, at home or away, my mother was there. It did not seem to matter to her whether I was a superstar or an also-ran; she was there. My mother was a constant in my world, which in my formative years was ever changing. **99**

Other children said,

> Mom was there everyday when I got home from school.

> When I came home from school, my first word was *Mom?*

In my own life, wherever Gladys is, I am home. Gladys means *home.* If she's out of town, our house is empty and lonely, but even a hotel room is home if Gladys is there. That haunting phrase, "going home," conjures up powerful memories—not of brick and wood—but of people: people with smiles, tears, and talk—lots of talk—and people who welcome you, recognize you, and own you as an indispensable part of the clan.

When we asked the children what they remembered most about their moms, we got responses like these,

> I just remember that she was *always there, always smiling,* and *always a comfort.* If there was one thing we could all count on, it was that Mom would be there and that she would always make things better.

> The biggest thing I remember is she was always there for me, like when I fell and got hurt or when someone called me names at school.

> My mom always forgives me, loves me, and believes in me.

Cheerleader

In order to be a cheerleader, you have to be at the game! Over and over we got the sense from these families that Mom was right there involved in all the kids' activities. She was their encourager, their enthusiast, and their support.

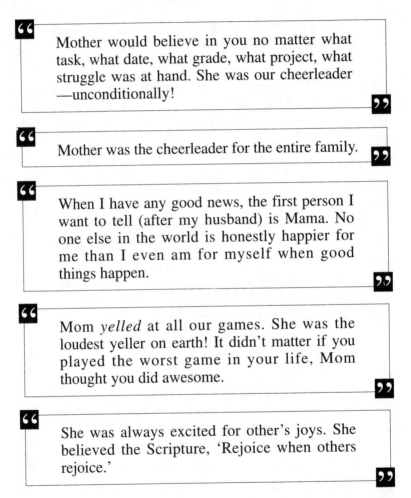

> Mother would believe in you no matter what task, what date, what grade, what project, what struggle was at hand. She was our cheerleader —unconditionally!

> Mother was the cheerleader for the entire family.

> When I have any good news, the first person I want to tell (after my husband) is Mama. No one else in the world is honestly happier for me than I even am for myself when good things happen.

> Mom *yelled* at all our games. She was the loudest yeller on earth! It didn't matter if you played the worst game in your life, Mom thought you did awesome.

> She was always excited for other's joys. She believed the Scripture, 'Rejoice when others rejoice.'

Do you get the idea that these moms made their kids feel special? Is it any wonder that so many of them have grown up to be responsible, godly men and women with good families of their own? The encouragement and support that came from Mom was evident in every family we interviewed.

> Mom always tried to make everyone feel important. She *never* put down any of my ideas. She always encouraged me.

> She wasn't slow to tell us we were smart or good looking. She let us know she thought we were wonderful and capable of doing whatever we chose. She was proud of us.

> She has stood by me with encouragement and support, only offering advice when asked, and loving me when I wasn't entirely lovable.

> One thing I know for certain, regardless of what I do or become (or don't do), Mom will always be proud of me. I *know* she will!

> Mama believed in us so much that we were convinced we could do anything. I don't know how she managed it, but she made each one of us certain that we were the absolute brightest, best, most godly, most talented kid in the whole world.

Before we leave this idea of Mom being a cheerleader for her children, I have to tell you that these women were cheerleaders for their husbands as well.

These significant women understood some of the special pressures that their husbands faced. Many of their husbands were in high pressure jobs—the kind where there's always another test, always more quotas to fill. More productivity is pushed, and finally if one year the company doesn't raise the quota, it's liable to cut the territory in half the next year; and they fear that they'll not be able to provide for their family. One administrator said to me, "You never finish." And as Dr. Robert Weiss, an authority in this field has said, "The stress these fathers feel from work is often severe." [2] These women understood the particular pressures their husbands faced and were their constant support.

While Gladys and I interviewed one of the physicians, he leaned over and took his wife's hand and said to Gladys and me, "You'll never know how much I appreciate this dear lady. I don't know how many of our regular Thursday night dates got canceled. We would get all dressed up to go to out for an evening and the phone would ring. It would be the emergency room saying that the doctor who was covering for me was overloaded and asking if I would please come and help out. And my wife, this sweet lady, would turn to me and say, 'You need to go.' And she would go back and take off her nice clothes and put on her robe and get a book or spend time with her children."

▼

These significant women understood some of the special pressures that their husbands faced.

Some of these husbands worked long hours (fifty to ninety hour weeks were not uncommon), but the wives understood that this was what their jobs required, and as you will see in the next chapter, they also knew their husbands had the family at heart. These women made sure their children knew that they supported and admired their husbands and were 100 percent behind them.

One son spoke lovingly about his mother,

> **66**
> Whenever Dad was on a trip, Mom would talk about how wonderful Dad was and how lucky us kids were to have such a wonderful father. I used to think, 'I can't wait till I'm old enough to go on a trip and have Mom say all those wonderful things about me.'
> **99**

One mother said,

> I not only 'let' him work those long hours, I was an encouragement to him, because I knew and he knew that neither of us liked it, but we also knew there were some things we had to put up with in order to get a business started.

Positive support and encouragement was typical of these women. One husband said, "You'll never know how much it meant to me, more than anything in the world, that she never complained about my long hours and time out-of-town."

One of the neatest expressions of this support was when one of the children said there were "no long sighs" in our house. In other words, the mother would not sigh and say "Will these long hours ever stop?" or "Why can't you spend more time with me?"

Mom was the cheerleader for the whole family.

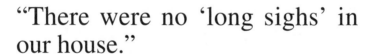

"There were no 'long sighs' in our house."

Prioritizer

No doubt about it—*family came first* to these moms. Their lives were full and productive, but *nothing*—except the Lord—came before their families.

One daughter said,

> I don't really remember Momma running around with other women friends. She was in the business of raising a family of four daughters who were going to have to get out in the world one day—and that she did!—with flying colors!

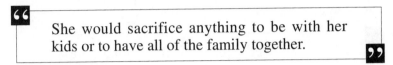

> She would sacrifice anything to be with her kids or to have all of the family together.

One son said,

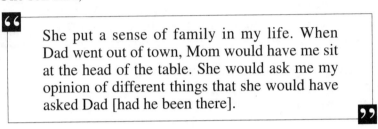

> She put a sense of family in my life. When Dad went out of town, Mom would have me sit at the head of the table. She would ask me my opinion of different things that she would have asked Dad [had he been there].

This mom knew how important it was to instill a sense of family in her children, even when Dad couldn't be there. What an esteem builder for that son!

One daughter eloped when she got married—didn't even tell her mom and dad about it beforehand. But she told us that when she and her new husband came home, Mom greeted them with a hug and a broad smile. The daughter said,

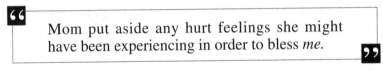

> Mom put aside any hurt feelings she might have been experiencing in order to bless *me*.

One of the other kids said,

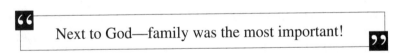

> Next to God—family was the most important!

One way that these moms made it evident that family came first was by their servant attitude, and they taught their kids how to serve others by their example.

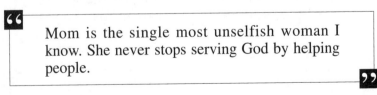

> Mom is the single most unselfish woman I know. She never stops serving God by helping people.

> " Without a doubt Mom is the most unselfish person I have ever met. She consistently puts everyone else's needs and wants above her own. "

One of the kids told us that one of his earliest memories of his mother was going with her when he was three or four years old to visit an elderly shut-in woman from church.

> " I recall being frightened of the woman at first, but Mom made me talk to her, and we all ate lunch together. We ate chicken noodle soup, and this elderly woman 'slurped' her noodles! Mom and I were so surprised! The woman laughed and made us promise not to tell anyone. It was a neat experience and a great introduction into caring for other people. "

▼

A spirit of fun ran thoughout these families.

Humorist

The fact that so many of these kids said their moms were fun to be with comes as no surprise. A spirit of fun ran throughout these families.

> " Mom's excitement was extremely contagious. She brought her excitement along on the yearly summer family vacation that Mom would carefully plan, pack, and prepare for. What adventures! "

One family had a particularly fun mom. All the brothers we spoke with said similar things:

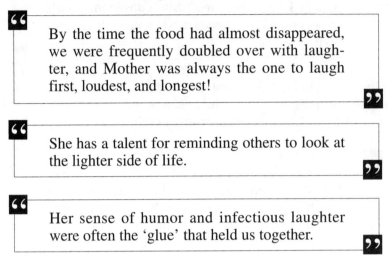

> By the time the food had almost disappeared, we were frequently doubled over with laughter, and Mother was always the one to laugh first, loudest, and longest!

> She has a talent for reminding others to look at the lighter side of life.

> Her sense of humor and infectious laughter were often the 'glue' that held us together.

And the most beautiful thought on the *benefits* of laughter came from one of these sons. He was explaining how he and his brothers would try to outdo each other in their attempts to entertain Mother, and he said,

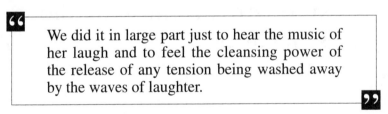

> We did it in large part just to hear the music of her laugh and to feel the cleansing power of the release of any tension being washed away by the waves of laughter.

"The music of her laugh," and the "cleansing power of release"—Wow!

A boy from another family laughingly told us about seeing his mom climb a tree after his younger brother who had already broken his leg three times. She was determined he wasn't going to fall out of that tree and break it again, so she went up after him.

Unique Attributes of Mothers

In case some of you haven't noticed, God has made men and women different! Women do seem to have some special attributes that are especially useful in the home.

Sensitivity

Men and women are just wired differently. Women are wired at about 440 volts. I mean, they've got four hundred wires sticking out all over their heads—reaching out to touch and contact other people. Men on the other hand, seem to be wired at about 12 volts. (Well, men *are* wired at high voltage in *one* area.) Other than that, men have one or two wires sticking out, and they tend to be bent.

▼

Mothers just naturally have big eyes and big ears and long sticky antennas.

Mothers just naturally have big eyes and big ears and long sticky antennas. They have that sixth sense, that sensitivity, that awareness, that big picture, that allows them to know what's going on with their kids—wherever they are. But fathers tend to have little eyes and little ears and little or no antennas. Men do have the ability to focus, but their focus tends to be linear, like a laser beam. Their concentrated focus can help them accomplish great things; but in rearing children, mothers have the advantage of being able to "receive" the bigger picture on their sensitive antennas.

A report in *Time* magazine talked about the "corpus callosum," a portion of the brain. This research indicates that some of these differences are physical and that

> the corpus callosum, a thick bundle of nerves that allows the right half of the brain to communicate with the left, is larger in women than in men. If it is, and if size corresponds to function, then the greater cross talk between the hemispheres might ex-

plain the enigmatic phenomena like female intuition, which is supposed to accord women greater ability to read emotional clues.[3]

Lewis Smedes well describes that special sensitivity that most women have.

> They visit good friends and hear delicate signals that all is not well; so they guard their tongues, and say nothing that could make things worse. She senses that her husband is keeping something from her, that he is secretly sulking behind his usual grumpy exterior, and she soon catches faint hints that he is having trouble at the job; so she makes sure that she does not blurt out something that could make him feel worse.[4]

▼

Mom always knew what they had been doing and where they had been.

Children are often amazed at how mother seems to know all that is going on in their lives. Several of the children we interviewed said Mom always knew what they had been doing and where they had been. Sometimes they laughingly admitted that maybe she knew too much about their activities. When one son would ask his mom how she knew these things, she would always say "Oh, a little bird told me."

One of the sons was telling us how important truth was to his mother, and then he said,

> 66
> She *always* knew if we weren't telling the truth.
> 99

Switchboard

Another unique gift God gave to mothers is the ability to keep the family *connected*—to keep the different members in tune with each other.

One of our mothers said,

> I'm always like the switchboard in the family—keeping people hooked up to each other.

You hear mothers saying things to their husbands like, "Can you take Ken with you this morning?" or "We really do need to go see Aunt Clara this weekend, we haven't been with her lately." She may ask Dad to take the kids to school just so he can be with the children. Women are more inclined to write letters to family members, to send cards and thinking-of-you notes. In fact, in many families, the wife is the one who keeps in touch with her *husband's* family, as well as her own.

These moms knew how to keep the family connected, even when they were apart. One thirty-year-old man was recalling how his mother kept them connected with his father when he was away.

> She spoke for our daddy when he was away. She would say, 'Now, your daddy thinks you are doing great. He is so proud of you.'

After she talked with Dad on the phone at night, she would let the kids know that she and Dad had been talking about them. She kept the family close even though there was a distance in time or place. Mom provided the hooks that held the family together.

One way the moms we interviewed kept the family in touch was to plan activities for the family to do together. One child talked about the family nights that mom initiated and planned. Another family told us how they would get together with the extended family for lunch on Sunday afternoons. The brothers in one family recalled raking leaves in the yard with mom. This, too, was a way for the family to be together.

Communicator

Moms are often better at communicating than men. This unique gift is another way to keep the family close and connected. One son said,

> Mom always tried to draw details out of me—whether it was about my day, a game, or a date.

Another son told us how he and Mom used to go on walks together and *talk*. Walking together is often an ideal way to initiate communication. Sometimes, it's easier to talk when someone is walking *beside* you instead of standing *in front of you*. Perhaps this gives us a little space and a little less pressure.

▼

Their aimless "prattle" may seem a waste of our precious time, but we are storing up for the years ahead.

These moms were also good *listeners*. One daughter wrote this in a sweet note to her mom,

> You always listen to me brag to you, cry to you, and talk about myself.

One daughter told of going through a particularly hard time as an adult.

> My mom would listen and hug me and tell me that things would work out. She was such a good listener. I would fill up on my mother's love and would then have the strength to go on.

If we want our children to come to us as teenagers and young adults, we have to begin by listening to them when they are small. At that time their aimless "prattle" may seem a waste of our precious time, but we are storing up for the years ahead when their conversation will concern crucial life issues. You've got to start the habit of *listening* while they are young.

Systemic wonder

Another unique ability a woman has is the ability to manage and juggle several activities and roles at the same time—she's what I call a systemic wonder. She's like that circus guy who spins plates on those long sticks—you remember. He gets one started, then another, then another, and he keeps all those plates spinning on the top of those sticks until he gets fifteen or twenty or thirty of those things going. Women are much like that. They can keep all kinds of plates going—driving the car pool, taking care of sick kids, helping with homework, preparing meals, doing housework and church work, and often holding down a job.

▼

She's like that circus guy who spins those plates on those long sticks.

Men on the other hand, because of their single vision and their focus, which is intense and powerful, usually pick out one plate to spin—but, boy can they spin that plate! And when they spin it, they are so proud of their plate, and they want to spin it harder and faster than anybody else. They say to their wives, "Hey, honey, look at my plate!" And their wives (keeping their eyes on their fifteen plates) reply, "Oh, yes, sweetheart, you are doing *such* a good job!" (In all fairness to men, some of their plates really are *big* and heavy and do require a lot of focus.)

I remember an experiment a professor did in his class. First he described the following scene: A man comes in the front door and sees his wife standing at the kitchen sink. The sink is stopped up, the soup is boiling over, one child is on her hip and another screaming child has pulled her shorts down to her knees. Then the professor asked the men: "What would you do?" Almost in unison they said "Why, we would ask if there was anything we could do to help." The women responded in unified disgust, "Kill the guys!" In their estimation, the men shouldn't have to *ask* what needs doing, it should be *evident*. Somehow, women are able to see and feel what needs doing and move in that direction.

One daughter summed up what we heard from many of the kids.

> 66
> My dad did (and still does) travel a lot, and my mom handled that situation well. She was always in control, and she always managed to go to everyone's games and recitals and manage the house at the same time. My mom was often the authority figure, but she was always a great friend to all three of the kids. I did a lot of stuff with my mom—we often played tennis together, shopped together, and ran all of our errands together, even all the way through high school. My mom was also a mom and a friend to all of my friends. It seems like our house was the community house—our friends would come and just sit around and talk with my mom. Everyone loves my mom!
> 99

Motherhood actually requires highly efficient management skills. Sally Helgesen, author of *Megatrends for Women* says,

> Increasingly, motherhood is being recognized as an excellent school for managers, demanding many of the same skills: organization, pacing, the balancing of conflicting claims, teaching, guiding, leading, monitoring, handling the disturbances, imparting information.[5]

Helgesen goes on to say,

> The ability to tolerate ambiguity and juggle many things at once often attributed to women, is a vital, but often underrated, management skill.[6]

In other words, businesses are beginning to recognize that the skills required for motherhood are valuable in management of business, as well as the home. Peter Drucker, the management guru, once said that his nominee for president of General Motors would be Frances Hesselbein, the top executive for Girl Scouts of America. Hesselbein brought *networking* into top level management, and this is now the management style of preference for the twenty-first century.

▼

"Motherhood is an excellent school for managers."

One interesting observation comes from researcher Carol Gilligan about the difference in how men and women define their identities.

> These highly successful women do not mention their academic and professional distinctions in the context of describing themselves. If anything, they regard their professional activities as jeopardizing their own sense of themselves. For a woman, identity is defined in the context of relationships.[7]

A woman's style is relational, bridge-building, systemic. That's why she is so vital in the role of connector and communicator in her family.

Strengths

We found that the women we interviewed were an incredible source of strength and fortitude. They had a quiet strength and sense of purpose that was a major support for their families. We heard these comments from some of the children.

> 66
> I believe that Mom is the only reason Dad kept trudging through some difficult times at work; for several years, she was his strength.
> 99

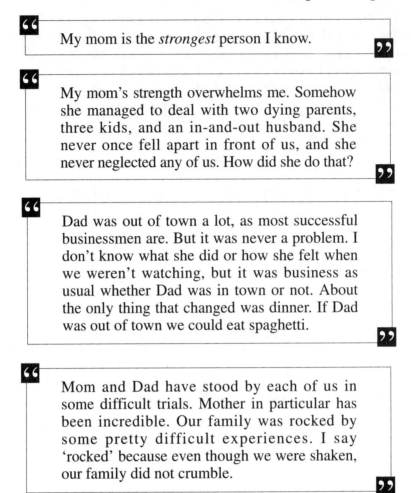

> " My mom is the *strongest* person I know. "

> " My mom's strength overwhelms me. Somehow she managed to deal with two dying parents, three kids, and an in-and-out husband. She never once fell apart in front of us, and she never neglected any of us. How did she do that? "

> " Dad was out of town a lot, as most successful businessmen are. But it was never a problem. I don't know what she did or how she felt when we weren't watching, but it was business as usual whether Dad was in town or not. About the only thing that changed was dinner. If Dad was out of town we could eat spaghetti. "

> " Mom and Dad have stood by each of us in some difficult trials. Mother in particular has been incredible. Our family was rocked by some pretty difficult experiences. I say 'rocked' because even though we were shaken, our family did not crumble. "

What a remarkable testimony to the strength that Mom can provide. "We were shaken, but we did not crumble!"

My own mother was an amazing source of strength. During the depression when Dad couldn't find a job and times were really tough, my sister developed an infection that the sulfa drugs of that day couldn't kill. (It was before the days of penicillin.) My sis had had seven operations and twenty-one blood transfusions. Before it was all over, she had a number of ribs and one lobe of her lung removed—those were tough, tough times. Lying in her hospital bed, Sis overheard my parents talking to a doctor. (They didn't know she could hear them.) The doctor said that there was no more they could do for her there. Her only hope was to go to a specialist in St. Louis, which was clear across the country.

▼

"We were shaken, but we did not crumble!"

Jean heard my daddy say, "There's just no way we can afford to do that. I don't have a job, we've borrowed all we can—all the money is *gone.*"

But mother said, "Somehow, this child *will* have the help she needs." Soon, an unexpected opportunity came that enabled Mother to go to St. Louis—free! She *walked* all the way across that city to see a top physician who did the kind of surgery Sis needed. Through this visit she learned that a qualified doctor was moving near our home, and Mother made all the arrangements. A woman with no clout, no power, and no hope, worked it out for Sis to have that operation after seven long years. Mother willed it, and it came to be.

Fortitude of single mothers

Single mothers really have it tough. Whether they are widows or have been divorced, they are usually left to care for two or three children—alone. I have talked with hundreds of these mothers in the last few years, and they're growing in number because of the increased divorce rate. I want to take just a moment to tip my hat to them and to challenge the rest of us to do what we can to help these special mothers. We need to reach out to them with a helping hand. We can become surrogate grandparents, aunts, uncles, brothers, and sisters.

Business sometimes deals especially harshly with single moms. A close friend of my research assistant was fired for staying with a sick child who was in the hospital. She was divorced and had no benefits. Sure, the company needed a worker who would be there consistently; so that just means that some of us have to pitch in and help out—these children are our most precious commodity.

Let's take a moment to look at some of the ways the amazing grit and fortitude of the women we interviewed came shining through.

Trained children for independence

While it is true that these mothers poured themselves into their children, they did not produce clingy, dependent adults. On the contrary, while the families ties remained *strong,* the children nonetheless could stand on their own. One daughter said,

> **66**
> Mom has always wanted us to 'fly.' She says, 'Go on now. I've done what I can to raise you all—stick close to your husbands. Yes, I am your mother, I always will be, but now you have a family of your own to take care of. **99**

A beautiful explanation of how a mother teaches her children to "walk alone" was written by Danish philosopher, Soren Kierkegaard.

> The loving mother teaches her child to walk alone. She is far enough from him so that she cannot actually support him, but she holds out her arms to him. She imitates his movements, and if he totters, she swiftly bends as if to seize him, so that the child might believe he is not walking alone. . . . And yet, she does more. Her face beckons like a reward, an encouragement. Thus, the child walks alone with his eyes fixed on his mother's face, not on the difficulties in his way. He supports himself by the arms that do not hold him, and constantly strives towards the refuge in his mother's embrace, little suspecting that in the very same moment that he is emphasizing his need of her, he is proving that he can do without her, because he is walking alone.[8]

Managed discipline

These mothers were not weak, dependent women, but strong women who could manage their children. They were disciplinarians, yet their grown children obviously feel love, respect, and admiration for them.

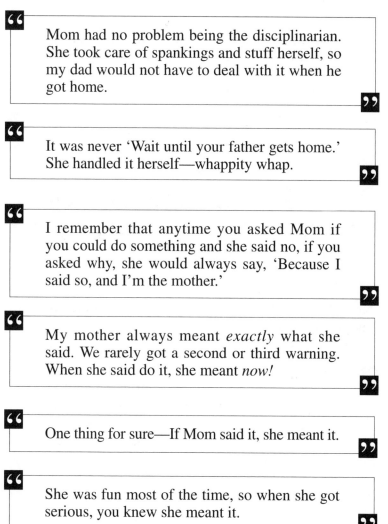

> Mom had no problem being the disciplinarian. She took care of spankings and stuff herself, so my dad would not have to deal with it when he got home.

> It was never 'Wait until your father gets home.' She handled it herself—whappity whap.

> I remember that anytime you asked Mom if you could do something and she said no, if you asked why, she would always say, 'Because I said so, and I'm the mother.'

> My mother always meant *exactly* what she said. We rarely got a second or third warning. When she said do it, she meant *now!*

> One thing for sure—If Mom said it, she meant it.

> She was fun most of the time, so when she got serious, you knew she meant it.

Insisted on high goals

These moms were a big force in pointing their children toward the stars. They expected them to do their best and would accept no less.

When one of the kids brought home a seventy-eight in Algebra on his six weeks report card, Mom stepped in to help.

> " That kind of grade was not an option in our house. Mother was good at math and decided that home study was for me. Every evening we spent an hour at the kitchen table working on algebra. "

▼

They expected their children to do their best and would accept no less.

This boy raised his grade by twenty points in the next six weeks and said that he never did poorly in math again. These moms were take-charge kind of women!

> " One thing my mother would not put up with in me was underachievement. I did not have to be perfect, but I was expected to do my best. If I settled for less, and I often did, Mom would get really perturbed at me. My high school years probably drove my parents crazy! "

> " Mom helped us with our homework and pushed us to do our best in it. "

> " Mom hated it if we didn't do our best at whatever we were doing. "

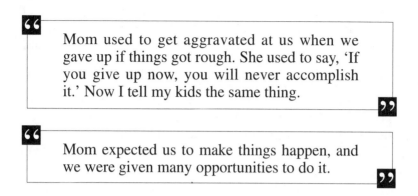

> Mom used to get aggravated at us when we gave up if things got rough. She used to say, 'If you give up now, you will never accomplish it.' Now I tell my kids the same thing.

> Mom expected us to make things happen, and we were given many opportunities to do it.

Expectation and a whole lot of opportunities to succeed. What a combination! And it works!

Served others

While the first and primary ministry of these women was family, they also carried their strengths outside the walls of their homes and into the lives of others.

One of the mothers had a telephone ministry. She would call people who were hurting or wrestling with problems in the morning before they went to work to encourage and uplift them. Others in her church picked up her idea, and soon, there were dozens of people who were being ministered to every morning.

▼

This was a part of town where only one man in two city blocks would have a job.

Another of the women we visited had a ministry in a Cincinnati housing project. This was a part of town where only one man in two city blocks would have a job. The self-esteem of the children was low and the violence was high. Many of these children weren't even going to school, so this woman taught mothers how to home school their children, and in the process taught the mothers, who had never finished school themselves. Several of the other neighborhood children saw what was going on and wanted to get into that "private school." This woman had the opportunity to teach character and integrity and self-esteem to the mothers and to the children, most of whom had never traveled beyond the three or four blocks of where they were born.

She would also take them to the wholesale store and help them buy peanuts and candy. She taught them how to price their goods and resell them for a profit. She taught them how to open a bank account, how to put money into savings, how to spend a little of it, how to give 10 percent to the Lord, and how to reinvest some of it back into the company so they could buy more candy. It was a wonderful ministry.

Another woman was a Court Appointed Special Advocate (CASA). These special volunteers serve as advocates for children who are bounced from one agency to another. They are a source of stability in these children's lives. Other women volunteered in a jillion other ways.

Modeled

The passage in Proverbs 31 well depicts so many of the women we interviewed. "A wife of noble character who can find? She is worth far more than rubies." This woman took care of herself, her children, and her husband. She ran her own business, she purchased her own land, and she served others. She is described with words like *strength* and *dignity* and *wisdom.* Women like the one in Proverbs 31 *do* still exist today. They're still here, they're still modeling, and they're still beautiful. "Her children [will] rise up and call her blessed."[9] The children of some of these beautiful women told us,

> ❝ In my Bible, next to the heading 'The Wife of Noble Character,' I have written my mother's initials. Each time I read this section of Scripture, I think of her. ❞

> ❝ My mother is the modern version of Proverbs 31. ❞

These women were a beacon of light, a model of what a godly woman is to be.

> I try everyday to hold on to that way of my mother. I know that what I am is sometimes hidden for now, but I know that I, in my mother's likeness, will shine through one of these days.

> My mom is the last of a dying breed. But as far as the next century goes, there will be four girls walking this earth who will be a shining likeness of that woman.

> I could not have had a better example of how to live a life for Jesus than my mother.

> Sometimes in the middle of my life and my job and all the confusion of all the things that go on in my world, I often stop and think of my mom and her simplicity. Will I ever be like my mom? How did she hold on to the simple?

Cherished role

These women cherished their role as mother and were not intimidated by some who might insinuate that motherhood is insignificant.

A friend of mine and his wife were in London, sharing an official meal with Lord and Lady So and So. The Lord and Lady had just finished telling my friend and his wife of their many accomplishments—one had been responsible for designing all the stage settings for the London theater, and the other was the curator for a large museum. Then they turned to the wife of my friend and asked, "And what do you do?" And she responded, "I have raised two wonderful boys."

▼

"Our success as a society depends not on what happens inside the White House, but on what happens inside your house."

A few years ago, Barbara Bush delivered the commencement speech at Wellseley College (a women's college). Several of the young women there were *not* happy that a "housewife" had been selected to speak. They wanted to hear from an entrepreneur or professional woman. But of course, this "housewife" had organized moves all over the world, had lived in twenty-nine houses, had raised five children, and had been through the loss of a child, sickness, and all the political turmoils that come with public service. She is a tough, good, loving woman, and this is what she said:

> As important as your obligations as a doctor and a lawyer and a business leader will be, you're a human being first, and those connections with spouses and children and with friends are the most important investments you will ever make. And at the end of your life, you will never regret not having passed one more test or winning one more verdict or closing one more deal, but you will regret the time not spent with your husband or your child or a friend. Your success as a family, our success as a society, depends not on what happens inside the White House, but on what happens inside your house.[10]

One of the mothers told the whole family in our presence,

I could have been a medical doctor, I could
have been a lawyer, but I chose to be a mother.

My own sweet wife, Gladys, jotted down some observations about these women that she wanted me to be sure to incorporate. But her statement was so compact and so well written, I think it's best left just like she wrote it.

Paul, emphasize these words in your book:
supportive, positive, warm
praising, smiling, cheerful
hugs, kisses, unconditional love
teaching, discipline
monitors, but trusts
raises children intentionally
humor, laughter, fun
positive "do" plans to take the place of negative "don'ts"
zest for life, creative
love of God in nature that rubs off on the family
sees the good, the lovely, the exciting side of life
serves family and others, hospitable
spiritual, continual prayer life
involved in church
love of the Lord shows in her life
family and Lord are priority—not money, country clubs,
    social functions or climbing a social ladder
a simple life involving time with children valued
    above these things

I want to share a few more comments from these children that describe the kind of mothers we are talking about. These are some of my favorite quotes:

> What makes me the proudest of my mother? My mom was willing to change, learn, and grow. She allowed me to fail and make my own mistakes. Mother is still there to pick me up and hug me, even though I am an adult. That's the best example of mothering I can think of! My mom is my friend! Although singing her praises is long overdue, I 'rise up and call her blessed.'

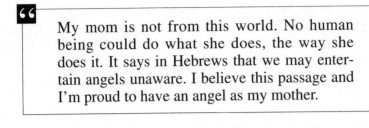

> My mom is not from this world. No human being could do what she does, the way she does it. It says in Hebrews that we may entertain angels unaware. I believe this passage and I'm proud to have an angel as my mother.

> My mom had the magic. I don't know where the magic comes from or how you get it, but mom had it. It's the magic that makes a house a home.

I'll never forget the closing of one early morning interview with one of the top executives in the Northeast. He had already left the room, but he turned around and stuck his head back in the door and said, "Mom really hasn't received enough attention. *Be sure you remember my mother.*"

Someone has said it well, "Mothers are the first book read, and the last book put aside in every child's library."

When I come home from work and see those little noses pressed against the window pane, then I know I'm a success.

11

THE INTENTIONAL FATHER

"Are there any men in his life?" I asked her.

There was no one. She had no brothers, her father was dead, and her ex-husband's father lived in another state.

She looked up at me, her eyes hopeful. "Will you talk with him?" she asked. "Just speak with him about what he's doing. Maybe if it came from a professional . . ."

Christopher Bacorn, a psychologist, was facing a fifteen-year-old boy and his mother. The boy was sullen and angry. He sat on the couch silently staring out the window. His mother was on the verge of tears. In her mid-thirties, she was thin, worn, and tired from too many nights spent worrying and waiting for him to come home. She described her "boy's heartbreaking descent into alcohol, gang membership, failing grades and violence." It had all begun four years ago, when his father had walked out on them. He

115

had recently gotten in a fight and hurt someone. It was then mandated that he talk with a counselor.

> I did speak with him. Maybe it didn't hurt, but like most counseling with 15-year-old boys, it didn't seem to help either. He denied having any problems, everyone else had them, but he didn't. After half an hour of futility, I gave up.
>
> I have come to believe that most adolescent boys can't make use of professional counseling. What a boy can use, and all too often doesn't have, is the fellowship of men—at least one man who pays attention to him, who spends time with him, who admires him. A boy needs a man he can look up to. What he doesn't need is a shrink.[1]

▼

"A boy needs a man he can look up to. What he doesn't need is a shrink."

Fathers Are Desperately Needed

Children need their fathers

In a study of male prisoners by Dr. David Blankenhorn, he found that the one thing they all had in common was the absence of a father.[2] He also found that while most of the prisoners asked for a card to send to their mothers on Mother's Day, none of them asked for Father's Day cards. What does this tell us about the prisoners' relationships with their fathers? Would these men even have been behind bars if a good father had been in their lives?

> What would happen if the truant fathers of America began spending time with their children? It wouldn't eliminate world hunger, but it might save some families from sinking below the poverty line. It wouldn't bring peace to the Middle East, but it just might keep a few kids from trying to find a sense of belonging with their local street-corner gang. It might not defuse

the population bomb, but it just might prevent a few teenage pregnancies." [3]

Just as the absence of a father can have an immensely negative impact, the presence of a father can have a powerfully positive effect. William Raspberry, a *Washington Post* writer, after a study of Martin Luther King Jr., made this observation,

> The main body of Martin L. King's belief and attitude can be traced neither to the university nor to his undifferentiated "Georgia roots," but to the influence of the late Rev. Martin Luther King Sr., "Daddy King." . . . I have come away with a renewed sense of how much it matters what fathers teach their sons, by precept and by personal example. Daddy King's legacy included: the quiet refusal to knuckle under to racism . . . the ideas taught from the pulpit; the firm discipline at home. The son simply would not have been who he was had not the father been who he was. [4]

"Like father, like son" is a truism, as is "The acorn doesn't fall far from the tree." Fathers make a tremendous difference.

> Children who grow up without their fathers are worse off— economically, educationally, psychologically, *every way we can measure*—than children who grow up with their fathers. [5]

▼

"The son simply would not have been who he was had not the father been who he was."

Fathers need their children

Not only do children need their fathers, fathers need their children. Judith Wallerstein began her longtime studies on children of divorce thinking that children were strong enough to adjust to their parents' divorces. But she found out that kids have much tougher adjustment problems than had first been recognized. In her research, she also discovered that children were not the only ones who suffered developmentally:

Young divorced fathers, separated from their children, seem to have their development blocked. Some never recover a sense of purpose or direction: they cannot grow up into fully mature men outside the structure of the family.[6]

Years ago, the Bible offered the same insight:

I will send you the prophet Elijah before the great and dreadful day of the Lord comes. He will turn the hearts of the fathers to their children, and the hearts of the children to their fathers.[7]

Dr. David Blankenhorn, author of *The Good Family Man,* says,

Children endow a man's life with a larger meaning. They confer a special blessing on his worldly endeavors, endeavors that might otherwise seem small and unworthy. Children make it possible for a man to believe that he has lived a good and purposeful life.[8]

Most men have a basic desire to *generate,* to produce a child that will come after them and link them to future generations. They want flag bearers. Those men who cannot bear children because of their infertility become so devastated, according to one study, they can't even talk about that experience.

The medical clinics explained that their average male infertility patient did not return for a second appointment, often avoiding even the simplest evaluative procedure.[9]

Fathering has more to do with caring than begetting. Begetting is so often selfish, while fathering is never selfish. Begetting can happen in a moment of passion, where fathering takes dedication and sacrifice.

Society needs fathers

Not only do children need their fathers and fathers need their children, but society needs fathers as well.

Neighborhoods without fathers are neighborhoods without men able and willing to confront errant youth, chase threatening gangs, and reproach delinquent fathers. . . . The absence of fathers . . . deprives the community of those little platoons that informally but effectively control boys on the street.[10]

The principal of Arlington High in Indianapolis was having all kinds of problems with vandalism, violence, and general misbehavior. Gangs and the threat of violence had become so bad that the school was unable to have any after-school activities, like basketball and football, or any kind of field trips. The school administrators had resigned themselves to giving up all extra-curricular activities. Finally, the prinicpal came up with an idea that turned the situation around. She armed a group of fathers with T-Shirts that said, "Security Dad." These fathers, wearing their T-shirts, showed up at football games, dances, and school-sponsored activities. They took turns walking the halls and the campus. They didn't particularly *do* anything. They were just *a visible presence*. And because of the father's participation, this principal was able to restore that school to normalcy.

▼

They didn't particularly *do* anything. They were just *a visible presence*.

Gladys and I had an experience that impressed us again with the power of father figures. We had stopped to eat at a rather non-descript hamburger place in the lower part of East Dallas. As we walked in, my eyes were drawn to the back of the place, where two boys were sitting. One had his hair combed straight up, and it was stuck together—kind of like a shark fin. The color was like one of those rainbow snowcones that has a little bit of each kind of syrup on it—multicolored all the way down. Oh, it was *bad* looking. The boy sitting next to him had more normal looking hair, but he was dressed kind of weird, and his face was painted completely white.

We ordered our food and sat down near a table where an older black gentleman was eating. As we waited for our food, I thought to myself that this was gonna be one of those *interesting* experiences—I always enjoy seeing and doing things that are little different.

Sure enough, in just a few minutes, a young black man came in, with about four or five of his gang buddies. When he looked back and saw those two fellows I just described, he proceeded to tell them, loud enough so that everyone could hear, just what they looked like. (And the truth of the matter is, I thought he did a pretty good job.) But of course, the guys in the back felt compelled to tell him what he could do with what he just said. Now the gang leader was getting mad, and he was moving toward those boys with another insult in his mouth, when the black man seated right near him stuck up his hand and one finger. He shook his finger and said, "Uh uh. None of that." That was it. That was all he did. One finger up in the air, and an "uh uh." That big ol' boy turned, gave one loud cursing shout to the whole establishment, and left with his buddies. The older man was able to do with a few words what no one else could.

On our way out, I stopped and told the gentleman that I was an admirer of what he did, how much he was needed, and how much I appreciated him. I realized that there are many situations where my two master's degrees and doctor's degree can't hold a candle to a powerful influence like his.

Major Tasks of the Intentional Father

Dads are needed *so* badly. *No one* can take their place in the home—not the mother, not the grandparents, not the school system, certainly not the government, and not even the church. Dad is essential. If his job isn't done *by him,* it just won't get done.

This is not to say that all children without a father are doomed to be psychologically depraved. Heaven forbid! We have seen too many fatherless children who have overcome. But they have done so *in spite of* their loss, not *because of* it. Thomas Edison became a world genius without an elementary school education, but who would suggest that because genius exists without an education, a lack of education should become the norm? *Besides,* we are not looking for the "norm" in fathering, we are looking to be the "best" fathers possible.

This next section, then, is to inform us how great fathers accomplish their "task" of fathering. Don't let the word "task" throw you. We sometimes equate that word with drudgery, duty, or compulsion. But the task of *fathering* brings joy and fulfillment.

Protector

"My daddy can whip your daddy" is a child's way of laying claim to the important concept that "My daddy is going to protect me."

While we do have women in the military and in the police force, we don't see many women lining up to fight the heavyweight boxing champion, there aren't any women in the NFL, and women still tee off from different markers on the golf course.

▼

The tougher things get, the more likely it is that Dad will be the one to handle the problem.

Women are just as smart and capable as men, can withstand pain as well or better than men, and generally outlast men; but women are more vulnerable physically, with regard to all the things that go along with her ability to bear children—childbirth, breastfeeding, and hormonal fluctuations. Men, unlike women, are trained in almost every society to defend their countries and families against all foes, even to the point of death, if necessary. The physically protective nature of men is the impetus for the moral commitment that protects society as a whole. As Gilmore says,

> [Manhood] must show a . . . moral commitment to defend the society and its core values against all odds.[11]

"Daddy fix it" (or "Daddy fits it" as it came out with my daughter's childish lisp) was the catch phrase in our family whenever anything went wrong. The natural tendency to turn to Dad in time of trouble has been documented by the research of Robert Weiss. He found that there is a correlation between the seriousness of a problem and the likelihood of male involvement. The tougher things get, the more likely it is that Dad will be the one to handle the problem. There may be a few clods out yonder who hear a bump in the night and push their wives out of bed to "check it out," but it *ain't natural.* God made the difference, nature made the difference, and thank God there *is* a difference.

Provider

Moses exemplified to the tenth power the father's burden in his complaint before the Lord.

> *What have I done to displease you that you put the burden of all these people on me? . . . Why do you tell me to carry them in my arms, as a nurse carries an infant, to the land you promised on oath to their forefathers? Where can I get meat for all these people? They keep wailing to me . . . I cannot carry all these people by myself; the burden is too heavy for me. If this is how you are going to treat me, put me to death right now.*[12]

Moses is talking about that provisioning role that God had given him, and God gives that same provisioning role to every father. The Bible also says that if a person doesn't provide for his own, he is worse that an infidel.[13]

Traditionally, men have often expressed their love by performing, protecting, and providing. Mario Cuomo wrote of his father that "the overwhelming impression we got was that this man was offering us his life; he didn't have to put his arm around you."[14] The fathers of the last generation or so often gave their lives to providing. While they may not have been very demonstrative in their affection, they expressed their devotion by working long hours to provide for their families. In today's world, fathers have learned not only to provide, but to be affectionate as well.

Moral leader

In the Old Testament, God placed the burden of teaching children about him upon the fathers:

> *He decreed statutes for Jacob and established the law in Israel, which he commanded our forefathers to teach their children, so the next generation would know them, even the children yet to be born, and they in turn would tell their children.*[15]

The Jewish father was considered to be a

> teacher and nurturer. Being a father was central to the identity of the Jewish male. The responsibilities of fatherhood . . . were a balance of practical and spiritual roles: training children for

an occupation, transmitting Jewish tradition, and teaching the skills of survival.[16]

There is no question that throughout the Old Testament and right up through modern society, the father has been responsible for the moral tone of the home. John Demos explains some history of the role of the father.

> In colonial America, fathers were seen as primary and irre-placeable caregivers. . . . Well into the 18th century, for exam-ple, child-rearing manuals were generally addressed to fathers, not mothers. Until the early 19th century, in almost all cases of divorce, it was established practice to award the custody of children to the father rather than the mother. Throughout this period, fathers, not mothers, were the chief correspondents (senders and receivers of letters) of children living away from home.[17]

Until the 1940s and '50s, fathers had traditionally taken a more active role in parenting. But in the 1950s, the weight of the role shifted toward mothers. This out-of-balance shift has left children without the male leadership they need.

▼

Church attendance is one area where the father has the big clout.

Fathers have a very significant impact on their children, espe-cially their sons. One place this influence is evident is in church attendance. If both mother and father go to church, 72 percent of the children will go when they're grown. If only the father goes, that percentage doesn't drop too much: 55 percent of the children will go to church when they're grown. But now notice what hap-pens when only the mother goes. If only the mother goes to church, only 15 percent of those children will go when they're grown. So while mother has a greater influence on children in some respects, church attendance is one area where the father has the big clout. Just look around in your own church. You'll see that the young boys will come to church with their mothers up through about junior high, but somewhere in junior high and high school, if Daddy's not going to church, the boys will drop out, as will many of the girls.

The families we interviewed understood the importance of the father's role as moral leader. One CEO of an international company said,

> The father must be the moral standard, the moral head of the home—not the mother, not school, not church, not grandparents.

The moral leader sets the tone of the home. One young man we interviewed said this about his father:

> My dad just has a way about him. He can help us keep things straight. Dad had the uncanny way of keeping things in perspective. I'll never forget him for it.

To illustrate what he meant, he told us about his very last high school football game. It was the last game, the last play, and the last quarter. There was time for only one last play, and he had to throw the ball. If the pass was good, he'd be a hero; if the pass was bad, he'd be a goat. He threw the pass, the pass was intercepted, and the other team ran it all the way for a touchdown. He was the goat. That boy came home late and *hurting.*

▼

And the moral leadership of the father comes from the foot of the table.

His dad was waiting up for him. "Son I'm sorry the game was lost tonight, but let me ask you a question. You know Brice? [Brice was the little grandson.] If we could reverse the outcome of the game by cutting off just the very tip of one of Brice's little bitty fingers, would you be willing to do it?"

"Oh, no, Dad! I would never do that."

And then the dad said, "I didn't think you would. So I guess winning the game wouldn't have been worth even the tip of Brice's little finger, then, would it?"

And the young man told me that when his dad said that, he felt like a tremendous weight had been lifted off his shoulders.

And the moral leadership of the father comes from "the foot of the table." He leads not as a dictator, but as a servant. While expecting others to do their fair share, he does his fair share (or more), including maybe carrying out the trash or cleaning the ring out of the tub. This is the kind of leadership that was modeled by Jesus, and it still works today. It's not the kind of "leadership" one man practiced when he drug his wife down the aisle after one of my talks. This man *pushed* his wife in my direction and said, "Tell my wife what the Bible says about the husband being *head* of the home." And the fleshly man in me wanted to slap him, because it was obvious from his tone and the way he handled his wife that she was a pawn. He was neither a moral leader nor a servant to his family.

▼

"Fathers are crucial in making men of their sons and women of their daughters."

Model of manhood

What *is* a man, then? That's what real fathers teach their children—both their sons and their daughters. The father plays a major role in developing the sexual identity of their children.

Fathers are crucial in making men of their sons and women of their daughters. And contrary to the popular image, it is not the aggressive, macho man but the competent, caring, loving father who does this best.[18]

Confirms femininity of his daughter

By modeling manhood, fathers actually confirm their daughters' femininity as the "other-than-mother figure who provides a second source of steadfast love."[19] "Girls secure in their femininity tend to have fathers who encourage their feminine adjustment."[20] In contrast, daughters who have little or poor interaction with their fathers often have a difficult time knowing how to relate to men.

One study showed that when the biological father was living in the home, girls were 42 percent less likely to make a sexual debut before age sixteen. A father needs to communicate that he respects, admires, and takes seriously his daughter who is becoming a woman. One of the best things a father can do is just to be around and available for unhurried conversation.

▼

Daughters who have little or poor interaction with their fathers often have a difficult time knowing how to relate to men.

Negative and distant relationships with Dad or abusive experiences with Dad can cause real problems in the ability of women to relate to other men. As we looked through a photograph album of family memories, we found the following note from a daughter who is now grown and married—a testimony to the fact that growing up in a loving, close, and positive relationship with her dad was a powerful factor in how she related to her husband.

Dad—
Thanks for shaping me with your wisdom and love into the faithful woman I am and giving me the ability, because of our relationship, to love Larry and be a good wife to him.

All my love—Connie

The father/daughter relationship is a too often neglected aspect of the "men's movement." One writer, Victoria Secunda, reports in

Women and Their Fathers that she "has yet to see the subject of being a father to a daughter addressed, except in passing," in periodicals, including *Wingspan* and *MAN*.

One daughter we interviewed said,

> " My father was a point of reference for how a man should be. "

Your daughters will look at you and say, "Oh, *that's* what a man is like. So *that's* how a man looks, acts, smells, and talks. *That's* how a man treats women, that's what a father is, that's how a man cares for his family."

One mother, in order to help her husband get to know his teenage daughter better, insisted that he go clothes shopping with the daughter when school started. The husband, of course, objected, saying that no way would the daughter want to go shopping with *him*. But the wife stood her ground and explained that if the daughter wanted new clothes, she would have to go with him. Well, naturally, the daughter protested, but when the father said, it's me or no new clothes for school, she finally capitulated.

This was quite an experience for Dad. He found out who wears what kind of clothes and what's in and what's out. He also found out that there's no cheap way to dress a teenage daughter! He found out who her friends were and who her friends weren't. Many of the details of her life that had previously been shared only with Mother became Father information as well.

One of the daughters said that the happiest moments in her adolescence were when her father received her dates at the front door and asked about their families, their interests, their schooling, and their plans. She said,

> " He let them know in a genial but firm way that he was going to be home when they brought me home and that he thought they were lucky to be able to share my company. "

Another daughter confided,

> I hated some of Dad's rules and his continual questions, especially when I wanted to stay out late, and he wouldn't let me. But as I look back, his standards were the ones that influenced me when I was on my own. The values he set were so clear-headed that I felt sure he would like the man I eventually chose to marry, and he did.

Mentors manhood for his son

The Bible says, "Stand fast in the faith, quit you like men, be strong."[21] This passage tells men to *conduct* themselves like men. Boys need their fathers to teach them how men conduct themselves.

At some point in his life, the boy must become a man; childhood dies. Boys eventually separate from their mothers in search of their maleness. Think of it like a person swinging on a trapeze. The time comes when he must change from one trapeze to another: the boy has to let go of his attachment to Mom and look more to Dad (or a "surrogate" father) as his role model. If he lets go of childhood and Dad isn't there for him, what then?

▼

Boys need their fathers to teach them how men conduct themselves.

Clinical studies as well as anthropological investigations . . . confirm the process through which boys separate from their mothers in search of the meaning of their maleness. In this process the father is irreplaceable. He enables the son to separate from the mother. He is the gatekeeper for the son, guiding him into the community of men, teaching him to name the meaning of his embodiment as a male. In this process, the boy becomes more than the son of his mother, or even the son of his parents. He becomes the son of his father.[22]

As Samuel Osherson says,

If father is not there to provide a confident, rich model of manhood, then the boy is left in a vulnerable position: having to distance himself from mother without a clear and understandable model of male gender upon which to base his emerging identity.[23]

He continues by saying, "There is compelling evidence that fathers remain . . . very significant figures for men far into their adulthood." Frank Pittman concurs. He believes that many men grow up yearning for better connections with their fathers. That ache reveals itself through their inability to adapt well to society. He says these men "dream of a father who will come and teach them how to be men, or just tell them that they're doing all right."[24] If Dad is not around the house, then the men in the extended family or the church need to be there to help that boy into manhood.

One of the sons we visited with had obviously seen manhood modeled by his father. I'll let him tell you how he felt in his own words to his father.

To My Dad

In water skiing he was a champ,
    "That's my dad on the water ski ramp."
And when I'd meet people I'd always say,
    "My dad's the best in every way."
I can remember as a little lad,
    I hoped to grow up just like my dad.
Well, fun times come and fun times go,
    And my love for my dad continues to grow.
He went to Washington and met the Prez,
    But that was nothing, so he says.
He built his business and made some money,
    But best of all, he still calls Mom "Honey."
His name's real big, as big as can be,
    But his family is what counts, he says to me.
Things come and go, and some are a fad,
    But I still hope to grow up to be just like my dad.

Dads play roles that aren't lost or won,
   They're just there for their son.
Well, I had a little son too, and a dream I had,
   Was that he'd grow up to be just like his dad.
We played together, and there were things I'd teach,
   And he always made sure he was within my reach.
But my little son died just a week ago,
   And now there's no one to say, "Like my dad I'll grow."
Something special happened in my time of need,
   Cause my dad was there in lightning speed.
He helped me through a difficult time.
   He said, "Don't worry Stew, the sun will shine."
"You'll have another son and things will work out."
   He gave me advice and a book so I would win this bout.
What a great guy to help me through this time so sad,
   The only thing I can say is, "I hope to grow up just like my
   dad."

What Every Family Craves From Dad

Be around

The first thing families crave from Dad is his simple presence. Come out of hiding, get out from behind the newspaper, leave your work at work, don't fret your public image—be available! Some fathers come in at the end of the day, plop down in the easy chair, watch TV, and snooze. Soon, the evening is gone, and very little, if any, time has been spent with the family.

One wife we interviewed complimented her executive husband by saying,

> He reads all the time, but when he is reading at home and one of our children comes in to him, he puts the book down immediately. Then when they are gone, he picks it back up.

Time is like oxygen: there's a minimum amount required for survival. We can get by with a little less oxygen as we climb a mountain, but if we go too long without an adequate supply, we suffer brain damage. There is a point at which the consequences of deprivation are severe. As Kent Hayes, an adolescent criminologist, has said, "It is difficult for youngsters to grow up when their parents are too preoccupied to parent." He went on to say, "If family and home take a backseat in every situation, no book or professional can help you out."[25]

▼

Kids can't bond with a moving target.

If you want your child to be a "chip off the old block," then you need to be around for your child to chip off of. Kids can't bond with a moving target. They can't become attached to someone who is not there or is only occasionally there. Erma Bombeck put it this way,

> I never knew what to do with the daddy doll, so I had him say, "I'm going off to work now"; and I put him under the bed.

Fathers who are preoccupied with their jobs, themselves, or their problems are not available to their children. "The curse of fatherhood is distance, and good fathers spend their lives trying to overcome it."[26]

Every once in a while in a basketball game, we see somebody chunk the ball all the way down the court to attempt a last minute score. How often does that work? Not very. The farther you are from the basket, the less likely it is that the ball will go through the hoop. The chances of hitting the basket from the opposite end of the court are virtually nil, and from half court, they are still extremely small. But if you get right under the basket, you can dunk it. You can get it in almost 100 percent of the time. So it is with kids. The closer you are, the easier it is to infect them with your principles of the good life.

And the time you spend with the kids needs to be unstressed, relaxed time. Don't always be looking at your watch or shaking your head. Don't have that glazed-over look in your eyes that says, "I really don't want to be here and my mind is somewhere else."

While these dads did not have a lot of discretionary time, the secret of their success was that they submitted what time they did have *to their families*. It seems that making a commitment of time, even short amounts time, and being *faithful* to that commitment was enough. The certainty, the consistency made up for the short duration. Many of the sons mentioned time spent hunting or fishing, playing games or building models, and the daughters talked about music recitals and camping. Whatever recreational time was available was spent on the *family's* choice, not the dad's.

▼

The closer you are, the easier it is to infect your kids with your principles.

One problem many fathers have is they think that if they get involved with their kids, their whole evening will be shot. The truth of the matter is, our children's attention spans are so short that we're lucky to get in a few good minutes every day. So when you daughter says, "Daddy would you do it *now?*" Then, jump up and do it *now!* Get down on the floor and play a short game, or go to her room and read a book, or go outside and push her on the swing, because soon she'll be ready to do something else, and you can get back to your paper or your book or your work. As Bill Hybels put it, "Hurried men tend to *skim* life, *skim* wife, *skim* kids."[27] Don't cheat yourself and your family.

Some men out there are still rationalizing that they can't spend any more time with their kids. They're saying, "When my boy's old enough, then I'll play ball with him. We'll camp, and we'll fish, and we'll do a lot of things together." The sad truth is, boys aren't born playing baseball. What your child may need right now is diapering. Furthermore, not all children are boys, and not all boys can play ball. Make sure to interact with your children based on where they are *now* in their development and according to *their* abilities and interests, not based on your personal expectations and preferences.

For some of the fathers who are reading, it's decision time. Where are our priorities? While the thirty families we interviewed have proven that it is possible to achieve both career and family success, we've got to decide which comes first—our job or our children. What is at the center of our hearts? And that brings us to the second thing that families crave from their fathers.

▼

For some of the fathers who are reading, it's decision time.

Have the family at heart

Some of the fathers we interviewed had to be out of town quite a bit, but their absence did not have the negative effect you might expect. When we asked about this, we kept hearing, in different forms, that Dad had the family at heart. Some of the comments we heard from the mothers were,

> " When he's home, he's home. "

> " He never brings the job home. "

We heard the same thing from the kids. One of the children put it this way.

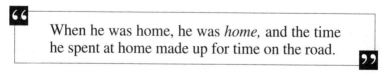

> " When he was home, he was *home,* and the time he spent at home made up for time on the road. "

And the family could tell the difference between a father whose heart was with the family and one whose was not. One mom said that she'd seen other fathers who would make an appearance at their children's game, but they'd talk about business the entire time. She continued, "The children and the mom know what's going on."

One father told me he had to learn to leave work at *work* the hard way. He was a manager in a major automobile manufacturing company. The union workers were very hostile toward management. On more than one occasion, when the union members knew he was going to be in the plant, they would pour buckets of urine on him from various places in the ceiling. He would have to go home and change clothes in the middle of the day. But he said, "I decided I was never going to allow any kind of resentment or anger to get into my family." When he crossed a certain bridge on the way home, he dumped all his anger and frustration right there. And everyone in his family agreed that he really did. He was one neat, fun guy to be around when he was home, even though his days on the job were extremely trying.

▼

"We could tell by the twinkle in his eyes."

The family of the football coach we interviewed said that when Dad's team lost, even on his way home with the family, he was up-beat. He left his worries at work.

This same coach worked *long* hours—ninety-hour weeks, eleven months of the year. And so this intentional dad set aside a whole month every year to spend just with his family. They would go out to their farm, where the only phone was in the barn, and spend quality, family time together for four weeks. By the way, when I asked the four daughters of this family who their hero was, they all immediately said "Daddy is." It was obvious that he had touched their hearts. *He had his family at heart.*

Family vacations seemed to be an important way for many of these dads to communicate their love for their families. One son said,

> I believe that our family vacations helped off-set Dad's time away from home. **"**

The father of one family from Mississippi worked about a sixty-hour week. After I had gotten to know this family a little, I asked the girls, "How does this good family come out of a guy who works sixty hours a week?" And they said, "We just knew that the family came first."

"How did you know that?" I asked. And they said, "Well, we could just tell by the twinkle in his eyes." But I wanted a more specific answer, so I asked, "How can you tell by a twinkle in his eye?" "We just can," they countered. "But what do his eyes say? How do you read them?" Finally two or three of them just kind of burst out all at once, and this is what they said,

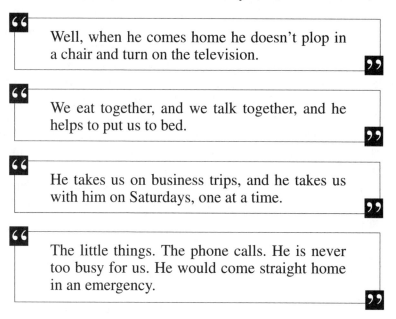

> Well, when he comes home he doesn't plop in a chair and turn on the television.

> We eat together, and we talk together, and he helps to put us to bed.

> He takes us on business trips, and he takes us with him on Saturdays, one at a time.

> The little things. The phone calls. He is never too busy for us. He would come straight home in an emergency.

So when they said, "we could tell by the twinkle in his eyes," there was a lot more to it than just a twinkle. All the things he did with and for them put the twinkle of love in his eyes because he had the family at heart.

One guy showed his family how important they were to him every Sunday morning. He would let his wife sleep in, and he would get the children up and ready for church. He bathed and dressed them, he fed them breakfast, he even brushed their hair. The mother could sleep in and take her time getting ready for breakfast and church—a fair trade for getting everyone else off on time five days a week. It was a real vacation for Mama. But the girls did finally take a vote on one matter. They voted that maybe

Daddy didn't need to help them fix their hair. Mama might be willing to do just that one thing.

Another father took special care of his family whenever they had to move to a new town. Moving time is usually an extremely difficult time, and when this mother told me that Dad always made moving fun, I had to find out more. When they moved into a new place, he would scout everything out first. He would find the best doctors, the best plumber, the best school, the best church, the museums, the libraries, and all the fun things to do. Then when the family came to town, he would give them a tour and take them to all the best places and make their first week a really great one.

One of his daughters really wanted a piano of her own. So he made a deal with her that if she would learn to play the piano and then practice hard and do well with her lessons for one year, he would buy a new one for her. A year passed and she had done well, so he came in one day and said, "Surprise! Guess what I bought you!" It didn't take long for her to guess—"A new piano!"

And she was so excited, and she asked, "Well, where is it?"

And he said, "It's in Detroit, Michigan!" Detroit was a thousand miles away, but her dad's creativeness made her actually look forward to the move.

▼

When this mother told me that Dad always made moving fun, I had to find out more.

Four of the husbands fixed breakfast every morning for the family. And I said, "Well, I do that too, you know. I fix the coffee and toast."

And they said, "No, Paul, we mean biscuits, eggs, bacon, whatever you want." And if Dad had to leave before the children got up, then he'd leave it warm for them in the oven.

One of my favorite stories comes from Stephen Bly in *How to Be a Great Dad*. He tells a story of a father who heard his son throwing up in the middle of the night. Now most of us fathers would wiggle and squirm enough to wake up our wives so they would hear the child and get up and take care of it; but not this great dad. He sneaked out of bed and went down the hall to take care of his son. The child had thrown up all over the bed cover and the floor; he had even managed to throw up all over the family cat. And of course the cat was wild and climbing the walls. This daddy cleaned up his son, gave him a bath, changed the bed covers, and took the sheets down to the washing machine. Then he gave the cat a bath and dried him with the blow dryer. He did all this without waking his wife. *Now that's some dad.* These guys who claim to be fathers, but who are really just headstrong and selfish are not really being *men,* they're more like *mules.*

▼

What size shoe does your son wear?

Grow antennas—be aware

Being an intentional dad requires developing a trait that is often overlooked by men—sensitivity. Insects use antennas to sense their surroundings. Daddies need to develop some antennas. They must watch, listen, ask questions, and be attuned even to nonverbal clues. What size shoe does your son wear? Who are your children's Sunday school teachers? Who is your daughter's best friend? What television shows do your kids like? Do they like okra and squash? How well do you know your kids?

One of my friends is a trial lawyer, and when she has a problem with a jerk of a husband, who won't pay child support or is fighting for custody he really shouldn't have, she always asks him who his child's pediatrician is—by name. Then she watches him squirm—these guys rarely know their children's physicians. But when your children are top priority in your life, this is the kind of thing you will know immediately.

A big part of developing sensitive antenna is knowing the difference in what it takes to succeed in your career, as against what it takes to succeed at parenting. And there's really quite a difference. Just look at the following lists:

Qualities Needed to Succeed in a Chosen *Career*	Qualities Needed to Succeed at *Parenting*
A constant striving for perfection	A tolerance for repeated errors
Mobility	Stability
A need to be free from time constraints to pursue an independent life	Plenty of time for family activities
A goal-oriented attitude toward the project	An acceptance of the seemingly capricious nature of the parent-child relationship
A total commitment of yourself	A total commitment to others
A stubborn self-will	A softness and willingness to bend
Efficiency	A tolerance for chaos
A belief that succeeding must always be the top priority	An understanding that failure promotes growth
A concentration on essentials	An ability to digress just to smell the roses
A concern about image	A relaxed acceptance of embarrassment
Firmness	Gentleness
An ability to create a family that is supportive of your chosen career	An acknowledgment that children have their own agenda
A preference for concise information	A willingness to listen patiently to prattle to help develop a child's articulateness
An insistence on high standards	A genuine tolerance for the lack of certain abilities

As you look down these lists, you'll notice that there's a big difference in what it takes to succeed in your career and what it takes to meet the needs of your children. You can succeed at both, but entirely different skills are required for each one. Don't forget where you are and treat your children like an employee or a business deal.

The kind of awareness we're talking about is the ability to pick up on the clues that your children give off concerning their feelings, their worries, and their fears. Lewis Smedes explains this so well:

> Some people always seem to notice things that other people miss; they catch little touches that are terribly important but seldom obvious to people who never look beneath the surface. They see subtle shifts in body language, hear delicate messages in other people's tones of voice, catch quiet hints that less sensitive people never notice. They have discernment.
>
> If you are discerning, you take your time. You do not act until you catch an insight into what is going on in other people's feelings, into what is really on people's minds, into what people really need at the time. You wait, you check your impulse to shoot from the hip, you do nothing, say nothing, until you have gotten a sense of what the situation really calls for.[28]

While serving as governor of Tennessee (he has since served as secretary of education under President Bush) and living in the governor's mansion, Lamar Alexander's antennas picked up a subtle clue from his children. In his book, *Six Months Off*, he tells how he noticed that over a period of time, his children were turning their chairs more and more toward their mother's end of the dinner table. He discerned from this clue that he had lost touch with his children. When he finished his second term in the governor's office, he took six months off and took the whole family to Australia. His purpose was to turn those chairs back a little bit toward his end of the table. Isn't that an insightful observation on his part? A real demonstration of *awareness*.

Not too long ago, I read a copy of a letter of resignation from the president of Steelcase. The third paragraph of that letter to his employees read:

> I am leaving Steelcase to put the balance back in my life. Since rejoining the company five and half years ago, the time I have had to devote to family, personal interests and spiritual growth has gradually diminished. I now find the only way to regain that balance is to leave the company and sway the pendulum back the other way. This is the right time for me to do this: I am 43 years old, my children are young, and they will not be young again.

This man's antennas picked up that his life was out of balance and his family was suffering. And he did something about it.

Remember Von—the dad I told you about in the Introduction who resigned as president of AGC to spend time with his children? When Von announced his resignation, a fifty-year old man came up to him after the meeting and said with tears in his eyes, "If I had done that years ago, maybe my daughter wouldn't be an alcoholic."

▼

This man's antennas picked up that his life was out of balance, and he did something about it.

Spotlight special times

This means that when your daughter or son has a special event, *you are there.* A major executive of Disney Films was trying to schedule a meeting with Warren Beatty concerning the casting of Dick Tracy. The respective secretaries agreed upon a meeting time, not knowing that it conflicted with the Disney executive's daughter's birthday party. For this particular father, there was no contest between his daughter and Warren Beatty. Beatty got stood up—and you just don't stand up Warren! Beatty wanted to know what could be more important than an appointment with him, and when he was told that it was a birthday party, he was so impressed that he went to the party himself—he just had to meet the little girl who had more clout than he did.

When Pat Cash won the 1987 Wimbledon, beating Ivan Lendl, he climbed up the seats in the stadium, almost to the very top, until he found his father. He took his father in his arms and hugged him. This dad had probably spotlighted his son's special events for years, and now his son was spotlighting him. The announcers were touched and broken, and one of them said it was enough to make a grown man cry.

Another father who knew how to spotlight his son was the father of Derrick Redman. You remember the scene at the Olympic Games in Barcelona. When Derrick, who was favored to win the 400 meters, pulled a hamstring and fell suffering on the track, he refused the help of several who tried to get him off the track. He just kept limping toward the finish line, saying that he wanted to finish the race he had begun. He had managed to hobble about fifty yards around the track, virtually hopping on one leg, when a big, burly man came out of the stands wearing a *Just Do It* hat and a T-shirt that read, "Have You Hugged Your Son Today?" He pushed his way to the struggling boy and when he finally arrived, he leaned over and said, "You don't have to do this, Son." But Derrick said, "Dad, I just want to finish the race." So the father put his son's arm around his shoulder and with a three-legged wobble, escorted him the rest of the way around the track. The father's comment was, "We began together, and we'll end together." That's spotlighting your child.

▼

"We began together, and we'll end together."

Another father was willing to pay high prices for spotlighting his children. He was invited to join the board of one of the largest retail companies in America, but when it came time for the first board meeting, he told them he couldn't be there—it conflicted with his son's football game. The corporation's response was that if that was where his priorities were, he really didn't need to be on the board at all. But the father's head was not turned. He also chose to go to another son's football game instead of to the grand opening of one of his units, even though the Japanese who funded the program were present.

One of the boys we interviewed told us how his father spotlighted his football games. Now you have to know that this father is a *very* quiet man. He doesn't say much at all, but when he does say something, it counts. In all the years I've known him, I've never known him to raise his voice. But his son told me that when he was playing football, his father would shout so loud that he could hear him clear across the stadium. *That's* spotlighting special times.

My father, too, was a quiet man. Though I never heard him *say* he loved me, there was no doubt that he did. He came to some of my track meets, but he couldn't get off work to come to many. But on one occasion he drove a hundred and fifty miles with my mother to attend a conference meet where I was to throw the javelin. My girlfriend, Gladys, was sitting by him. I'd had a terrible time. It was a slippery, wet day, and every time I tried to plant my foot to throw, it would slip out from under me. Finally, on the last throw, I was able to get a steady foothold, and as the javelin took off, I knew it was a winner. Gladys said my father jumped up like he was shot out of a cannon and shouted, "That's my boy!" I don't think he was even aware of what he was doing. I'll never forget that day. It was the day I felt most owned and blessed by my father. Every child needs the spotlight turned on them as often as possible.

Spotlight each child

One boy said that he and his dad made a list of one hundred things they could do together. Then everyday they would roll the dice to see what they were going to do. And when they got to the hundredth one, they'd have a special celebration.

▼

That one day spent with her may have saved her years of trouble in school.

One father told us about a time when he took his six-year-old out of school for the day. His daughter's teacher had sent a notice home saying that the little girl hadn't been wearing her "listening ears" lately. Dad decided he would take her out of school for the day, spend some time with her, and see if he couldn't figure out what the problem was. So they spent the whole day together: they did one thing he needed to do, then one thing she wanted to do, then one thing on his schedule, then one for her, and so on throughout the day. He listened to her and watched her carefully, and at the end of the day he said, "You know, I believe you have really *good* listening ears. I think that your problem is not your ears at all, but that you're not following through with what you are told. You are not being a *responsible* listener. You're not making responsible decisions with your information."

So when she went back to school the next day, she went up to her teacher and she said, "I think my *ears* are okay, my problem is that I am making irresponsible decisions."

That dad knew how to spotlight his child at a really crucial time in her life. That one day spent with her may have saved her years of trouble in school. Taking your child out of school for a special day with Dad can be a real education—for the both of you.

Another father noticed that every evening when he came home, his daughter wanted to go through his briefcase and examine everything in it and talk about what she found. Finally, it dawned on him that his daughter needed her own briefcase. So now, when he comes home, they go though their briefcases together. He found a meaningful way to spotlight his daughter.

Another daughter said,

My father never missed a recital at the music club, even though he hated that kind of music.

Other fathers would take their children with them on business trips. The truck drivers who work for Wal-Mart are allowed to take their families with them one week a year. It's my understanding that the J. B. Hunt drivers are expected to call home every night when they're on the road and that when a new man is interviewed for a job, they interview his wife as well.

I am told that when Michael Eisner was being considered for an executive positive with Disney World, he was late for an appointment with the men who came to talk to him about that job. When they came to his house, the man who answered the door confirmed the fact that they did have an appointment with Mr. Eisner. But he informed them that this was the time of day he took his children for ice cream and assured them that Mr. Eisner would be back shortly.

Another one of the fathers we interviewed told us about a speech he had recently delivered at an insurance salesmen's convention. His daughter had been in the audience, and in the middle of his talk he had turned to her and asked, "Sweetheart, do you remember the time I won the million-dollar roundtable three years in a row?"

And she said, "No, Dad, I don't guess I do."

And then he asked, "Well, do you remember when we used to have those Dairy Queen dates?"

And she said, "Oh yes!"

And then he turned to the audience to make the point that daughters don't remember when you sell a million dollars worth of insurance, but they do remember your special dates.

Other dads called home evey night when they traveled, and they talked to *every* child. An executive for Ford Motor Company, who had to spend months overseas, was questioned by his superior about his phone bills, which were running as high as a thousand dollars a month. He told his boss, "We're a close family. I need that phone time to keep in touch with my family. I'll pay the bill myself if I have to, but I need all that time." His superior said, "No, that's okay. We'll pay the bill. You go right ahead and take care of your family."

▼

One father wrote a letter to his kids everyday he was out of town.

Some of the children told us about the special letters they got from their fathers. One father wrote a letter to his kids everyday he was out of town. One of his kids said his letters were "awesome, special, and *long.*" Another family of kids who received letters from their father said his letters were "pages of affirmation, meaningful, and well thought out."

But I guess one of *my* favorite letters is from a submarine lieutenant who came up with some ingenious ways to bless his little boy, Matthew, and his wife while he was out in the submarine, under the oceans, defending the country. I think you'll agree.

Dear Paul,

I am a lieutenant in the U.S. Navy and have been on the submarine force for the past twenty-five years. Out of eight years on board a submarine, I have spent about four years under water. I was on the fleet Ballistic Missiles submarines, which made no port calls and would avoid all contact with other vessels.

To keep in touch with my wife and son (age four) while I was at sea, I learned some great ways to show them my love.

1. While I was home, I would have my wife take pictures of the things Matthew and I would do together—sliding down a slide, swinging, building with blocks, playing with cars and trucks, wrestling on the living room floor, et cetera.

   I would tape these pictures on the refrigerator about 3 feet from the floor (eye level for Matt), so as he played he would see and remember doing enjoyable things with Daddy—not just an eight by ten glossy photo of what Daddy looks like.

2. I would write fourteen letters to my wife and son in the three days before we would submerge for 70-90 days. Each would be addressed and stamped. I would put a date in pencil on one of the corners and have the chaplain on the submarine tender (a mother ship for submarines that would always stay in port) mail them when the date came up. This way my family got mail from me once a week. (If you think writing one letter is hard—try writing fourteen different letters in three days.)

3. I would also buy small inexpensive gifts for my son. I would wrap them and put a date on them, and my wife would give them to Matthew on those dates (about once per week).

4. I would leave cards, notes, or even those little yellow sticky memos throughout the house, that said "I love you," "I am thinking of you," or "Here's a big hug or kiss for you." I would place these cards or notes under their pillows, under their sheets, in the linen closet about four or five towels down (or in a towel), in a pair of rolled up socks in my son's drawer or in his jeans' pockets, in a pair of my wife's sexiest panties, with a special note for her (sailors will be sailors), in the tissue box about one-fourth the way down, in the

freezer (I would unwrap some frozen food and place a note there), under a doily and lamp in the living room (if she didn't find it, I'd know she hadn't dusted—ha ha), under the next bar of soap, in the bathroom closet, or under the last plate in the kitchen cabinet. These little time bombs of love would brighten their days and bring joy to their hearts.

Though I must confess there is some selfishness involved. During the three months under water, you sometimes fear being forgotten.

All of this may seem like a lot of work, but the dividends are pure gold. When the submarine crew finally comes home, I see some small children turn away in tears and scream at the man Mommy calls Daddy. But my son runs through the mass of people yelling "Daddy, Daddy," and jumps into my arms, with a smile that goes from ear to ear and hugs around my neck that no one can break.

And of course, it is like having a honeymoon with my wife every three months (I forgot to tell you that in one of those hidden cards was a movie ticket and babysitting money for a much needed break for my wife).

Is this lieutenant not a great dad! This is the height of intentional spotlighting!

▼

"My son runs through the mass of people yelling 'Daddy, Daddy!'"

Spotlight your wife

Most wives would give anything if their husbands would give them a little special attention. These fathers that we talked with *did*. One executive of a sixty-million-dollar company has two phones on his desk. The first one is for business, the second one is for the two women in his life—his mother and his wife. When that second phone rings, if he doesn't answer it within three rings, they know that he's in a conference and that he'll call them as soon as he can. Even his son didn't know that phone number until he became the president of the corporation.

▼

Do something special and unique—just for her.

One sweet, seventy-nine-year-old father still writes his wife a love letter every morning. It is so important to remember your anniversary, your wife's birthday, Mother's Day, and any day that is special to her. Take a little time to write something in your own words, maybe even a poem! Tell her what she means to you. Think ahead and make your anniversary a special day. Just like you plan for your important business deals, take the time and forethought to spotlight your wife. Do something special and unique—just for her.

Make it fun

If there's one thing that stood out with the fathers we interviewed, it was that they were a fun bunch of guys to be around. One of the kids said,

He's our daddy, and we just have a lot of fun.

The children of the coach laughed as they talked about the times their parents woke them up in the middle of the night with all the racket they made having fun playing ping pong down in the basement.

Another father, president of a university, makes pancakes every morning for the whole family. He doesn't just make ordinary pancakes—he makes them special! If it's St. Patrick's Day, the pancakes are green, if it's Christmas, they're red. One Christmas the pancakes just blew up! He insists that he didn't use gunpowder. The family laughed about those pancakes more than anything else we talked about.

I have a physician friend, one of the most skilled physicians in our city—who happens to be bald. This man has a very unique talent that he displays frequently: He can get empty coke cans to stick to his bald head. He may come to a party with four or five empty coke cans stuck on his head.

One wife of a prominent lawyer said of her husband,

> **"**
> He's just fun to be around, and he loves children. He's great at babysitting—but not just sitting, he's great at parenting. He loves it. **"**

I like what Michael Marks says about what it takes to be a father.

> Being a father means answering a question one more time when you're too tired to speak. It means towel drying a squirming, uncooperative body during your favorite TV show. It means a late-night trip to the drug-store for diapers when you've got only $4.67 in your checking account and you haven't yet paid the oil bill.

▼

"Being a father means towel drying a squirming, uncooperative body during your favorite TV show."

When I asked Gladys to summarize her observations about these fathers, she said,

> These men had an intense desire to be with their children. They enjoyed talking and playing with them. They did not make time for family out of duty, but truly because the family was at the top of their pleasure list. I saw in them an eagerness, a "can't wait to be with my kids" attitude that just came out of their pores. It was so obvious that they wanted to be home.

But I guess my favorite quote of all is from—you guessed it— one of the men we interviewed:

> **"**
> When I come home from work and see those little noses pressed against the window pane, then I know I'm a success. **"**

God as Our Father

He knows his children
>   As a shepherd knows his sheep (John 10:14).

He gives unconditional, sacrificial love
>   "I will lead them beside streams of water on a level path . . .
>   because I am Israel's father" (Jeremiah 31:9).

He supplies our physical needs
>   "Do not worry about your life, what you will eat"
>   (Matthew 6:25).

He is compassionate
>   "As a father has compassion on his children" (Psalm 103:13).

He bestows significance
>   "We wait eagerly for our adoption as sons" (Romans 8:23).

He provides security
>   Come unto me all ye that labor (Matthew 11:28).

He offers forgiveness
>   "Who is a God like you, who pardons sin and
>   forgives the transgression" (Micah 7:18).

He disciplines us as sons
>   "Those whom I love I rebuke and discipline" (Revelation 3:19).

He gives wisdom
>   "If any of you lacks wisdom, he should ask God" (James 1:5).

He is accessible
>   The Spirit himself intercedes for us with groans that words
>   cannot express" (Romans 8:26).

He is jealous for his children
>   "And do not call anyone on earth 'father,' for you have one
>   Father, and he is in heaven" (Matthew 23:9).

He grieves for his children
>   "O Jerusalem, Jerusalem, you who kill the prophets and stone
>   those sent to you" (Matthew 23:37).

He rewards his children
>   Come unto me all ye who labor (Matthew 11:28).

▼

Although role respon-
sibilities are changing,
priorities remain the
same.

12

DUAL-CAREER FAMILIES

Some special help is needed for families where both parents work. More and more moms are going to work, and family roles are shifting. But the fact that both parents work *cannot* blur our focus—when both parents work, we just have to work harder at keeping the proper balance, and it becomes even more important for families to prioritize.

Few of the women we interviewed worked out of the home, and all of the ones who did worked in their family-owned business or their own personally owned business. But as we discussed in "The Intentional Mother" chapter, "staying at home" did not mean staying at home. These women were often quite busy outside the home: they were volunteer servants to children of the community, to hospitals, to courts, and were involved in various Christian ministries. So the issue for us is *not* whether or not moms should work outside the home; rather, the issue remains one of *priorities*.

Many of the daughters of these women, who are now mothers, work out of the home (almost half of them). Some are professionals, lawyers, physicians, et cetera. Those who had daughters still at home knew that they may someday work out of the home to help provide for their families, and these women had no problems with this, even if they might have preferred differently.

▼

When both parents work, you just have to work harder at keeping the proper balance.

The one thing these women could not stomach was anything that smacked of not placing their children at the top of their "of critical importance" list. They understood that husband and wife roles are changing, but they would never minimize the "family first" principle. Anything else, including job, had to knuckle under to family. So, *if* mom worked out of the home, they simply felt that *both* homemakers (Mom and Dad) had to work harder at keeping things in the proper order and making sure that their children felt secure and cared for. They had to come up with new approaches, develop creative and spectacular initiatives, and plan more carefully to make sure that their children were at the top of the list. There is no adequate substitute for Mom and Dad.

Dr. Sirgay Sanger and John Kelley, in their book, *The Woman Who Works, The Parent Who Cares,* point out that some men want to have it both ways. They want the second income that the wife's work provides, but they don't want any of the personal inconvenience.[1] Studies have shown that when Mom goes to work outside the home and adds eight or nine hours to her day, the average father only contributes an extra *two* hours per week to the home—often leaving the woman with two *full-time* jobs.

Dr. Candice Feiring of the Educational Testing Service in Princeton found that a supportive husband actually helps his wife be a better *mother.*

> The sense of support and validation a woman feels when her husband helps with the chores transfers directly into her moth-

ering. . . . The more support a man provides, the more sensitive his wife's behavior is with their child.[2]

Furthermore,

> In practical day-to-day terms, knowing that he is in the basement doing the laundry or that he will take charge Saturday enhances a working mother's sensitivity because it gives her two fewer things to worry about when she sits down with her child. . . . A husband who accepts his fair share of household chores is telling his wife, "I support and applaud your decision to work"; a woman who gets this message night after night is going to have the kind of peace of mind that fosters a deeply attuned maternal sensitivity.[3]

So if a couple makes the decision that the wife will work, the distribution of the specific responsibilities will change, but the principles and strategies will remain firmly intact—for all kinds of families.

▼

The distribution of the specific responsibilities will change, but the principles and strategies will remain firmly intact.

One wise father we interviewed said,

> You can't have a pattern in one generation that will be the same for the next generation—except for the principles, the fundamentals. These never change.

Although role responsibilities are changing for some families, the messages and priorities remain the same.

Following are just a few, simple concepts that may help you as you work to achieve success without failing your family.

Use Time Wisely

The concept of "quality time" has been vastly overrated. It seems to carry the idea of doing as much as you can as quickly as you can. But what children need is a relaxed, spontaneous, unrushed atmosphere.

The book by Sanger and Kelly talks of "three evening touch points": dinner, shared time, and bedtime. Dinner is portrayed as an opportunity to "nourish the child's spirit." When it comes to young children, we often focus on the amount of food consumed; thus, dinnertime often degenerates into a "food fight," and we miss out on the opportunity to interact with our children.

▼

When both parents work, the evenings must concentrate on *family.*

"Shared time" as against "quality time" is your next evening touch point. Make sure that when you are with your children that the focus is on the child not the activity. The purpose of shared time is not to *finish* a project, but to enjoy the act of *doing. Quietness* is important—especially for small children. Turn off the TV and the stereo, and unplug the phone. Children need some quiet, relaxed time with Mom and Dad.

The final touch point is bath and bedtime.

> The last thing you should have to do in the delicate period leading up to bed is wrestle an overexcited two-year-old out of the bath, or chase him around the bedroom with his pajamas in one hand and a toothbrush in the other.[4]

A predictable bedtime routine will actually help you avoid many of the bedtime battles. When children get into a comfortable routine, each step along the way reminds them of what comes next, and they unconsciously begin to settle down.

Take advantage of these evening touch points. Don't come home from work so preoccupied that you can't concentrate on your children, and don't allow yourself to fill your evenings with extra activities. Especially when both parents work, the evenings must concentrate on *family!*

Be Sensitive

Sometimes the amount of time parents spend with their children is not as critical as how they react to their children's verbal and nonverbal signals.

> A young child's body language, the questions he asks, the requests he makes—often these clues will give a parent who knows how to read them a concrete and specific idea of what her boy or girl is thinking and feeling.[5]

Because so much time is spent away from home, extra sensitivity on the parents' part is absolutely essential. This is where those antennas we talked about in the last two chapters come in.

Your child needs to believe that Mommy and Daddy know and understand her better than anyone else. While a caregiver loves and provides for her, Mommy and Daddy know her best.

> Show your child you know how to read him. From a two-year-old's point of view, the Good Mommy is the Mommy who, even when he begins talking in midsentence, is able to tell what is on his mind. We call this capacity *reading*. Because of the eight- to ten-hour separations work imposes, tracking a child closely enough to read and join his moods is difficult, particularly since many of the clues he uses to signal those moods are obscure or cryptic.[6]

That's why it's so important to be sensitive to the multitude of little clues your child sends out. You cannot stay tuned to your child if you are distracted by community projects and social clubs and sometimes even excessive church work. Keep tuned in to your child—like you tune in a radio station. Tune in to your child's station and don't allow the static of outside distractions to pull you from your goal.

If you can get to the point where you can answer the question: "What does my child mean by that?"—regardless of what your child says—chances are you are truly *tuned* in.

In order to get to this point, you must put your work behind you when you walk in the door and concentrate on your child. Talk with your child, ask creative questions that will help draw him or her out. "What was the best part of your day?" "What was the worst part of your day?" Establish daily routines of talk time. Keep those antennas wired with sensitivity voltage.

▼

When you walk in the door, you must put your work behind you and concentrate on your child.

Concentrate on Communication

A creative strategy for converting a child's thoughts into words comes from an Oregon family. Dad is a regional sales manager, Mom is an executive secretary and homemaker and their six children are aged three through thirteen—that's a lot of childlike perspective to elicit. So Mom and Dad arrange mock television interviews between themselves, as interviewers, and the kids, as "stars." Like reporters anxious to reveal stars to their fans, they probe each child's opinions on most everything, and the kids, ever anxious to act like stars, give elaborate and revealing responses.

Talk to your children all the time. Because children of dual-career parents have to do more things for themselves, they end up being treated a little more like adults. This constant exposure to a more adult world mightily enhances their opportunities to learn and mature. Take advantage of this.

Maximize Mornings and Homecomings

Make the best use of morning time by taking care of necessary details the night before or by getting up thirty minutes before your children. View the morning routines as *opportunities* to interact with your children and express love. So many times, mornings are hectic and tension builds. You can't avoid all of this, but with some extra planning and a positive mind-set, you can make the most of this time. One mother remembered that her grandmother always used to say, "The hurrier you go, the behinder you get."

And this is doubly true for children. The faster we try to push them, the slower they seem to go. And so, this mother, even when she really is in a hurry, tries to *pretend* that she's not. She doesn't let that tension and frustration show.

Another mother suggested beginning an activity with young children in the morning and then finishing it in the evening. You could begin a Lego house or read part of a book. This kept her children looking forward to Mom and Dad's return. Knowing that they can pick up where they left off is a way of providing security and the promise of the parents' return.

▼

Even when you're in a hurry, try to *pretend* you're not.

Some helpful hints for dropping off and picking up children at day care come from *The Woman Who Works, The Parent Who Cares*. The main thing is that you focus your attention on your child not the caregiver. So many of us, in our efforts to be polite, completely ignore our children at these crucial moments. They also suggest that after you pick up your child in the evening that you focus your attention on the child during the drive home and the first few minutes at home—not on your errands and not on dinner preparation. One working mother went out of her way once or twice a week to drive by the fire station on the way home because her child loved the fire station. A little extra thoughtfulnesses can make a big difference.

Choose Professions Wisely

If at all possible, choose careers that allow you to work around your children's schedules. Women might consider having a day care in their home or selling personal care products, such as Avon or Mary Kay. Many mothers have found that working as a school teacher provides just the right solution. Their weekends, holidays, and summer vacations coincide with their children's—it can make a huge difference. Furthermore the profession itself trains these mothers in the most powerful and effective ways to interact with children.

Fathers might give some consideration to the vocation they choose as well. Jobs that demand less time away from home and that are more sympathetic to family needs are ideal.

According to national author, Richard Louv, America has become, in a sense, "anti-parent."

> Threatened by international competition, the nation's economic engine demands increasing devotion from its workers; the engine monitors its own production, but fails to monitor the stress on its parts. As the bolts and widgets are pushed, their metal fatigue grows, unseen.
>
> The central problems are not so much that the work places and institutions of the economic machine invade parental privacy, but that the institutions and work places operate as if family pressures do not exist.[7]

Even to talk about parenting in some work places is seen as nonproductive, a career hindrance. So modern-day parents need to seek out corporations that have a positive or pro-family stance. Then they can make an educated decision as to which corporation they will work for.

▼

Children are more important than a manicured lawn or an opulent house.

Put First Things First

The dual-career families I have known who were doing a magnificent job with their families used several "tricks" to get the job accomplished. One of the things they did was to reprioritize their lives. They simply made the decision that at this stage of their lives their children were more important than a manicured lawn or an opulent house. In fact, the children were more important than a *clean* house. "Hang the house, if it comes to children or house—

children win. Let's go the park, it is a beautiful day." Anyway, children are blind to dirt; and if they do see it, dirt is a *friend* not an enemy.

One assistant principal, who works in a tough public school district has reappraised her basic ministry in life and reassigned the last and best energies to her children and husband (who works longer hours than she does). This couple spends three hours every weekday with their children. On the weekends they spend even more. Many families with only one working parent don't spend this much concentrated time with their children.

Sanger and Kelly have an excellent formula for conserving energy for the most important thing—your family. They say that one reason many working mothers are exhausted is that they go about their tasks using a "flat-out style," meaning that they go at their day in one concentrated burst of energy, without discriminating which tasks really deserve their best efforts. Their three-part antidote is: (1) Give tasks the energy they require. Save your best energy for the most important tasks. Don't expend equal energy on tasks of unequal importance. (2) Build rest stops into your day. Tiredness makes problems look bigger. (3) Design your week so that it includes at least one "mini-vacation." Go for a walk, attend an aerobic class, do something you enjoy.[8]

▼

Save your best energy for the most important tasks.

Make Take-Home Meals Special

Children come before home-cooked meals. In dual-career families, diligence must be applied to job and family, not to hours of meal preparation—sorry about that. You may have to skimp on full-course meals, but don't skimp on time with the children.

Successful dual-career families often spend just about as much time around the evening meal table as those whose mothers stay home. The difference is in the food preparation. Working parents buy a lot of "take-home meals." In one family I know, one spouse calls the other to see which one is going to the cafeteria or Long

John's to buy the evening meal. But they don't just throw it out on paper plates when they get home. They prepare it further by adding some quick (and occasionally "not so quick") fixin's of their own and serve it in nice dishes and with real silverware (never plastic). The extra time saved is the time they use to make the family table fun and enjoyable. On weekends they sometimes "put on the dog," and the whole family pitches in to make special dishes. This also serves to teach the children how to "home" cook and "bake from scratch."

I believe that it *is* possible to rear fantastic families if Mom and Dad both work out of the home, but it seems to take an unusually determined set of parents. The intentional parenting mind-set becomes even more important—you must set your sights on your goal and refuse to be distracted.

STRATEGIES THAT WORK

SECTION THREE

Some of these spiritual strategies directly counter the dominant values of our culture.

INTRODUCTION

When you set out to build a house, a bridge, or anything, it is foolish to begin without a plan or strategy. Three things are necessary just to get started: dedication, vision, and strategy. Great accomplishments don't just happen.

When Stormin' Norman Schwarzkopf swept through the desert to whip Saddam Hussein's army in Desert Storm, he announced three components in his strategy to win the battle: initiative, mobility, and surprise. As the world soon learned, his strategies were amazingly effective.

God has a strategy to help us win our battles too—but it is a bizarre strategy in the world's view. God actually turns the world's value system upside down. For example, he would have us choose the foot of the table, not the head, the narrow way, not the broad. He would tell us that to live is to die and that it is foolish to invest in this world (instead of the next—the *real* world). He also said his teaching would divide households—put mother against daughter and father against son. This, too, sounds strange, but there are some things more important even than your family. Yet paradoxically, by following his teaching, we can all become *one* in the larger family—the spiritual family. And if the blood family is also one in Spirit, it is *twice one!*

So as parents, we have a difficult job trying to pattern our children's value system after God's when it seems so unnatural to them. And then—as if that job is not tough enough already . . .

Satan has a strategy too. Yes, there is opposition out there, an enemy. If parents don't believe there is evil, a Satanic force, then they are at a grave disadvantage.

One of our most difficult jobs is teaching God's unconventional philosophy of life to our children. In order to implement spiritual strategies, we have to directly counter some of the dominant values of our culture. Dolores Leckey suggests a needed shift in emphasis:

> to *being* from doing and producing;
> to *sharing* from possessing;
> to *creating* from consuming;
> to *self-worth* from status and privilege;
> to *reconciliation* from individuality and separation;
> to *equality* from domination.[1]

These timeless values of *service* have always been a part of God's strategy. The servant mentality calls for thinking of others before self, and that's tough; it *says* easy, but it *does* hard.

So we have quite a task. But don't feel too overwhelmed. Our children will help (they don't always go against the grain), God will help, friends will help, and this book and others will help—all the weight is not on your shoulders.

13

STRATEGIES OF THE HEART

Achieving success without failing your family requires a servant heart, just the opposite of what we usually envision when we think of success. The primary strategy of the great families we interviewed was to cherish and nurture the *heart* issues of family life. They poured their hearts into the hearts of their family members; they put others before themselves in service. These are unusual strategies, indeed, but they *work.*

The Core Dimension—Spiritual Devotion

If your children are devoted to God, the rest of their lives will fall into place. Passing your faith on to your children is your *fundamental* task. You must not depend on your Sunday schools or youth ministers to instill the way of Jesus in your children. As good as Sunday school teachers are, they only see your children about one or two hours a week—at most. This can't replace the round-the-clock modeling of Mom and Dad. Modeling your faith is one thing that cannot be delegated. Nearly 60 percent of Americans say they hold their current religious beliefs because of their parents' example.[2]

Walk-about, talk-about model

So we come again to *modeling*. We discussed it in "The Power of Parenting" chapter, and we'll look at it again in "Motivation." Modeling was a key strategy in the families we interviewed. And at the top of the list of what they modeled was biblical faith. Without such an underpinning for reasoning out the temptations of life, these parents felt their children would be left floundering and at risk.

Many Christian families have assumed that the best way to teach Christian values is to line up their children for evening devotionals. And they have felt guilty when they had trouble making it work. For some families, structured devotionals work, for others they create problems due to different children, ages, and schedules. Many of the families we interviewed tried to have formal devotionals when their children were young, but soon converted to what I think is a more biblical model—the walk-about, talk-about model. It just seemed natural to them, and it worked.

> These commandments that I give you today are to be upon your hearts. Impress them on your children. Talk about them when you sit at home and when you walk along the road, when you lie down and when you get up.[3]

The best way to spiritually influence your children is to talk of spiritual principles as you go throughout your day. When a natural model of goodness in "walk and talk" flows from your hands and tongue, it is "caught" by the children and it sticks.

As one mother told us,

We believe in living Christianity in all of life: in baseball, in cheerleading, in day-to-day living. That is more important than devotionals. Devotionals are important, but how you live the other twenty-three hours of the day is what really counts.

Devotional times that zing

The best way to make devotional times zing is to make them specific to each child. Many parents prayed with their children individually as they put them to bed. Some actually laid hands gently on their children and imagined the light of Christ healing any trauma of the day, filling them with peace. One child told us,

> **"**
>
> The best memories of my childhood were when my mom would come in after I was put to bed, and she would kiss me goodnight and sit there by me for a few minutes so we could talk. Then she would leave and my dad would come in, and he would kiss me and we would talk a little bit. I used to look forward to their coming into my room for those few minutes. I remember it like it was yesterday.
>
> **"**

Gladys found that a good time to encourage our children was early in the morning. She would go in and hug our sweet girls, and then she'd hug our two big ol' boys—even though they were in high school and well over six feet. It was kind of neat when Mom came in and awakened them with a kiss.

▼

"Pretty soon, Daddy, I'll be too big for you to carry."

Lamar Alexander, former secretary of education, governor, and university president, tells this story about his daughter Leslee: "One night when I was already in bed, Leslee (then about eight) wandered into our room and asked me to carry her to bed. I said that I was too tired. She said, 'Pretty soon, Daddy, I'll be too big for you to carry.'"[4] Kids *do* grow up, and these little windows of opportunity are available for such a short time. Go through them while you can.

The evening shouldn't be the only time we utilize for Bible study. One father in Dallas rarely ate breakfast, because he taught

his children Bible stories while *they* ate. He had a small black-
board that he put on the table, and each morning he taught them a
short Bible lesson. Other families have a Scripture-of-the-day or
study a proverb-a-day from the book of Proverbs.

Spiritual disciplines

These families were big on spiritual disciplines, such as Bible
study, prayer, fasting, meditation, and Scripture memorization.
Drs. Lewis and Dodd, in their research of over 3,000 teenagers,
found that the number one indicator for the *continuation of faith*
from one generation to another is the practice of spiritual disciplines by the parents.

Bible study

The Word of God took a position of honor in the families we
interviewed. Romans 8:28 was the inscription on the inside of one
husband's wedding band. Sometimes Mom and Dad studied the
Bible and prayed together.

A number of folks had neighborhood Bible studies in their
homes. Even though the studies were not designed specifically for
the children, this underscored to the whole family how important
the Lord and the study of the Word were to Mom and Dad.

Prayer

Almost every one of these families mentioned the importance
of individual and family prayer. One couple we talked with had
quiet times every morning in the swing or walking together. They
ended the day in prayer, on their knees. On the birthday of *every*
child and grandchild they spent an hour on their knees praying for
that child, and those children *knew* this.

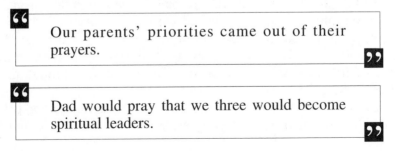

> " Our parents' priorities came out of their
> prayers. "

> " Dad would pray that we three would become
> spiritual leaders. "

When I asked one couple what advice they would like me to pass on to others, they said,

> Be consistent, turn off the TV, go do something together, pray together, and be real in your prayers. You can't hide from God or each other. Let your prayers be heartfelt.

Another family had an unusually well-developed family prayer life. They regularly prayed for family members and others. They kept each other informed of important upcoming events and special concerns and problems so that their prayers could be specific. They even kept a record of the way God had answered prayers in their lives, so they would always be conscious of his blessings.

A large number of the children we interviewed mentioned how remarkable their parents' prayer lives were. It was almost a theme throughout every family. They used words like "wonderful prayers," "awesome prayers," "really long, personal prayers."

These parents taught and modeled Christian stewardship of what God had given them.

Scripture memorization

Many of these families strongly encouraged each other to memorize Scripture—the parents as well as the children. Their children could quote a number of passages for us. They referred to Scripture often and creatively.

One high school boy told us about how he would set a goal to memorize a certain number of Scriptures every year. In our visit with another large family, we learned that all the children regularly memorized Scripture. While we were in their home, the dad called out some Scripture references and the children were able to recall them letter perfect.

Fasting

One family had a practice of fasting for a certain period around Easter. Even when some of the teenagers were going through a rebellious period, they still voluntarily chose to fast with the rest of the family, and this shared activity brought those girls back to their family.

The neglected curriculum—stewardship

These parents taught and modeled Christian stewardship. At a very young age, the children participated in giving to others.

By nature, most young children enjoy giving. If we can nurture this quality while they have a heart for it, this discipline can carry into their adult lives. One father was shopping with his small son for a canned food drive at their church. The father made his way to the "generic" canned food section and began loading his cart. The small boy watched in surprise, "Why are you getting that *cheap* stuff?"

"This is for the food drive at our church," the dad explained.

"But Dad," the youth protested, "we don't buy that stuff for us, why should we buy it for someone else?"

After only a moment's hesitation, the dad began putting the generic cans back on the shelf. The trip to the grocery store cost him more than he had bargained for, but the lesson was well worth it. Who learned the greatest lesson? The father or the son? The father blessed himself and his son by being vulnerable to the son.

The parents we interviewed believed the teaching of Jesus:

> *Give, and it will be given to you. A good measure, pressed down, shaken together and running over, will be poured into your lap. For with the measure you use, it will be measured to you.* [5]

They told us things like:

> 66
> I hope I can give more than I take. I surround myself with givers and I avoid takers. I always try to give more than I take.
> 99

> 66
> Success means that when you make it, you give it.
> 99

> I never expected to have enough to make it into retirement. If I quit working right now, I couldn't make it. We give enough away to need to keep on working.

> I haven't gotten used to anything I can live without.

> Dad and Pop [granddad] helped people, and the children never found out about their generosity from them; they found out through others. Dad was the kind of guy who didn't have to receive credit.

These attitudes have carried over to their children.

> I want to be just like my dad. He gave away 40 percent of everything he made.

> My mother and dad would be the same people if they lost everything tomorrow. Their priority is not money.

> Dad taught us that true success meant that when you 'made it,' you gave it.

Some of the families who could well afford any car they wanted drove used cars. They taught their children how to buy good used cars and how to shop at garage sales so they could be better stewards of their money. They allowed their children to know when they were making financial sacrifices and to participate.

What we saw in the families we interviewed seemed to harmonize with the findings of a study by Minear. He said,

> How you personalize your child's giving is a very individual issue. It will take some creativity, but it is worth the effort. The tender, generous side of children often goes untapped and unnurtured because adults don't devote time or thought to developing an attractive strategy of giving.[6]

One year a mother and daughter decided that they would give the money they had planned to use for new coats to a missionary instead. The daughter later commented to her mother about a neighbor who had a beautiful new coat, "Well, she may be rich in money, but we are rich in love, aren't we, Mom?"

▼
_____

The tender, generous side of children often goes untapped and unnurtured because adults don't devote time or thought to developing an attractive strategy of giving.

_____

It was common to hear these parents say, "After a *certain point* money is no longer an issue." These families found that money doesn't cure the major issues of life. (Of course, the "point" at which people make this decision varies—some who have very little of life's possessions choose to give away most of what they have.) Drs. Dodd and Lewis did some very interesting research on the relationship between family income and whether or not children take God seriously (see following chart). The children of families with low income (defined as $5,000) and high income (defined as $100,000) were the most likely *not* to take God seriously. The middle income parents had the children who were more likely to take God seriously. But surprisingly, like a bouncing ball, when the parental income skipped over the $100,000 mark, the children's interest in God shot up. The researcher accounted for this phenomena with the same logic I heard from these parents: "After a certain point, money is no longer an issue." Obviously, the children "caught the point" also.

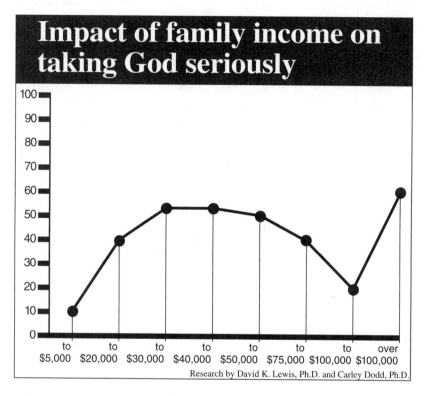

Impact of family income on taking God seriously

Research by David K. Lewis, Ph.D. and Carley Dodd, Ph.D.

So we see that it *is* possible to achieve financial success and not lose your children. But to have both, your sights must be set on Jesus, not money. The families we interviewed were well aware of the dangers of wealth and knew that, to paraphrase Jesus, those who acquire many possessions are often blinded by them and miss "the point" completely. And in time, many lose both their children and their possessions.

These families also understood the meaning of the proverb, "Wealth is worthless in the day of wrath, but righteousness delivers from death."[7] Covetous or greedy people never get around to prioritizing their children as the most valuable asset they possess. Sometimes, after they have blistered the world with success, they try "buying" their children with company privileges (if they own their own business). This usually backfires for one of two reasons:

first, the children are already bent out of shape for lack of parental models and couldn't manage a business if it was turned over to them; or second, they are so angry and resentful toward their parents that they wouldn't take the business—the thing they blame for separating the family—if it were dumped in their laps.

Spiritual principles in the workplace

These families were conscious of the need for high ethical standards in their businesses, as well as in their personal lives. Integrity and honesty were a part of who they were and how they lived. One of the men said, "Success is wrapped up in being a person of high integrity." These men and women did not leave their spiritual devotion at home—they also took it to work. One said,

> **"**
> I don't preach, but I believe they can see that I believe in high standards by my lifestyle, by my decisions, and by my talk. I think I am a better manager as a Christian than I would be as an atheist. **"**

One manager of hundreds of employees sent out a three-page letter telling his employees what kind of person he wanted to be. He said, "Please tell me if you observe me acting otherwise, because this is who I want to be." Another top executive sent his employees a Christmas letter (at his own expense), telling what Christ had meant to his life.

When we went to the office of a businessman who runs a company grossing over twenty-five million dollars a year, we noticed that there was a bronze plaque by the front door of his plant with the company motto inscribed on it. It was the twelfth chapter of Romans. These people didn't separate their faith from the rest of their lives.

Commitment to church

The commitment to the Lord carried over into a strong commitment to his people. Church was a top priority. Almost without exception, when we asked about their attendance and involvement in church, we heard, "Oh, we are always there. It is just a given that we will be there."

One of the men, an elder in his church, said he spends twenty-four hours in preparation for every one hour he spends in teaching.

And while these families didn't isolate themselves from their communities, they made their primary friends in the church. One father said,

> Our center of existence has been a set of principles found in the Bible and a set of friends found in the church.

For most of them, the church was the center of their social lives. They did not trust the values of the community at large and were willing to take the time to engender better moral values by spending more time working with their children at home and with other church people, people whose values they trusted.

One lawyer told us,

> I need to be around men who have a burning desire to serve. You really can't last long if you are a lone ranger. I need to be held accountable by other men.

Here is a guy, a top lawyer in an enormous city, who wants to be held accountable by *lay* people in the church. That is where his primary friends are—not in the legal profession but in the church. He likens his life to scuba diving in a hostile environment. "You always need a buddy with you." And he is not unusual in regard to the other families we spoke with.

Through the church, God has provided a "spiritual" family to fill in the gaps that we sometimes have in our physical families. For many of these folks, especially the ones who have had to do a lot of traveling, the church became a kind of extended family. One girl said point-blank: "The church *is* our family." Those who were far from grandparents, uncles, and aunts turned to the church to "adopt" a grandmother or grandfather, aunts and uncles. One wife said, "When my parents couldn't come quickly for the birth of our last child, our church friends immediately became the substitute parents."

Now, these were discerning people; they were not blind to the faults of people in the church. Even when they didn't agree with everything taught in the church they attended, they were keen on preserving a sweet spirit. One parent said he could remember very well his own mother saying, "Please don't ever be critical of the church."

▼

Covetous or greedy people never get around to prioritizing their children as the most valuable asset they possess.

Freedom in faith

The families we interviewed believed that each person has the freedom to search out his or her own faith. As one person said, we are "free in Christ." They all stressed that a relationship with the Father supersedes church attendance in importance, though none would ever miss services. This belief in freedom was extended to their children. They wanted their children to be able to think for themselves, to be autonomous in the Word. But freedom was always balanced with respect and consideration. The children were allowed to ask questions and raise issues, but never in a critical or ugly way. They did not want their children to be blind followers, but neither did they endorse "bucking authority." The children were expected to be polite and respectful of their seniors.

Of course, when children are allowed the freedom to make faith their own, there is always the risk of disagreement between parents and children. There were a few families with differences on religious issues. But these families were not factious. They didn't draw lines. They loved and respected each other deeply "where they were."

Time—Going, Going, Gone

Time, your most precious commodity

According to a survey by Massachusetts Mutual, Americans believe that "parents having less time to spend with their families" is the single most important reason for the family's decline in our society. [8]

Urie Bronfenbrenner found that the average father, who thinks he spends twenty minutes a day with each child, usually spends considerably less. In fact, his research indicated that the average father spends only thirty-seven seconds a day giving undivided attention to the child. That might be enough for a house plant, but certainly not a child. Talking about the modern, hectic lifestyle, Richard Louv writes,

> People are beginning to say, "This is crazy; we're not living, we're doing lunch." The rebellion is not against feminism; nor does it particularly support traditional roles. The rebellion is against time pollution, the feeling that the essence of what makes life worth living—the small moments, the special family getaways, the cookies in the oven, the night fishing with the kids asleep next to the lantern, the weekend drives, the long dreamlike summers—so much of this has been taken from us, or we have given it up. For what? [9]

One wise woman said,

> Have children only if you want to share your life with them. If you don't think they are going to be the best people in the world to spend your time with, don't have them. There are other things you could do.

Time is the most precious gift you can give your children. But unfettered, stable, consistent time won't simply materialize before your eyes. You've got to plan for it; it takes purposeful effort on your part.

Many moms are accustomed to rearranging their schedules to insure time with their children, but we also found several fathers who sacrificed their own desires and conveniences to make time to be with their children. These parents tended to choose activities that the *whole family* could participate in together. One dad gave up flying and golf because he couldn't do these activities with his family. Another family, with two children, started playing tennis.

One father arranged his schedule so he could spend two to three hours *every* evening with his family—including a family night every Friday, even though that was the regular "date night" in the children's circle of friends. This dad would spend from seven to nine every evening with the family, then when the children got ready for bed around nine, he would go upstairs to do his study and homework until midnight. He was up again around five o'clock the next morning to make his long commute to work. For years he slept less in order to spend more time with his kids, but his kids thought he was around all the time. Not until they were grown did they understand what their home life had cost him in terms of time and effort.

▼

"You are worth my time. I would rather be with you than anyone else in the world."

A lawyer in Los Angeles made a similar time arrangement for his family. He rises at 5:30 A.M. in order to study for about an hour or so until the kids wake up. Then he eats with the family, takes the children to school, comes home and walks with his wife, and finally goes to work after the traffic is down. He works a long day and comes home late in the evening to eat with the family. He and his wife made a joint decision that he would not work on the weekends, even though it affected his income. They felt it was worth it in the long run. Family priorities weighed more than business priorities. The message these parents wanted their children to hear loud and clear was, "You are worth my time, and furthermore, I would rather be with you than anyone else in the world."

Prioritize

One executive dad who worked long hours said: "I did three things: my job, my family, and church work." All else had to wait until the children were grown. This is the kind of prioritizing we are talking about.

The same dad also told us that he made sure that *his* recreation time was *family* recreation time. He didn't play golf all day Saturday with the guys. He planned things the family could do together.

Unfortunately, this dad and the dads we interviewed are exceptions to the rule. According to Gerald Kushel, president of the Institue for Effective Thinking, only 4 percent of executives put both work *and* family first. The vast majority make work their first priority. If you want to achieve both career and family success, you must be in that 4 percent minority.[10]

Of utmost importance was unrushed time with the children. Time when Mom and Dad were available and relaxed: talk time, question time, reading-to-them time, play time, fun time, not to speak of helping with homework, going to school productions, ball games, recitals, special family outings and trips, and then some one-to-one time with *each* child.

Brenda Hunter, in *What Every Mother Needs to Know,* emphasizes the educational implications of time spent with your child.

> Intelligence alone does not guarantee academic success. Some students with average intelligence perform at high levels while geniuses fail. The most powerful motivator for a child is time spent with a parent.[11]

But Urie Bronfenbrenner tells us that,

> Recent studies reveal that a major disruptive factor in the lives of families . . . is the increasing instability, inconsistency, and hectic character of family life.[12]

I know of only three ways to make more time for the important people in our lives—our children. (1) *Organize better.* You will never get *everything* accomplished. List your priorities (usually there is no need in listing more than five), then operate from the top. (2) *Delegate more.* Have someone else do every job that doesn't absolutely require you, and this may include hiring extra help. (3) *Eliminate all unnecessary activities.* Carefully evaluate what you do. Many activities can be cut.

Whenever I teach this three-fold approach, there are always those who tell me: "Well, I *have* organized myself, I *have* delegated all I can, and I *have* eliminated all the unnecessary activities

I can—now, what do I do?" To this I say, *"Nothing—*you are *not*
going to change. You are too bullheaded!" These are the same people who hide behind: "It's not my fault" or "I can't." They see
themselves as victims of circumstance and offer "when" and "if"
excuses as reasons: "when my vacation comes," "when I get a
raise," "if it weren't for my job," "when I get this project done."
Don't allow these excuses and postponements to cause you to neglect your family. *Prioritize family!*

Seize the early years

I can't adequately impress upon you how important it is to
begin early in training your children. Child developmental special-
ists and mothers have known this all along. But most parents don't
utilize the young child's learning potential. Maria Montessori, the
Italian physician and childhood development specialist, knew how
important the early years were—even the very first year. She
found that children as young as five years old could learn to speak
three languages.

The title of the popular book by Robert Fulghum says it in a
nutshell: *All I Really Need to Know, I Learned in Kindergarten.*
Things like sharing, manners, love, kindness, taking turns, getting
along with others—you know, the basics of life—all are learned in
the *early years.* If we allow our children to get by with selfishness,
ill manners, being ugly to others, and cruelty for their first six
years because "they are just children," we may not be able to reverse those traits later on.

Work with the hormones

I believe that by the time your child starts to school, your major
job as parent is half done, and by the time your child is twelve,
your job is about three-fourths finished. God has put a time bomb
inside children called hormones. These hormones begin to kick in
around the age of twelve or thirteen. You can't always teach children too well during this stage because the hormones get in the
way, and your children tend to take a "turn for the worse." Well,
not always, but they begin a very disruptive period of their lives,
partially because their systems are changing drastically. Hair begins to grow in funny places, pimples pop out on their faces,

voices change, manners tend to disappear, and attitudes can turn sour for no reason.

The most effective approach is to be more firm in our training in the first twelve years and then let up the next five or six. If you reverse this order, you are working against your child's incoming hormones and will likely run up against some heavy resistance. Those parents who wait until that funny stage of adolescence to enforce their parental authority are in deep weeds. It is extremely difficult, almost impossible, to bring them under reasonable control when they have been out of control during the formative years of their lives.

God has put a time bomb inside children called hormones.

The reason for this is obvious. Until children are about twelve, Mom and Dad (despite what the children may say) are their heroes. It is natural for children to look up to their parents—the parents are bigger, know more, provide food and transportation, protect and defend them from winter cold, summer sun, bad people, and ghosts and things that crawl in the night. So with minimal teaching, they are more *naturally* inclined to say "Yes, ma'am" and "No, sir" and "please" and "thank you." During these years, parents may be able to *control* their children without really *training* them—by yelling and ruling. But along about the sixth or seventh grade, when the hormones kick in, these tactics will no longer work, and the lack of childhood training will be obvious.

Hormones and the resulting personality shift are God's way, through nature, of preparing them to become self-governing, autonomous adults. And God is preparing them to be sexual beings—capable of bearing children, being mothers and fathers. In just five or six years, they will be out of your home—on their own or in college. Either way, they will be out from under your supervision—and glad of it, usually. So you just *hang on* through those teenage years as they develop their own styles of meeting life's demands, because in a few years they will have to steer their own bicycles without Mom and Dad's training wheels attached. Good parenting skills glide along *with* the hormones, gradually training and releasing parental authority as the children validate they can handle it, not abuse it.

Train for responsibility

The parents we interviewed understood the value of training their children to be responsible while they were young. One dad regularly took his son with him to bank board meetings. The president would sometimes frown on this, but Dad brought him anyway. The son told us in the interview,

> Dad would often turn to me after a meeting and ask, 'What do you think? What decision would you make?' By the time I was thirteen, I was responsible for thinking on my own and understanding what went on in those meetings.

That son is now on that same bank board. I wonder where the frowning president's son is?

Another junior high son was entrusted to trade baseball cards of high value on his own. His parents trained him to have a good sense of judgment about cards and a good system of cataloging them. He was responsible for thousands of cards.

In another large family, the thirteen-year-old daughter was given the responsibility of doing the entire family's weekly food planning and shopping. She was in charge of purchasing four hundred dollars worth of food each week. The grocery clerks were amazed.

One father told us a story about how his own father had trusted him by allowing him to write checks from the family checkbook at age fourteen. He said he would never forget the day when he had written a pretty sizable check and the banker called him aside and said, "Son, you have written a pretty big check here."

"Yes, sir, but my daddy said I could."

"Well, I know your dad said that, but this is a pretty big check. Would you mind waiting while I call your dad?"

"No sir," the boy said, hanging his head down a bit.

The boy waited for awhile, overhearing the conversation. Then he heard the bank officer say, "Yes, sir, I have ascertained that it is your son's signature on the check. Yes, sir, I will cash the check."

And the banker cashed the check.

The son (now in his sixties) told us that he felt so good that he walked out of that bank "with his buttons poppin'." He, in turn, allowed his own children to sign on the family checkbook when they were *twelve*. Of course, the family had trained their children for that responsibility by gradually teaching them how to be responsible with little things earlier on.

One of the fathers we interviewed trusted his son so much that at the age of sixteen, he allowed him to drive their best pickup truck, with their horse trailer and best horse in tow, to a vet in another town. Another father, when he heard about this, could hardly believe that a boy that young could be entrusted with such responsibility. "Why, I wouldn't let my *twenty-one year-old* son do that! I wouldn't trust him."

This reminds us of a twelve-year-old boy who was gone three days before his parents worried about him—why didn't they worry? I believe it was because Jesus was so responsible that his parents knew it would be foolish to worry about him. When they finally did go looking for him, they found him "conducting business" with the professionals—outlandish, but true—at twelve years of age.

But many parents today are still spoiling their high school and college students with, "Well, when you graduate from college and get out into the world, then you will have to support yourself." There is nothing wrong with helping those who help themselves, but when do they learn how to help themselves? They learn it best in the very early years of their lives.

Train for leadership

I am convinced that many conservative Christians have unknowingly held their children back instead of leading them forward. As a result, these children tend to be followers, perhaps following some bad examples of those who are taking the lead. Some hold their children back by saying, "You're too young to do . . ." So they hold their children back till everyone else is doing *everything!* Our children, to be leaders, ought to be *out front*—the first ones to do all the good and wholesome things. If it is right and possible, why not? Encourage leadership at an early age!

Train your children to think

Teach your children how to think. "Sometimes I would let them get into a bind, so they would have to figure it out for themselves," one father confided. This same father also knew when to stay close by his children's side. His daughter told us how her father helped her stay with a math and computer science program, when most of her classmates were dropping out. He helped her by working with her every step of the way. Both she and her brother gave their dad a lot of credit for teaching them problem-solving skills. Some parents hold to the "sink or swim" theory. They seem to think that the only way to teach children to stick with something or learn a new skill is to throw them out there and leave them on their own. But the dad we just mentioned helped his daughter stick with a difficult program by working closely with her. These parents knew when to walk alongside their child step by step and when to let them walk on their own.

Another thing these parents emphasized was the skill of decision-making. Teach your children to think things through for themselves at an early age, so they will know how to make the tough decisions later on when you're not around. Ask questions like, "Now, is that a good decision? Have you thought about . . . ?" Some parents even advocate allowing children to make all their own decisions by the time they are seniors in high school. This way, your child has the opportunity to make mistakes and fall, while you are still close by.

Precious Memories—Anchors for the Heart

Memories—good memories—are anchors to our past that provide stability for our future. Memories are a significant part of who we are. They are little snapshots of special times with significant people. If you haven't already noticed, you will soon notice as you grow older, that family reunions and memories of the past become more important with age.

Simple activities with parents create some of childhood's happiest memories. Psychologist Alida S. Westman surveyed college students to discover "what made them happy during childhood." Almost two-thirds (60 percent) identified "activities with one or both parents." Most of the activities mentioned were "simple things, such as taking a walk, going on a family picnic, or playing together." On the other hand, few students recalled "activities which would be difficult to arrange, such as vacations." Toys, it turned out, were not particularly important for childhood happiness: only 39 percent of the college students mentioned toys when identifying their fondest childhood recollections.[13]

▼

Try building a happy, stable mental scrapbook for your child.

Try building a happy, stable mental scrapbook for your child. Plan special events, vacations, and fun times. Arrange your weekly, even daily, schedules with your child's memory in mind as against your own short-term desires. Take plenty of photos (still and video). Your family will spend many hours reliving "precious memories."

Vacations can be great memory builders. The families we interviewed were big on vacations, and they took regular vacations together. One family took extra advantage of vacation traveling time by taking ACT and SAT test booklets along and asking questions to prepare the kids for the tests. One family had spelling bees in the car as they drove along. This helped Dad, as well as the kids, because spelling came hard for him. It also helped to pass the time.

One dad we interviewed felt so strong about vacations that he said,

> Take family vacations whether you can afford them or not.

A really great idea comes from the family who kept a tripod near the door with a big newsprint tablet tied to the top. The tablet became a kind of family journal, a collection of memories! Any time they had a problem they needed to solve as a family, they

solved it on this tablet. If they had lessons to be learned, Bible stories to be told, or privileges to be worked out, they put it on a page
of the tablet. We looked at pages that had names for their foster
babies, rules for spelling, things to do on vacations, a study of
Proverbs, and a page of things Dad wanted his girls to remember
when they went off to college. That big tablet is a journal of a hundred pages or more of family memories. Their memories were
down in black and white, so every time they looked through their
tablet, connected memories came flooding back to mind. It's a
beautiful record of that family's history.

▼

They liked leaving civilization and pitching their tents where they could fish and camp.

Being out in nature is another great way to create memories.
Many of the families we interviewed seemed to gravitate toward a
rural living environment, and they liked leaving civilization and
pitching their tents where they could fish and camp. These families talked about camping, scouting, traveling, canoeing, and scuba
diving. It wasn't all just fun stuff, though.

One family talked about hiking across the Grand Canyon in 120
degree weather. The best athlete in the bunch "flaked out" because
he hadn't drunk enough water. Another time they were stuck out in
a tent while it rained for hours and hours. The memory of bringing
back a carload of soggy clothes and mildewed equipment was still
fresh for a family that spent a lot of time in the summers camped
in Mexico and other places on mission trips. Almost all of these
folks remembered significant times in the out-of-doors.

Our own family had some of our most powerful experiences
while camping. On one camping trip in the Grand Teton National
Park, our little daughter, Connie, found a struggling lake trout on
the rocks. We knew that if we put him back in the lake, the waves
would throw him back on the rocks. Connie just *had* to save the
trout, so we found a little pond a few yards inland and put him in
it. But he wasn't doing too well, and our little one knew he was

sure to die. I had to do something—but what? Of course! Artificial respiration! So we carefully massaged the little trout—more out of respect for Connie than the trout. As "luck" would have it, the trout recovered—but not quite. He was swimming all right, but in tiny circles, so we feared the worst—brain damage. But before we could mourn, the little fella shot off straight as an arrow. It was a victory. We saved a life—and we made a precious memory.

▼

"I've gotten along without God so far—I think I can for the duration."

On that same trip we experienced one of the saddest moments of our lives. It was near dusk when we heard a "commotion" near us, but I wasn't sure what it was. About that time, our youngest son, Brad, came running over shouting, "Dad, there is a lady over here who needs help *bad.*" I ran over to find a university professor standing with two small children, wringing his hands. He pointed to his wife in the tent. I rushed in, and found her unconscious. She was not breathing, but I discovered that her heart was still beating and began immediately to give mouth to mouth resuscitation.

Soon, a physician who was camped nearby rushed in and took over. But it wasn't long before something happened that stopped all recovery possibilities and we had to wait—until her heart stopped beating. And then we waited much longer for the coroner. During the wait, I visited with the professor, sharing our hurt and concern and assuring him that God was very near, especially when tragedy strikes. I'll never forget his response: "I've gotten along without God so far—I think I can for the duration."

Later we took the professor and his two children to a cabin provided by the park service. It was a memory our children will never forget—the memory of a lonely man, walking into a strange cabin with two tearful children, without a wife . . . without a mother . . . and without a God—so far as they knew. It was a nightmare for us as well. We will never forget our helplessness. It was a sobering, penetrating moment.

Psalm nineteen says that "the heavens declare the glory of God and the earth shows his handiwork." So much of the time we surround ourselves with the things *we* have made until we lose touch with the *eternal*. When our children camp and hunt and fish, they are more likely to become overwhelmed with God the creator and with the power of the Almighty in the elements.

▼

"The heavens declare the glory of God and the earth shows his handiwork."

Dealing With Personality Differences

A final heart strategy for these families is that they valued and appreciated *differences* in their children. Personality, temperament, "wiring"—all these play into the individual differences that make up each child. They did not insist or expect that all their children conform to a certain mold. Effective families learn how to deal with individual differences in their children and turn these differences into assets.

The children in the families we interviewed knew that they were appreciated and loved—individually—*regardless of their abilities* or *looks* or *personalities*. The standard is that all children are of inherent value "just because they are ours"—not because they pay, not because they entertain, not because they earn anything or make good grades. They are loved because they are *ours.*

In many of the interviews, we asked parents, "What will happen if your children don't do as well as you?" The football coach said,

> 66
> I have always appreciated the second team player—the guy who doesn't have all the greatness of the first string player, but who puts his heart and soul into the game.
> 99

His children were well aware that they would be a success in Dad's mind whether they made the first string or not. This same family had a son, Johnny, with Down's syndrome, and every member of that family accredited Johnny with providing the family with balance and a sense of purpose. Even though his success may be less evident to those outside the family, he is a beloved, contributing, integral member of that family.

Actually, if our culture valued things like integrity, honesty, and sensitivity more than raw IQ, Johnny would be the valedictorian of his class. For example, Johnny's dad had told the family, "Don't cut across the field with the golf cart, because you will get the golf cart stuck in the sand. Come down the road instead." But as children will do, one day Johnny's sister cut across the field while Johnny was with her. Johnny said, "Dad told us not to cut across." But Sis said, "O, Johnny, I'll be *real* careful; it'll be okay." Sure enough, you guessed it, they got stuck, and it took a good while to get the cart out before they could continue on their way to the house. Now Sis tried to explain to Johnny that there was no need in telling Dad; but of course, Johnny would have none of that "'cause Dad told us not to cut across." Sis finally coerced Johnny into promising not to tell Dad. So as soon as they drove up in the front yard, Johnny hopped out in front of Dad and said, "Dad, Sis has something to tell you." He promised he wouldn't tell Dad and he didn't. Johnny is my pick for valedictorian.

The three sisters in another family said that as children they had talked about what kind of men they might marry when they grew up—perhaps a banker, a preacher, or a school teacher. They understood that their potential mates would lead them down different roads and put them in different socioeconomic circumstances; but they made a pact that they would never allow money, or the lack of it, to become a barrier. The key was that they would be faithful to the family, to the Lord, and to each other.

We met one family where the daughters were more financially successful than the sons, and this is happening more and more. One son was a clerk in a store and the other was trying to get a small business going; and although they were satisfied with their jobs, neither was set to make a high salary. Their sisters, meanwhile, had gone to school longer, and one was a lawyer and the other a psychologist. But this societal, or role, reversal made no difference to their family. They remain cohesive and powerful as a family.

I have five fingers on my hand. Four of them are very much alike, but one finger is really different. It is shaped differently, it looks different, and it works differently from the others. It is called a thumb. In almost all of the families we interviewed, somewhere along the line, we found a thumb or two. But thumbs are the very thing that gives the hand its unique effectiveness. Because a thumb, working in opposition to the other fingers, enables the hand to pick up things and to hold and use instruments.

▼

These families were able to turn individual differences into assets.

History has shown us that it is often the "different" ones who make the most significant contributions to society. Albert Einstein excelled at logical and mathematical thought, but had little interest in interpersonal intelligence, an area in which Sigmund Freud and Mahatma Gandhi both excelled. Pablo Picasso was below average academically but unmatched in visual-spatial skills. Igor Stravinsky was a master of music, T.S. Eliot of language, Martha Graham of dance and movement. The families we interviewed understood the value of "uniqueness" and were able to relabel their thumbs in such a way that the person's uniqueness became a strength rather than a liability.

One of the fathers—who was a strong, successful professional—has a free-thinking, laid-back son, and their differences naturally created some conflicts. As they have worked on their relationship, the father has become much less performance-oriented. He even allowed his child to be his teacher in the latest trends in music.

Some of the families had split religiously, and some of the children had left the family's value system for awhile. But these things were not allowed to splinter the family. They hung on to that person at all costs. One parent told me,

> "If our children don't turn out perfectly, we will still love them. We will not pressure them to be perfect. Even if our daughter got pregnant out of wedlock, we would still love her."

I guess what we are trying to say in reference to the beauty in our diversity is expressed in this little poem:

Swans don't run like the roadrunner,
Roadrunners don't soar like the eagle,
Eagles don't sing like the mocker,
Mockers don't fly in formation like geese,
No other bird can hover like a hummingbird,
Nor is any bird as faithful to his "wife" as the common
    sparrow.

God made children like birds.
There's no need in us comparing or wishin'
For a different set of abilities or gifts.
He wills that each child fly with his own set of wings
Designed just for them—with loving care.[14]

Every child has a special gift from God. Honor it!

▼

"Put the family in a good, healthy environment. Expose them to people who hold the same kind of standards you do."

14

STRATEGIES FOR LIVING

It was almost as if these families were listening in on each other's interviews, because we kept hearing the same message over and over—not in identical language—but the message was consistent:

1. Define your values and prioritize!

2. Set goals and plan strategies.

3. *Make it happen!*

These parents *made things happen!* They didn't just rock along and go with the flow of their culture. They set their own agendas and goals and "marched to their own drumbeat."

These parents managed their families' environment and influences. They strategically prepared their children for life. They had

195

a vision for their families, and they planned strategies to make that vision a reality.

Impart Life Skills

Skills for living have to be taught. Your children will not just learn them by osmosis. Following are some skills emphasized by the families we interviewed.

Inoculate for temptation

These children were conditioned for temptations early so they could be more successful in overcoming them. Their parents anticipated problem areas and tried to give their children alternatives. They practiced problem-solving exercises before difficult situations arose. Before one father allowed his son to use a family car for the first time, they had a conversation that went something like this:

"Now son, this is a good running little car, isn't it."

"Yes sir!"

"It'll be a temptation to see how fast it will run, won't it?"

"Uh, well, I hadn't thought much about that."

"It's kind of a natural thing. Chances are good that as soon as you get down to the red light, Tim (one of his buddies) will pull up next to you and rev up his motor and challenge you to dig out and see how fast that car will pick up. So, what do you think you ought to do?"

So he gets the son thinking about his temptation ahead of time with his rational head, not his emotional one. And sure enough, when Tim shows up and starts revvin' up his motor, Dad's words pop in his mind, and he has the willpower to resist.

Reframe negative circumstances

All of these families encountered some pretty heavy times along the way. Through the bad times, however, the parents taught their children to reframe those circumstances with a positive, optimistic outlook on life. One family recalled the time they were moved overseas, away from the children's friends and grandparents and cousins. They couldn't speak the language and felt kind of homesick and isolated, but they used that time to build strength in their family. They would pile into their little car and tour all over Europe. Getting lost was all part of the experience, along with singing every chorus of *Ninety-Nine Bottles of "Coke" on the Wall* several times and spending more time listening to the American country music station than they spent absorbing local culture. But they loved it.

Another family, who was plagued with all sorts of health problems, adopted the strategy:

> **"** We don't complain, because it is just expected that we will get well and go on. Nobody is allowed a 'pity party.' **"**

They focused on good health, on what they *could* do. Mom just wouldn't let them feel sorry for themselves. One Sunday at church, all the kids were gathered around while a tenderhearted soul was talking to the mother. This woman was just going on and on about how sorry she felt for their family and how tough their lives were. The children listened politely as long as they could and then finally just burst out laughing. They meant no offense, but seeing themselves as objects of pity was ridiculous to them.

▼

Survivors have learned how to reframe their setting.

The son of a CEO likes to remember the time he was on the rowing team in school. The crew captain was giving him a hard time, trying to force him off the team by generally making his life miserable. He almost dropped out, but with some encouragement from the coach, he stuck with it, eventually going on to become the commodore for the team. It was a miserable experience at the time, but he now says it was a real turning point for him because it gave him a heart for people who are in discouraging situations. He has reframed that experience as a character-building opportunity. It gave him more compassion.

Life-mate choices

> Choose your life's mate carefully. From this
> one decision will come ninety percent of all
> your happiness or misery.

How true! These parents put a high priority on who their children married. They knew that something this important should not be left to chance, so they gave their children lots of practical advice, beginning while the kids were very young, about what to look for in a good mate.

One group of brothers and sisters remembered that Mom was always telling them, "Don't ever marry someone who . . ." She might follow with something cute like "someone who smokes, because your kids will come out green." She was funny and playful, but she made her point. Her daughter said,

> Mom taught us to like certain types of people.
> She would point them out in public. She told us
> things to look for in other people like character
> and integrity. We would never think about
> bringing a really 'yucky' person home to her.

Another mom, from the Bible, also had strong feelings about who her children married.

> Rebecca said to Isaac, "I'm disgusted with living. . . . If Jacob
> takes a wife from among the Hittite women, my life will not be
> worth living." [1]

One father would invite the prospective husbands and boyfriends to come to the farm. He would put those boys to work, so his four pretty daughters could see which boys would amount to something and which ones were afraid of work. Once he had the boys put a fence through the end of a pond instead of around it, so he could see how they handled the "mud and the muck and the snakes." These dads were not afraid to put a little pressure on prospective suitors, like the father who greeted a future son-in-law with "So you are the one I have been praying for all these years."

Many of the families let their children know they prayed every single day for their future mates.

> **"** We prayed every day since the children were born that they would meet and marry a Christian. **"**

Manners—a must

Webster's defines *manners* as "morals shown in conduct." Effective parents teach their children skills that enable them to be at ease in social situations. Children who have good manners and are pleasant to be around get positive strokes from others, not only their parents, and learn how to interact well with others.

> Kids want to be liked, and manners make them likable—not just to grown-ups, but to one another as well. Not victorian, but at least "thank you," "please," and "excuse me"; not interrupting; shaking hands and greeting people pleasantly when being introduced and looking people straight in the eye and listening to them when they speak. [2]

From the children we interviewed we heard comments like,

> **"** This family is big, big, *big* on manners, like 'yes sir' and 'no sir' and 'ma'am' and 'please.' **"**

> **"** Mom would not put up with her children being disrespectful or 'smart alecky' to her or any other adult. **"**

> **"** One of the main things my mom would never put up with was us 'talking back' or being disrespectful. **"**

The meaning of work

These parents understood the value of hard work, and they taught their children the dignity and sense of accomplishment that comes from honest labor. A number of the children told us that they were shocked to learn that they were considered "rich" by classmates or friends, because they had to work just like everybody else. One girl said,

> **"**
> It really made me mad that some of my classmates thought I never had to work hard. I earned all my spending money. **"**

Even though most of these children did not work outside the home, almost all of them had job responsibilities. The parents taught them real work skills—some children helped make plumbing and electrical repairs in the home, some worked in the family business. In one family the children spent hours putting price tags and labels on products that the family business sold. One dad bought an old car to take apart and put back together. Mom said it was a great experience—the whole family working on that old car.

Two Harvard psychiatrists, Drs. George and Caroline Vaillant, report that

> success in adulthood is more related to a child's capacity to work than his intelligence, social status or family background. . . . Those who worked hardest as children developed into the best-paid and most satisfied family men. Their work as youngsters had usually consisted of household chores, part-time jobs, sports and studies. [3]

Having to earn certain things and learning work skills prevents kids from developing the sense of "entitlement" that is prevalent in the children of the wealthy. Robert Coles[4] and Andrea Brooks[5] observed this trait in their research of children, and both felt it was detrimental to the ability of the children to adjust to adulthood. We didn't see that sense of entitlement, the notion that the world owed them something, in the families we interviewed, because the parents made sure that work was a part of the children's daily lives.

Manage Family Influences

All of us are susceptible to the influences around us—some of these influences are good, and some are not so good. As intentional parents, your job is to take a look at these influences and *manage* them. You certainly can't control all the influences in your children's lives, but there is a lot you *can* do. Here are some of the ways the families we interviewed managed what influenced their children.

Choose your house with your children in mind

Managing your child's environment will, of course, require sacrifices on your part. Instead of choosing a neighborhood suited to *your* desires, you must consider the social, educational, and church needs of your children.

▼

Managing your child's environment will require sacrifices on your part.

The families we interviewed chose their houses based on where the best schools and churches for their children were, not their own personal desires. Their house choice was not based on being in the "right" part of town or the availability of golf courses and tennis courts. Their own conveniences were secondary. And they chose churches where the children could be active participants, not just spectators. They looked for positive, *praising* churches where they could receive encouragement and give time and energy in service.

Many parents searched for communities or neighborhoods that were less hectic than average, in order to give their children a healthy atmosphere. They looked for places where family time was encouraged.

One family, who lived in the Washington, D.C., area became concerned at the number of children in their neighborhood who were left entirely on their own during the day. They began looking around for another place to live and eventually moved thirty miles away from the city to a small community with a family-friendly lifestyle and a church the *children* were excited about. Their final decision was made when they saw how the school introduced the football players at the game—they had the whole family stand up when the players were introduced. Even though it cost the father an extra hour coming and going to work every day, they moved to that community for their children. This is the kind of intentionality that is required.

▼

They said their happiest times were when they moved out "to the boonies."

A number of the families we interviewed lived out in the country, even if only for the summer. They said their happiest times were when they moved out "to the boonies." One mother pointed out, "It is a whole lot more work for me out in the country, but it is a fantastic place for healing." It was worth the work to her. Many distractions that pulled family members in opposing directions were eliminated, and everybody had to learn to associate with everybody else and develop a responsibility not only for each other, but often for crops and animals as well.

Many of the children understood the benefit of the small town atmosphere. One of the boys said the best advice he ever got from his parents was to date a girl from a small town, and when he finally did, he married her.

Open your home to your children's friends

The Bible teaches us to be hospitable, and this hospitality needs to be extended to our children's friends, as well as our own. Romans 12:13 tells us to practice hospitality, and 1 Peter 4:9 says to "offer hospitality to one another without grumbling."

Wise parents open their homes to the friends of their children by providing a safe, fun place. What better place for your children and their friends than your home? Several of the families called attention to the need to know the names of their children's friends. One dad said, "If you don't know the names of all your children's friends, you are too busy." His wife added, "Yes, and you need to know even more than their names."

In these families, the action revolved around their houses. As one family told us, "The door is never locked. Everybody eats at our house and swims in our pool." They didn't have to worry much about where the children were because, for the most part, they were *at home.*

▼

Wise parents open their homes to the friends of their children by providing a safe, fun place.

And speaking of opening your home to your children's friends, we just have to mention the gambling party that was thrown by a church leader. High school graduation night at his children's school traditionally included a big dance, which unfortunately included drinking and drugs and after-dance possibilities for trouble. This guy and his wife decided they just had to do something. So they told the kids that they could go to the graduation dance if they wanted to, but at *their* house they were going to have a gambling party, and everybody was invited. This was a *real* gambling party, with all the big equipment—the roulette wheel, the craps table, blackjack, the professional dealers, the whole works—everything but slot machines. As you might guess, just about everybody in the high school decided that the gambling party sounded like a whole lot more fun than the dance, and they had a great turnout. When the kids came to the house, they all were given $25,000 in Monopoly money and sent off to try their luck. The kids came back to the host at about ten o'clock, and since everybody was running out of money, he gave each one an additional $25,000.

About midnight, he called everybody in to see how rich they had gotten. He asked everyone who had $5 million or more to stand up. All the professional dealers stood up. Then he asked for those with $1 million. Still only the dealers were standing. He finally found one person who had broken even with about $50,000, but most of the kids who were there had lost all their "money." And they could look around the room and see that the ones who ended up with all the money were the dealers. It was pretty obvious who the big winners were.

"Does that tell you anything?" he asked them.

"Yep."

"Anybody want to try gambling with your own money?"

"Nope."

Then they conducted a special devotional before everybody left. There's no question in my mind but that the kids who were there learned a whole lot more about gambling that night than they would have learned from the best sermon on the subject on a Sunday morning.

Expose kids to potential heroes

These parents brought others into their homes who were role models and mentors. They believed in the importance of having "heroes of the faith" around their dinner table—preachers, missionaries, local leaders, physicians, anyone their children could look up to—talking with their children and influencing them. One of the fathers said,

> 66
> Put the family in a good, healthy environment.
> Expose them to people who hold the same kind
> of standards you do.
> 99

One of the sons said about his parents' hospitality, "That is how we developed our heroes."

Some of these children said,

> 66
> We met and made our best friends at our own
> table.
> 99

One family had a study group of about thirty people in their home every Monday night for years. Another had a dozen or more people over every Sunday after church for dinner. A young woman said,

> Mom and Dad always had great friends, so we knew what made good friends.

Protect children from negative people

We noticed something else in the lives of several of the families that surprised us a little, but actually, it correlates to the strategy of exposing your family to positive people. These effective parents tended to avoid the influence of people who had a negative impact, even when those people were close relatives. On several occasions, we heard them mention a parent or a brother or sister who was not a particularly good influence, maybe because of an alcohol dependency or a disrespect for values that the family held dear. The strong families didn't spend much time with those folks, and they didn't encourage their children to be around them. Of course these families displayed kindness and love toward the "negative" family member, and those weaker relatives were cared for when necessary; but the parents purposely steered their children in other directions, almost like isolating an infection.

▼

We couldn't find a single family that allowed the children to watch TV before *all* the homework was done.

Monitor intrusions

Whether we like it or not, the influences of our corrupt world are sometimes brought right inside our homes and up close to our families. The parents we interviewed actively monitored these intrusions to the best of their ability.

They regulated the influence of the media by limiting and monitoring the television and movies their children watched. We *couldn't find a single family* that allowed the children to watch TV before *all* of the homework was done. Several families told us that they would love to have cable because of the sports, but there was so much other garbage on cable that they did without it. There were even a couple of families who didn't own a television. They might rent a set to watch a movie on their VCR or for special occasions like the Olympics, but their general policy was to have no television.

We spent five hours with one such family—a family of seven children. We were amazed at the warm, networking, cordial, peaceful environment we saw there. This family was different—beautifully different—and the parents told us that one of the reasons the children were so calm was that they were not programmed by a jumble of thirty-second advertisements and twenty-five minute drama formats, that many times include violence, sex, and emotional ups and downs and tension.

One of the parents said,

> Television is too restrictive. It takes away from games and talking and play and reading and walking. It keeps us from sitting on the front porch and visiting.

Research tells us that television strongly interferes with family interactions.[6] Television has actually altered about 60 percent of the people's sleeping habits and about 55 percent of their mealtimes. It tends to give many deceptive, if not downright false, messages. Television does not tell our children to do something useful, it tells them what to acquire. One survey tells of a ten-year-old child who could name only one president (George Washington) but could identify and spell correctly Michelob, Jack Daniels, and Heineken.[7] Over 3,000 studies have linked TV with violence, and several studies connect TV and poor school performance. Furthermore, television is a passive medium. Regardless of the content, it reinforces passive rather than active responses.[8]

No scientific study is required to document another disastrous effect of television: it has all but displaced reading as a leisure activity. It also shortens the attention span. William Bennett has done some interesting research that found that programs like "Sesame Street" actually have a negative effect on a child's attention span. The short segments and hopscotching format of such programs is detrimental to the development of concentration skills. He says that reading stories to your children and programs like "Mr. Rogers' Neighborhood," which has a much slower pace and more continuity, teach children to pay attention and concentrate for longer time periods.

If you do have a television set, it's important that you monitor what your children watch and that you use it for character-building videos like *Hoosiers, Gandhi, Chariots of Fire*, C. S. Lewis' *Chronicles of Narnia*, National Geographic specials, "Wilderness Family" series, or the Disney classics.

Many of the same charges against television can also be levied against uncontrolled electronic games. While such games can be fun, consideration must be given to the amount of time spent on them and in some cases, their content.

Movies were also closely screened by these parents. None of the children were allowed to see whatever movie they wanted—regardless of the rating. The parents tried to protect their children's innocence and high ideals as long as they could by knowing the kinds of movies that were good for their children and which ones were not, and by exercising control over what the children were allowed to see.

▼

None of the children were allowed to see whatever movie they wanted—regardless of the rating.

Most of these families regulated how the telephone was used. One family made a vacation home by moving two old, small houses together on their farm. They spent a whole month at the farm every year. The only phone was in the barn about half a mile away. Their four teenage daughters could hardly stand it, but these parents didn't want their vacation time to be spoiled by a lot of interruptions. Some of the families limited the number of calls the children could receive and also the amount of time they could spend on the phone for each call.

Postpone initiation into the workplace

It was also a little surprising to find that many of these parents kept their children at home rather than allowing them to work as young teens. They didn't want them getting out of the home too early and going to work too soon.

The teenage workplace can provide some very powerful, negative influences in your child's life at a time when he or she is most vulnerable, or "tender." Chances are good that your child will meet other kids who are "on their own" too soon, kids who are older and have "new" ideas for your child. This can encourage activities that do not fit in with your standards. And then there are the late hours that many fast-food restaurants require, causing your child to miss out on family time and to be "too tired" to do their homework. They may also begin to like the "night life." We need to rethink this issue and make sure that we gather all the data before we encourage, or even "allow," our children to work out of the home in the evening.

▼

The teenage workplace can provide some very negative influences in your child's life.

Other considerations are pinpointed by some rather interesting research by Minear:

> A number of studies have been done on the so-called workspend ethic . . . a trend that involves spending a lot of . . . time at jobs in order to earn money for excessive purchases. . . . There are some big problems with this trend. First of all, children who work too much at an early age often find that they don't have time for other activities that will be much more vital

to them in the long run. . . . Another drawback is the tendency to lose sleep, eat poorly, and experience work-related anxieties too soon.[9]

The *Journal of Home Economics* reported on a study that found that "the majority of employed high school students indicated that they worked chiefly for the money, rather than to gain experience or skills."[10] This same report suggested alternatives to the typical teenage job. They advocated establishing mentoring relationships in healthy work environments that would allow adolescents to work with adults in their regular daily activities. The interaction with mature adults in business settings provides fantastic insight and wisdom. Or how about encouraging your children to work in community volunteer programs that encourage youth service, such as Meals on Wheels and Habitat for Humanity (a national volunteer organization that builds houses and sells them to needy families at no interest and no down payment).

▼

Many of these parents kept their children at home rather than allowing them to work as young teens.

Instead of allowing their children to work in the evenings at fast-food restaurants or teen hangouts, most of the parents we interviewed paid them to do extra jobs (besides their regular chores), around the house, such as cleaning or yard work. Some of the parents even went in with the children on business ventures or involved the kids in the family business. The farm children learned how to make extra money by inventing a way to pick up the loose cotton after the stripping was done. They used cyclone fencing and the hood of a car.

One family bought a lot with an old metal building on it. The children told about tearing down the building, sorting through the junk, and coming on hundreds of *rats*. They were in "stitches" as they told about watching Mom hauling tin and killing rats left and

right with her rubber boots and pry bar—and this was the wife of a
CFO of a top ten company in the Fortune 500.

A lot of these folks used their creativity to find family projects
and ways of making money so that the family could be together
and earn money at the same time.

We even met some families who home schooled their children.
This served a double purpose of educating the children *and* tying
the home closer together. Only a few of the people we interviewed
had experience with home schooling, but those who did felt very
good about it. One of the major criticisms of home schooling is
that the children tend not to develop good social skills. I think
Christian families can avoid that, and the ones I met have done so
by allowing their children to become active in social activities,
civic groups, sports programs like T-ball, Little League, Pop
Warner football, and soccer, and by getting together with other
families who home school for field trips, tours, and recreation.

Minimize harmful competition

I must set the stage here by reminding my readers that I am a
competition freak. You don't need to encourage me to be more
competitive. Since I was a child, I have been in competition. I was
recently inducted in my alma mater's Athletic Hall of Fame. I took
the award and ran before the committee could find out they had
made a mistake. Nevertheless, I am growing less and less enam-
ored with our almost unending push of competitive athletics.

▼

Life doesn't terminate at the end
of our peak physical condition.

The cost alone is a considerable factor. Today's children can't
be satisfied with basketball shoes—they have to have a famous
athlete's signature on them, at twice the price. Then, they must
have the "right" hat, glove, bat, etc. In my day, when we played
sandlot baseball, we would turn our undershirts wrong side out
and call ourselves "The Fruits of the Loom." (I'm not knocking
good, protective athletic gear.)

But the monetary cost is minor, very minor, compared to other considerations. Coaches are telling me that many young boys and girls are encouraged by their parents to start too young and to work too hard. Their muscles are not developed enough to handle strenuous pitching and throwing, and their joints and bones are not able to withstand the heavy contact that occurs in some sports.

The psychological cost is high too! I remember the ten-year-old catcher with three hundred dollars worth of gear on, trying to catch a wild pitch. There was a man on second and third. If they got *this* out, they would win the game. But as luck would have it, the pitcher threw one in the dirt. The ball scooted past him in a cloud of dust, and by the time he recovered the ball, both runners had crossed the plate, and his team lost the game. The memory that lingers in my mind twenty years later is this little boy sobbing, as a ten-year-old child ought, walking with his mother's arm around him saying, "I lost the game." Mom said, "No, honey, it wasn't all your fault. The ball was thrown in the ground." But he sobbed, "They [his own teammates] said it was all my fault!" *I* say, the family paid too high a price for the privilege of playing baseball that day.

▼

And must we win? And must we win at all cost?

And must we win? And must we win at all cost? Vince Lombardi is reported to have said: "Winning isn't everything; it's the only thing." That's ridiculous! Even the ultimate athletes—the Babe Ruths, the Michael Jordans—outlive their victories. Our children must be prepared to live a *whole* life. It's a false philosophy that implies that life terminates at the end of our peak physical condition. It is as juvenile as the sensualist believing that life should end in one immense orgasm.

Tocqueville, the great French writer, visited the U.S. in 1830 to write about our great success. But he noticed a "restlessness in the midst of our prosperity." And I think his following quote is still true today.

> In America I have seen the freest and best educated of men in circumstances the happiest to be found in the world; yet it seemed to me that a cloud habitually hung on their brow, and they seemed serious and almost sad even in their pleasures. [They] never stop thinking of the good things they have *not* got.

This restlessness and sadness in pursuit of the good life is intensified, says Tocqueville, by "the competition of all. . . . Their minds are more anxious and on edge." How could such restless, competitive, and anxious people sustain enduring relationships, when they "clutch everything and hold nothing fast."[11]

Harmful competition also occurs in the classroom. An assistant principal of an elementary school told us about the intense pressure that parents put on their children to get in advanced or gifted classes. She went on to say that the competition doesn't end there. Many of these parents want their children to be the "best of the best." One parent wouldn't accept a grade less than ninety-five from her child in an advanced class. Parents often expect too much, too soon.[12]

▼

Parents often expect too much, too soon.

Thankfully, Vince Lombardi later said, "I wish to h--- I'd never said that d--- thing. . . . I sure as h--- didn't mean for people to crush human values and morality."[13] But this is exactly what can happen when winning becomes everything.

And another thing, when playing with your children, please let them win—not just sometimes, but maybe most of the time. "Redneck" fathers have said to me: "Well, they gotta' learn to play it tough, nobody's gonna' give it to 'em." I agree, there is a time (and they will learn it soon enough) to face the big boys. But when they are in training with Dad, who is years older and years more experienced, he needs to let them experience winning. They know you could beat them if you really wanted to. And don't deny your child that unforgettable day when he or she will be able to beat you, even when you are trying with all your might. Allow your child these victories.

This "gotta win" attitude creates real and lasting mental problems for those children who are not athletically inclined. Some children are just not built that way. Even the country boy knows that you wouldn't attempt to train a Border collie to be a coondog. He knows to find out what the dog's special gifts are and go with them. Use the same wisdom with your children. You can't force special aptitudes on children, so don't try. Please, before you follow the crowd of other parents who are taking their children from tennis to voice lessons, from ballet to baseball, find out what each of your special children's aptitudes are—then begin with them in mind.

▼

Your children need a higher ratio of "winning" than is normally available in "too early" competitive sports.

In a nutshell, I just believe that your children need a higher ratio of "winning" than is normally available in "too early" competitive sports. In baseball, football, basketball, soccer, etc., half of the boys and girls that walk off the field are losers. The ratio of winning to losing is 50/50. I would like to create a higher ratio of winning. That is why I presently favor sports like hunting, fishing, camping, roller blading, biking, and hiking—because the parents can be active participants with the child. Some days you catch 'em (fish), some days you don't. And no one considers it a personal failure to not catch a fish. Neither is it considered a personal failure to not shoot the buck or the duck. And the fact that sometimes the child can catch "the big one" increases that winning ratio even more. There just seems to be something in hunting and fishing that encourages friendships, long talks, and basic together time beside the camp fire and on cold mornings. These are lifelong sports that the whole family, young and old, can engage in, not just young super athletes.

Let's cherish our children for who they are. Let's make sure we're not subconsciously trying to reenter the sports arena, or any other competitive arena, through our children. It isn't fair to the child, to say nothing about the fact that it doesn't work.

I know that most of you are going to continue in Little League with your children, and that is okay. Little Leagues all over the country are recognizing what I am trying to say and are changing their emphasis. But I do hope I have given you a little broader perspective concerning the needs of your children and family over a life span.

Participate in Education

School is the work of children. It is their primary childhood responsibility. But it is far more. It is their future. School forges the work of the adult-child—her career choices, challenges, even satisfaction.[14]

If school is as important as Guarendi says it is, we had better take a close look at our children's learning environment. Insuring that your children get the best education possible is your responsibility. It's not enough to just send your kids off to school and hope for the best. You've got to be informed about and involved in their schools, and you need to monitor and help with homework.

And even before they start to school, you can be "education-minded." Simply the way you talk to your child can make a lot of difference in his or her attitude toward learning. James Kavanaugh, former chief of pediatrics at St. Elizabeth's Hospital in Boston, has some helpful suggestions for relating to young children in his book, *Basics: A Program Designed to Help You Recognize and Enhance Your Child's Abilities.* [15]

1. Begin talking to children in infancy.
2. Include children in activities.
3. Don't interrupt an enthusiastic storyteller to make corrections. There will be plenty of time for grammar later. When you do make corrections, be positive, not critical.
4. Reinforce learning by association. Example: "That bird is like the one we saw yesterday. What did we call it?"

5. Be specific in your choice of words. Say: "photographer," not "the lady with the camera."
6. Converse each night at the dinner table. As children mature, play word games with them and discuss new ideas and events.
7. Read: *to* your children, *with* them, *in front* of them, and talk about what they are reading. Don't stop reading aloud to your children when they begin to read on their own; rather, move on to more challenging material—stories, poetry, plays, etc.

Emphasize reading

Jim Trelease, a reading expert, emphasizes the importance of reading aloud to your children. His book, *The Read Aloud Handbook,* is often described as the "Read Aloud Bible" and is an excellent resource.

The parents we interviewed instilled in their children the desire to read and taught them how to read well. Mom and Dad loved to read, and their love was contagious—the children caught it. Mom and Dad read to the children even after the children could read well. The children sometimes read or told stories to Mom and Dad. Reading was a highlight of the child's day—a time of fun and enjoyment. One parent referred to reading as "food for the brain." These parents encouraged their children to read broadly— art, music, science, literature, history, classics, and biographies. Books were all over the house in inviting places—on tables, desks, shelves, and beside chairs and beds.

Reading to your child develops a closeness in the parent-child relationship, as well as the educational and spiritual value it provides. Research isolates one factor for reading readiness—parents reading to kids.

In one family the father told us,

> **"** All of our children are exceptional readers. We taught them to read, and read well. **"**

This dad read to the children in front of the fire at night from books like the Bible, *The Call of the Wild* (by Jack London), horse books, religious books—all were read as bedtime stories.

Mark Twain said that the man who *does not* read has no advantage over the man who *cannot* read. Many parents don't really know what to read to their children, so I have listed in Appendix Two what I call the "classics." This is not an exhaustive list, by any means, but these are books that every child can benefit from.

Involve yourself

The children we talked with told us that their parents not only taught them to love reading, but were also very involved in their schoolwork. These parents didn't just send the kids off to do their homework, they often tutored the kids themselves when they needed assistance. If the parents were not able to help, they found someone who could. One dad, when he was out of town, would help his child work out math problems over the phone.

▼

"The man who *does not* read has no advantage over the man who *cannot* read."

In Japan, if a child has to stay home because of illness, oftentimes the Japanese mother will find someone to stay with the child, and she will go to school and sit in that child's chair to make sure she can teach at home what is covered at school in the child's absence.

Encyclopedias, educational videos, *National Geographic* magazines, and other resource information were either in the home or would be quickly obtained for a project. Now that computers have come down so much in price, many families purchase a computer and child-level software to prepare the young minds of their children for the next century. There are some great hypercard programs for children that will feed their curiosity as well as educational games, such as "Where in the World Is Carmen San Diego?" that teaches geography while the child is having fun.

Encourage creativity

One family told us about their regular "model night." They would make model airplanes or cars or a paper clock or the latest kind of paper airplane. When I was a kid, I learned how to make darts out of matchsticks, needles, and a piece of paper. It's hard to do it right, and it takes expertise, but it is great fun to learn. We made all kinds of things out of shingles. We made little toy tanks out of spools of thread and matchsticks and rubberbands. Those toy tanks were special because they were something we made together, not just something somebody pressed in plastic that Daddy bought and brought home.

I'm not suggesting that you should use *all* of these particular strategies in your family, I'm just giving you a multitude of ideas and examples. Select a few that fit your situation and your family, and add them to your daily routines. And remember, the number one strategy of Jesus is modeling *service*.

DISCIPLINE THAT EMPOWERS

SECTION FOUR

▼

"Children will do just about what you expect them to do—for good or for ill."

INTRODUCTION

The concept of intentional parenting calls for a premeditated decision concerning the way we discipline our children. Our methods of discipline must not be chosen at the last moment when we have "had it up to here."

Intentional discipline, as the name implies, relys on forethought, planning, reading, and prayer. It is preventive before it is corrective. It looks to the future and is based on a vision of what we want our children to be in God's kingdom.

15

MOTIVATION—
Preventive Discipline

I have a lawyer friend who has tried cases on Wall Street and negotiated contracts in China, yet she says it is more difficult to motivate and persuade her three-year-old child than it is to negotiate contracts in China and on Wall Street.

Many of us go at motivation as if we were hammering a nail. We figure the harder we hit it, the more likely it is to go where we want it to go. So when our children fail to respond as we think they should, we try to *force* them to do it our way. We threaten punishment, we yell, we demand; and while this may get partial compliance from our children, it won't really touch their hearts.

When the lusty King David was finally convicted of his sin with Bathsheba, he remarked to God, "I know what you want. What you really want is a broken and contrite heart."[1] And folks, that's exactly what we're after with our kids. We don't want to break their *spirits,* but to somehow *so touch them* that they have a broken and contrite heart. When disappointing Mom and Dad makes their hearts hurt, they'll be motivated from within to do what's right. And isn't that what we're after?

Let's see if we can't find some ways to touch our children's hearts.

Walk Your Talk

> There are only three ways to teach a child: the first is by example, the second is by example, and the third is by example.[2]

Albert Schweitzer is making a powerful point. And I want to make the same one. If there is only one thing you remember about motivating your child, remember this: "You've got to walk your talk and practice what you preach." You just can't expect your children to listen to your advice and ignore your example. One of my favorite quotes is, "Children have never been very good at listening to their elders, but they have never failed to imitate them." How true.

The parents we talked with practiced what they preached, and the kids knew it. One father told us about watching in amazement as his son expertly put in a fence. He asked his son, "How did you learn to do that so straight?" The son pointed his finger right back at him and said,

> Everything you did in the garden and in the lawn was perfect. I learned to do it right the first time *from you.*

One married son wrote this note to his parents on their fortieth anniversary. He obviously understood the power of modeling.

> Dear Mom and Dad—
> Congratulations on forty years of marriage. Hopefully, with the influence y'all have had on us through your relationship, we will be counting many more anniversaries ourselves.
> Love—Brad

Worthy models *draw* us to them; they draw just like a *magnet.* I saw this when I interviewed these people. It was so *obvious.* I was drawn to them by their servant hearts, by the way they talked, by their actions, by their spirit.

Remember the children who knew how devoted their mom was to the Lord because they saw her knee prints in the carpet and her worn Bible on the night stand? Even though Mother wasn't aware of it, those children never forgot the knee prints. Those kids' spirits were shaped by her *example*. There's no better teacher.

One IBM executive selected the twelve guys who reported directly to him partially because they had never been divorced. "If they can't manage their own homes, how can I expect them to manage the corporation?" I think what he meant was if you don't keep your promises and vows at home, you can't keep your promises and vows at work, either. He expected his men to be consistent in their walk and in their talk. Only then could they build a greater IBM.

▼

The example of Mom and Dad has more power than all the rules and punishments piled together.

God knew the power of example when he sent his own son as a model. Jesus draws us to himself like a magnet. He said "When I am lifted up from the earth, [I] will draw all men to myself."[3] The example of Jesus has more motivating power than all the biblical commands put together!

And the example of Mom and Dad has more power than all the rules and regulations and punishments piled together.

Love Them

"God so loved the world that he gave his only begotten son."[4] How does God motivate? Love! And notice the little word *so*. God *so* loved. That's what draws us, what motivates us to love the father—the fact that God's love is so great toward us. If love is what motivates *us* to do right, surely it will motivate our kids just as powerfully. That sweet little children's song, "Jesus loves me this I know . . ." has motivated millions all over the world.

But if we're going to make the most of the motivating power of love, we've got to understand the difference between love and *perceived* love. You may love your children with all your heart, and you may tell your children over and over that you love them; but until your children actually *believe* you love them, it is all in vain. Your children's *perception* of your love for them makes all the difference. It is not so much what you *say* as what they *hear* you say.

Researchers now tell us that the combined effects of perceived love and perceived trust (we'll talk more about trust in a minute) actually provide the antidote to the two major negatives in children's lives: *peer influence* and *conflicts with Mom and Dad.*

Stephen Glenn, author of *Raising Children for Success,* addresses the relationship of perceived love to peer influence.

> Children who have strong perceptions of closeness and trust with significant adults are very resistant to peer influence.[5]

Fred Streit did an in-depth study of children's *perceptions* of their parents' love for them and found that perceived love has a major impact on kids. Even though the influence of peers is great in adolescent years, the power of perceived parental love can *counter* peer influence. The values of Mom and Dad are bolstered by the child's perception of their love.

The second thing that happens when children feel loved (and trusted) is that there are fewer conflicts at home, because the children see the rules as boundaries of love, rather than hard-nosed and unreasonable demands. They know that beyond any rules or policies is genuine love—a love that is *bigger* than the rules, and a love that is actually the *reason* for the rules. In one family, the kids said,

> **"**
> We didn't like some of the decisions that Mom and Dad made, but we knew that whatever decision they made, even if it was a bad decision, it was made in our best interest, because they loved us. **"**

A friend of mine told me about an experience with his daughter. When his daughter first began playing baseball, she was really good. In fact, in the first couple of weeks she knocked two home runs. This so enthused her father that he began shouting for her and cheering her on from the sidelines. But then she went into a slump. She struck out over and over again. And finally, a few weeks into the season, her father asked her, "Sweetheart, what do you hear me saying and doing over here on the sidelines?" And the daughter said, *"Fussin'."* So you see, her perception and his intent were completely different. This good father explained to her what he *intended* to communicate, then modified his behavior to validate that he really did love her. Only after this explanation could she reframe his "fussin'" as fatherly love and encouragement.

And the kind of love that motivates is *unconditional.* Whether we intend to or not, what we often communicate is, "I'll love you *if* you knock home runs, I'll love you *if* clean up your room, *if* you win, *if* you make As in school." But that's not how it works. The kind of love that *really* motivates is not performance based. Unconditional love means I love you *just like you are.*

One parent summed up the motivating power of love this way,

> It's all based on love . . . not regimented, not forced. You can't force love. It is an art. It's an image in the mind's eye. It's not because you read it in a book. It's an attitude. It's an investment early on. And it pays off, one way or the other, good or bad, later in life—way out of proportion to what the original investment was.

Trust Them

Trust is just as important as love. In fact, one of my colleagues bumped trust right up front when he said that trust really *precedes* love, because you can't have love without trust. The parents of one family we interviewed would put it this way, "I'll give you my trust, and if you break it, we'll talk about it then." They didn't wait to see if their children would be responsible, they just *assumed* they would be. And the uncertainty the kids felt about what would happen if they broke that trust added some mystical power to their motivation. They didn't know *what* would happen, and they didn't want to find out.

One of the fathers said,

> If they told us where they were going, then that's where they were. We never were very good at being detectives.

One executive told me an amazing story about trust. One day, one of his employees walked into his office with his resignation in hand. This employee was resigning because, just the week before, he had been responsible for losing a million dollars of that company's money. So he came in, tail tucked between his legs, prepared to take the grief he was sure was coming. He was ready to resign and get the million-dollar nightmare behind him and get on down the road. But to his surprise, his boss said, "I'm not going to accept your resignation. I trust you to do better in the future. I have a million dollars worth of experience invested in you now, and I need you to help me get it back with interest." The trust that boss had in his employee absolutely turned his life around. That young man would have scaled Mount Everest for his boss.

▼

A powerful motivation for these kids was the high expectations their parents placed on them.

Have High Expectations

If we heard it once, we heard it a zillion times—a powerful motivation for these kids was the high expectations their parents placed on them. They *never* said their motivation was fear of punishment, fear of retaliation, or the fear of failure, but rather fear of letting their parents down. The agony of knowing that they would disappoint their parents who loved and trusted them so very much is what kept them in line.

Let me just share with you some of what we heard.

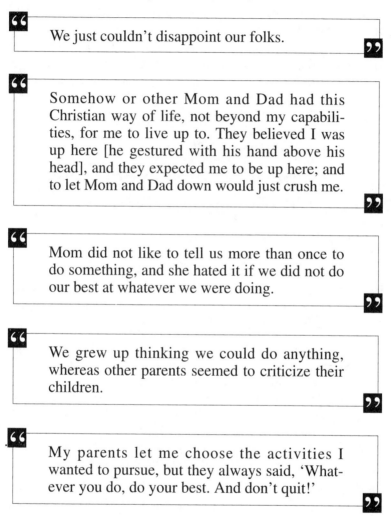

> We just couldn't disappoint our folks.

> Somehow or other Mom and Dad had this Christian way of life, not beyond my capabilities, for me to live up to. They believed I was up here [he gestured with his hand above his head], and they expected me to be up here; and to let Mom and Dad down would just crush me.

> Mom did not like to tell us more than once to do something, and she hated it if we did not do our best at whatever we were doing.

> We grew up thinking we could do anything, whereas other parents seemed to criticize their children.

> My parents let me choose the activities I wanted to pursue, but they always said, 'Whatever you do, do your best. And don't quit!'

Now, mind you, the expectations of these parents weren't out of reach; they were attainable. They never expected the children to be anything beyond what they were capable of, but they *did* expect their children to do what they *could do* and to *try* to live up to their potential in whatever their interests and talents were. And these parents provided opportunities and created ways for them to pursue their interests and develop their talents. The children told us that Mom and Dad's highest and most important expectations had to do with character, purity, honesty, "doing the right thing"—Christian virtues. That's what the Lord is looking for, and that's what these parents were looking for.

In setting expectations for your children, it's important not to keep "raising the bar" above performance ability. If you have expectations beyond your child's abilities, your child will respond with frustration and discouragement: "I just can't ever do enough to please my parents, so why even try any more."

▼

Knowing that they would disappoint their parents is what kept them in line.

Ray Guarendi's study of successful families revealed that these parents were "noncompromising in their expectations that their youngster reach for his limits."[6] In another place he said,

> Every child is born with tremendous potential. Excellent parents believe this. They also believe it is *their duty to make a child explore his potential, sometimes initially against his will.* Regardless of their unique talents, all children possess the ability to behave a cut above the crowd. Settling for average—in morals, manners, or character—is not something these parents are comfortable doing. They have too much respect for a child's resources to allow them to lie unfulfilled.[7]

One son I talked with told me something about his father that really impressed me. When the son was making a career decision, his dad advised him, "Don't sign on with Ford Motor Company. It's a privately owned company, and no one outside the Ford family will ever be selected as president." Now that may sound as if the father was placing too much burden on his son; but you see, this father believed his son was presidential material, and he didn't want his son to limit himself in a company where he couldn't become president. What a wonderful demonstration of the high expectations he had for his son! The father, however, was mistaken—outsiders *could* become president. And the truth of the matter was that this guy was one of the final five being considered for that very position. But before that selection took place, this man resigned, against many protests, in order to go to Florida and bless others by serving in an elder hospice (a place where people in the final stages of terminal illness go to die). The father saw in him a genius, and the son rose to the occasion.

I like what Sam Walton said, "High expectations are the key to everything." Another lady said, "Children will do just about what you expect them to do—for good or for ill."

▼

The father saw in him a genius, and the son rose to the occasion.

Make Them Feel Significant

Another thing that motivates children—wonderfully—is a feeling of significance. It would please God immensely if all our children could say: "I'm making a contribution. I'm a significant person. I am needed. I am wanted. Without me, this family wouldn't be the same, and maybe the world wouldn't be the same. God even knows the hairs on my head and gave his son just for *me*. If I'd been the only person in the world, he would have died for me—just for me!"

Alfred Adler, the great psychiatrist and friend of Freud, commented on what happens when children *don't* feel significant. "If they don't find significance, people adopt crazy behavior."[8] Now, isn't that interesting? That statement was written years ago, but you find it ever present in almost every newspaper across our nation today. When human beings do not feel a sense of belonging and significance, they find mistaken and crazy ways of behaving in order to draw attention to themselves. You've seen the kids with the green hair sticking straight up or with rings in their noses.

These kids are looking for some sort of significance. They want to be noticed.

Fred Craddock tells the story of a young boy from the hills of Tennessee. His mother, as a young woman, had gotten pregnant out of wedlock. She had the child alone and was rearing the young boy by herself. It was not always a pleasant experience. When they would go to town, the cruel townspeople would try to guess who his father was, and he would often hear, "I wonder whose son he is?" School was tough too. At recess time he would rather play alone than be called "those" names. In spite of all the taunting remarks, this lad still went to church, but he always went late and left early to avoid any questions about who his father was.

The preacher was a big man with a booming voice and a full beard. The boy was in awe of this man of God and was a little bit intimidated by him too. As "luck" would have it, he didn't leave quite early enough one Sunday, and he got stuck behind a fat lady who blocked the whole aisle. He tried to squeeze past her, but before he could get around her, he felt a big hand on his shoulder, and he could tell by the powerful voice that he had been "caught" by the preacher—he was scared stiff. He heard the big voice ask the dreaded question, "Now let's see, whose son are you?" The little boy wished he could disappear into the floor.

▼

When human beings do not feel a sense of belonging and significance, they find mistaken and crazy ways of behaving.

But then the preacher continued, "Oh yes, I know whose son you are. You are a son of God!" Then the preacher whacked him on the rump and said, "Now, go out there and claim your inheritance."

And he did. You may know the boy. He grew up to be Ben Hooper. He became so loved and respected in Tennessee that the people of the state elected him governor for two terms.

How do you go about setting things up so that *your* children feel significant? Here are six ways.

1. Give them responsibility

One of our fathers put it straight, "Children don't always want to play." I think what he meant was that children like to be contributors, to be responsible. Sometimes we coddle them long beyond their days when they should be coddled. One father, who had nine children, reprioritized his life at age forty and decided to go to medical school. Because he was a successful entrepreneur, he thought he could manage without having to work or borrow money, but he wasn't completely sure. When he expressed this concern to his children, they looked him straight in the eye and said, "Dad, if you need help, *we'll* put you through med school." How significant do you think those kids felt? Significant enough to believe they could put their dad through medical school.

The children of another family said,

> Our family home is *everyone's* home, so Mom and Dad made it everyone's responsibility to keep it clean, even down to the youngest member.

Another father, the founder of a large multi-million dollar grocery store in the northeast, assigned his eight-year-old daughter the responsibility of caring for farm animals in a little animal farm out in front of the store. But he didn't just give her the responsibility of the *work,* he encouraged her to feel ownership in the project by allowing her to select and place the little animals—she got to choose! And don't you suppose she was less resistant to the *work,* since Dad gave her the *fun* part of the responsibility too?

One dad we interviewed had what he called a "character-building pea patch." This man planted fifty acres of black-eyed peas (can you imagine *fifty* acres!), and if any of the kids needed any extra spending money, they could "pick peas, shell 'em, and sell 'em in the market." Some of the kids from other families sold magazines or lemonade or greeting cards or watermelons—you name it! The parents involved them in all kinds of responsibilities. Is there any better way to instill feelings of capability, independence, and maturity?

Now, when we give our children responsibility, we have a responsibility too. Our responsibility is to *prepare* and *train*. We must give them the *ability* to measure up to the responsibility. Too often we assign jobs to our children that they are ill prepared for, and then they fail, and then they feel bad. If we don't prepare them, we're setting them up for a fall.

Stephen Covey, in his book *Seven Habits of Highly Effective People*, tells how he trained his son for success. Covey had decided it was time for his son to learn how to cut the grass. But he didn't just tell his son, "Go out there, boy, and cut that grass. The gas is here and the mower's there." What *did* he do? For two weeks, he and his son went out and looked at the yard, but they didn't cut anything. For two weeks, he explained to his son what the job called for. It called for just two things: it had to be *green* and it had to be *clean*.

▼

When we give our children a responsibility, we have a responsibility too.

"Do you see our neighbor's yard?"
"Yes, sir."
"How does his yard look?"
"Well, Daddy, it looks green."
"And how does our yard look?"
"Well, part of it looks kinda brown."
"What else do you notice about his yard?"
"It's clean."
"How does our yard look?"
"Well, it's dirty. Its got some paper and sticks and rocks in it."
"Okay, so we're looking for green and clean."

Then he told the boy he could do this job any way he wanted to. "You can use the water hose, you can bring out buckets, you can spit on the grass, if you want to. Whatever you want to do to make it *green*. Now, if I were you, I'd turn on the sprinklers, but you can do it however you want.

"Okay son, who's going to be responsible to see that this job gets done?"

"You are, Daddy."

But Daddy said, "No, son, *you're* responsible."

"But Daddy, I thought you were the boss."

"No, you're the boss. I'm your helper. Why don't the boss and the helper get a little run on this job?" So they got a couple of trash bags, and they cleaned up half the yard.

"Now," Dad said, "this is clean. Look around. You don't see any sticks; you don't see any trash. This is called clean and that (pointing to the neighbor's yard) is called green.

Well, after two weeks of training, he finally delegated the job to his boy, and he expected it to be done in a certain time. Well, the allotted time went by, and nothing was done. So finally, he called his boy and said, "Let's go out and look at the lawn and see how things are going."

The little boy started out the front door and his bottom lip began to quiver, "Daddy, it's just so hard."

▼

He knew his son hadn't done anything, so how could it possibly be *hard?*

"Well son, what do you mean?" He knew his son hadn't done anything, so how could it possibly be *hard?*

"Being responsible for all of this."

"Well, you know . . . you've got a helper."

"You'll help me?"

"Yeah, that was part of the bargain." So they got a couple of sacks and began to clean up. And in the midst of this cleaning, the son began to buy the philosophy that it was *his* responsibility and that Daddy was just the helper.

But notice how much time it took and how gently the father worked with him so that the son could succeed. By the way, he only asked his daddy to help two or three more times during the whole summer, and it was just as green and as clean as the neighbor's.

But now, what if this daddy had skipped the training or threatened to spank him when he was slow to catch on. That's exactly how so many of us operate, and as a result our children never buy the responsibility.

2. Encourage them

One thing is certain—you *don't* motivate through criticism. Speaking in Tantera, Missouri, at a convention, I asked the five hundred or so who were there for a show of hands. "Do you work better with encouragement or constructive criticism?" And boy, the hands shot up on *encouragement,* but there wasn't a single hand on *constructive criticism.* If that's true for adults, I guarantee it's true for kids as well.

▼

One thing is certain—you don't motivate through criticism.

When the parents we interviewed saw their children taking responsibility, they encouraged them big time, and in some cases rewarded them. I remember one father, an insurance salesman, who lived out in the country on a place that required a lot of work. While he was off selling insurance, his kids really pitched in and helped take care of the place. One year he was selected as best salesman, and his company gave him a trip for two to a fancy ski resort in Austria. But this dad knew the value of encouragement, so he asked his company if he could exchange the trip to Europe for a ski trip to the Rockies that the whole family could enjoy. And he told his family that they were just as responsible for his success as he was, because they were the ones who cleaned up the shed and took care of the cows and the horses and the fields while he was out selling insurance. Did those kids feel loved and significant? Don't you know they were motivated to continue helping?

While we're talking about encouragement, I need to stress that there is a big difference in *encouragement* and *reward,* and while both have their place, encouragement is *better* than reward. Let me explain. Encouragement is when you're cheering for your child in the *middle* of the race or game or homework or piano practice or any endeavor, or perhaps during a tough time in his life—in the middle of it! Not at the end and not only if he or she wins or does well. When your son finishes the race and wins, you *reward* him; when your daughter finishes the semester and makes As, you *reward* her. What we're saying is that reward is not nearly as good for the child as encouragement. Rewarding is not bad, it is just not good enough. There are a lot of kids who *don't* win the race, who *don't* make straight As, and they need encouragement. They need to hear us say, "I'm so proud of you." "I know you must feel good about what you've done." "You never give up." "You're a great kid!"

▼

Encouraging our children to make better and bigger decisions as they grow—while we stand beside (or behind) them—is a terrific builder of self-esteem.

---

3. Allow them to make decisions

I love the story that Gordon MacDonald—famous lecturer, author, and pastor—tells about his almost-adult daughter. She was trying her very best to make a tough decision, and she was having a hard time. Finally, sensing her struggle, Gordon asked his daughter, "Honey what do you feel like right now, an oak tree or a tulip?" She didn't understand his question, so he explained. "If you feel like a strong, independent oak tree, I'll stand back and let you make the decision yourself. But if you see yourself as a tulip right now, I'll build a fence around you and fend for you and help you." Now *that* communicates! Encouraging our children to make better and bigger decisions as they grow—while we stand beside (or behind) them—is a terrific builder of self-esteem.

4. Bombard them with empowering words

"You can do it!" "I trust you." "I respect you." "You're good at that." "I've watched you grow up handling tough things." "I'm proud of you." "Go get 'em tiger!" These are the words children love to hear. When the apostle Paul wanted to communicate his concern for a group of Christians, he said, "We dealt with each of you as a father deals with his own children, encouraging, comforting, and urging you"[9] That's what great parents do—*empower!*

The opposite of words that empower are negative "nametags" that strip our kids of confidence and lower their self-esteem. In fact, our kids tend to live up to those nametags. Tags like "lazy," "fatty," or phrases like, "Can't you ever do anything right?" "Will you never grow up?" "Why don't you lose some weight?" "You're just like ____." "What's wrong with you?" What do those tags imply? You don't quite measure up; you haven't got it all together; you're not mature enough. Those negative, ugly nametags, *even when given in jest,* stick like a mud ball on the wall. (Even after the mud ball falls off, the spot remains.) And they are always interpreted as put-downs.

▼

"We dealt with each of you as a father deals with his own children, encouraging, comforting, and urging you."

One family, wanting their children to feel significant, had a big, portable sign for the front yard that could be changed to suit the occasion. So they would tell the whole neighborhood when something great happened: HAPPY BIRTHDAY! or WELCOME HOME CHAMP! This was a way of shouting to their children: You are significant! *What you do counts!*

5. Listen to them

Another thing you can do to make your children feel significant is to listen to them. Give them your full attention. Get behind their eyes; walk down their spines; look up from the newspaper; turn off the TV—listen! And while you listen, look them in the eyes. There's an amazing power in the eyes, a power that flows from the parents' eyes to the children's eyes. Our eyes can say not only that we love and trust them, but that we believe in them. Our eyes, as well as our hands, can tell them that they are deeply loved.

Eyes are also a great revealer of what's going on inside our children's heads. One dad said,

> **66**
> Read your children, look into their eyes. See if there are problems, ascertain those problems. This is hard, and to be frank, I'd rather not do it. **99**

But this dad recognized its importance, and he did it anyway.

6. Put a ring on their finger

Put a ring on their finger? I know that may sound strange, but I'm talking about the story of the Prodigal Son in the Bible. When this prodigal returned home, the father put a ring on his finger. This was no ordinary ring. This was an *unusual* ring. It represented *trust*. It would be like giving a kid today a credit card. This ring was a *signet* ring that made an imprint in the father's behalf. It said, "This is my son, and what he signs for, I'm good for."

Remember the father we talked about earlier who allowed all of his children to be put on the family checkbook at age twelve? Of course, this was done with great deliberation and training, but my, how significant it must have made those children feel. It made them feel like they had *rings* on their fingers.

Monitor Them

Monitoring means being aware of what's going on in our children's lives. It doesn't mean snooping—because we're not trying to catch them doing wrong. We are monitoring to catch and congratulate them for the many positive things they do *right*. Researchers Grace Barnes[10] and Michael Farrell say, "The findings confirm that parental support and monitoring are important predictors of adolescent outcome."[11]

But for many families, the sad reality is revealed in a survey by Louis Harris: "Parents rarely know what's going on with their kids." Thirty-six percent of the parents surveyed thought their children had taken a drink, while sixty-six percent of students admitted they had. Five percent of parents thought their children had used drugs, while seventeen percent actually had.

We've got to work hard not to be a part of those statistics.

Lamar Alexander, past secretary of education and president of the University of Tennessee, said it *best* when talking about his own childhood,

> There was always something to do and always someone watching. Not only watching but encouraging and helping and clapping and trying to put your picture in the paper almost any time you did anything that amounted to something. This was all done with great enthusiasm and seriousness by almost everyone in town.[12]

▼

Monitoring does not mean trying to catch them doing wrong.

The kids we talked to said, "We were definitely monitored." They were talking about television, dates, curfew, et cetera. One way these parents monitored was by volunteering to help in their kids' schools. They wanted to understand the power and the influences and nuances of the schools where their children were. Some volunteered as assistant teachers, some took students on bus trips. They sought out ways to be involved. One of the fathers knew his kids so well that when his son didn't come in when he was supposed to, the dad went out, after midnight, and *found* him—in a city the size of Houston. How could that dad even *begin* to know where to look? He had been monitoring his son. Needless to say, the son was in on time almost all the rest of his days at home.

Another mom and dad we talked with celebrated their 20th wedding anniversary in a big way—they flew to another city and planned to spend two or three romantic days together. As soon as they landed at their destination and checked into their hotel, they called home. They found out that the child-sitter had been talked into allowing the daughter to go to a teen hangout on a weeknight. The daughter knew the parents didn't approve, and though it wasn't dangerous, it *was* a breach of the pact the parents had made with the children. The parents immediately returned to the airport and booked passes home. This kind of monitoring and high priorities shouted, *screamed,* that the parents were willing to pay a high price for the good of their children, and it told the children how important it was to be consistent and honorable and to keep their promises.

Another friend, an M.D., received a call from his wife, telling him that their son had been unusually disrespectful to her. The son thought he could get away with it because he didn't think his father would dare leave his practice to come home to do anything about it; but the father did, leaving his nonemergency patients waiting. And it made an impact on his son for the rest of his life.

Two of the most beautiful statements we heard about this monitoring business came not from a textbook or a professional, but as usual, from our neat families. Rather than the usual negative statements we heard:

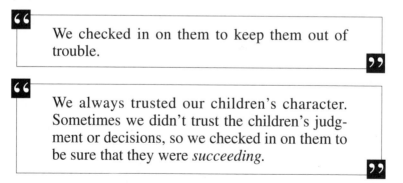

We checked in on them to keep them out of trouble.

We always trusted our children's character. Sometimes we didn't trust the children's judgment or decisions, so we checked in on them to be sure that they were *succeeding.*

Wow! Did you catch the positive ring of that last word? He wanted to be sure they were *succeeding!* A beautiful summary statement of what we've been trying to say in this section.

Build on Natural Motivation

Another thing that helps motivate our children is to build on their *natural* motivation. Find out what your child is interested in and motivate with that. One night, four brothers were scuffling and fussing and making all kinds of racket in their bedroom. All of a sudden they heard Dad coming up the stairs, and they heard some strange tinkling noises coming with him. They were sure they were in big trouble! But when Dad opened the door, he didn't have a switch in his hand or a scowl on his face; he had a tray with four glasses and a jug full of his special "milkshake" made of milk, cinnamon, sugar, ice, and his own "secret ingredients." Next night, you'd expect a repeat of fighting and fussin'—back to normal— but not so. They had another milkshake instead. And it became a tradition. What a wonderful way to motivate good behavior. The boys now say they can still hear Dad coming up the steps, ice tinkling in that jug. And today, one of those boys is fixing the same milkshake for his kids—except, he says, he can never fix it as good as his dad did.

▼

When Dad opened the door, he didn't have a switch in his hand or a scowl on his face; he had a tray with four glasses.

One of the entrepreneurs we visited explained how to build on a child's natural interest by telling me the story of how he motivated a young man to work for him. When the young man came in to inquire about the job, this man asked what his interests were, and the boy said he *loved* to water ski and what he really wanted was a ski rig. So the potential employer said, "What kind of rig would you like to have?" Of course, the boy told him. "Well," said the employer, "what kind of a trailer would you need for that rig, and what kind of pickup would you need to pull that rig?" And of course, the boy spelled it all out; he could just see it. His mouth was watering for that ski rig.

And then the employer said, "Well, I think I can help you get that ski rig." Now, do you think he had that boy's attention? "If you are the kind of worker I think you are, and if you can stay with it and be persistent, and if you get a couple of promotions, which I think you will, you may have that ski rig before you ever thought you could."

Well of course, the boy was just delighted to be able to go to work for the man, because that wise employer had built on the young man's natural motivation. This is the kind of thing we need to do with our children. Find out what they are interested in. What makes their mouth water? And then see if you can't help them bring it about.

But what if that boss had said instead, "What's a ski rig got to do with a job here!? I pay this much, and I expect you to be on time and to keep your nose to the grindstone!" So much depends on how we go at it. Motivation is inside out.

Make It Fun

Finally, as you have noticed in many of our lessons, we end with *humor.* Make life around the house fun. I read a story about a mom who used humor and creativity to motivate her kids. One day, when her children came home from school, she was feverishly working around the house, and she had a big sign hung around her neck. The sign read,

---

Human Time Bomb

If irked or irritated,
WILL EXPLODE

Company's coming,
help URGENTLY needed!

Now I ask you, What kid wouldn't pitch in and help out with a sign like that, with a mom who has a sense of humor like that?

Or what about the executive whose son had left college because he wasn't doing too well. He had decided to come home and work for good ol' dad. And he did okay for awhile, but then things began to deteriorate, and he just wasn't doing as good a job as he could; but after all, he was the owner's son, and he thought he could just slip by. One day when he came to pick up his check, his father's secretary told him she didn't have his check, that his father had it. Well, the son just rejoiced, because he knew that anytime his father gave a raise or wanted to congratulate an employee, he kept the check so that when the person came in to get it, he was able to encourage and brag on him as he gave him his check with a raise included.

The son was highly expectant of good news. His father said something like this, "Son, you know I wear a number of hats. I wear the president's hat, I wear the father's hat, I wear the board chairman's hat. Right now, I have on my boss's hat, and I've got to tell you that you're fired. But wait a minute! Let me put on my father's hat." Then he said, *"Son,* I heard you just got fired. What can I do to help?"

▼

Make life around the house fun.

Now, how about that! This great father was able to say to his son, you are being irresponsible right now, and that's not good for you or the company; but you are my son, and I'm going to do whatever it takes to help you become responsible. Since then, he has gone back to another university, has married a neat woman, has come back to the family corporation, and has been put in charge of a highly efficient grocery business—partially because his father knew how to couch discipline in humor and fun. And the son, years later, is able to tell the story on himself with hilarity.

Without discipline, love is incomplete; without love, discipline is irrelevant.

16

DISCIPLINE:
Principles and Styles

Motivation and discipline go hand in hand. I remember one little guy who had really been acting up, and after repeated warnings, his mama finally decided he needed a stronger motivation to straighten up. So she chose a large closet, turned on the light, and put him in it. In about fifteen minutes, she came back to check on him. She opened the door and asked, "Well now, how are you doing?" And there the little guy stood—arms crossed and eyes determined. "I've spit in every shoe in the closet" he reported, "and I'm waitin' for more spit."

Now, I'm not sure this mom got the results she was after. What she was really after, and what we're really after, is a *changed heart.* Our ultimate goal is to motivate our children to be the kind of people God wants them to be—in time.

Many of us have a mistaken understanding of the word discipline. When we talk about *discipline,* we think only of *punish-*

ment—spanking, time out, grounding, depriving—all negative actions. But the Greek word for *discipline* doesn't mean punishment;
rather, the Greek *paideia* means teaching or instruction or guidance.

▼

Discipline doesn't mean punishment at all; rather, the Greek
paideia means teaching.

Now of course, just like the little guy in the closet, if teaching
and instruction are ignored, there comes a time when actions must
back up our words, but let's make sure we get things in the right
order and put the emphasis where it belongs—on training.

Begging for Boundaries

We know from hard-won experience that the parents who provide the appropriate structure in their home have the happiest,
most secure children. Secure children do not act out, run away,
fight, or resist authority as much as those who never know the
rules or what might happen next.[1]

There's no question about it: from the time we're born until the
time we die, we all need boundaries. Kent Hayes lays down a simple but profound truth: a definite pattern of rules in a family actually allows more freedom for the individual members. It's kind of
like driving. The stop signs and speed limits allow us the freedom
to travel in relative safety. Warning signs and guard rails and speed
bumps are for our own good and the good of others. Boundaries
and rules are essential to our happiness as adults, and certainly are
essential for our children—whether they know it or not.

The impressive thing is, that in most cases, children *ask* for discipline. In fact, Ralph Minear says that "children ask, indeed beg
for moral and spiritual guidance from their parents."[2] Yet, many
parents are afraid to set limits on their children. Maybe it's because they've been scared by a few authorities who warn that they

will ruin their children if boundaries and limits are imposed. I think just the opposite may be true.

One study reported:

> The young people told us time and time again how much they needed family structure, how much they wanted to be protected, and how much they yearned for clear guidelines for moral behavior.[3]

Current research validates that not only is appropriate discipline not harmful, but that it is essential to the happiness and well being of your child. One set of researchers said, "parents today are too lenient and permissive with their children."[4]

William Raspberry, a columnist for the *Washington Post,* said,

> We delight in the sophistication that tells us there are no absolutes, no moral authorities, and one result is that we confuse and frustrate our children, who keep telling us (though not usually in words) that they want rules: consistent, reliable guidelines for running their lives.[5]

Boundaries and rules are essential to our happiness.

So as Ralph Minear says,

> There has to be a bottom line. . . . There has to be a point where the parents make it clear: your freedom is limited. These are the outside boundaries, and you have to operate within them.[6]

John Rosemond doesn't mince words:

> Expect your children to obey. Stop apologizing for the decisions you make in their lives. Get back in touch with the power of "Because I said so." Stop thinking that you can persuade your children that your decisions are for their own good, or even that you need to try! Essential to a child's sense of security are parents who are authoritative, decisive, and trustworthy—in a word, powerful! So, get with it folks! Your children are counting on you.[7]

I think the best quote of all is one all of us know by heart, "Thy rod and thy staff, they comfort me."[8] But what does that mean? Well, a rod is used for nudging, prodding, and pushing. The shepherd uses it to get the sheep to obey and go where they ought to go. He pushes and nudges them for their best good. A rod is not used for harsh punishment; rather it comforts, guides, and keeps the sheep in line. So with our children. When children know that Mom and Dad will prod and guide them away from danger, a child is *comforted.* Proper guidance makes children feel safe and loved. It's like a fence around the playground that keeps the children out of the street.

▼

Boundaries are as wholesome as the skin on your body.

A Source of Power

Containment and structure are sources of power. A good firecracker has to be contained for it to explode. If the powder is left out in the open, just lying around, it won't do much of anything but burn up. The internal combustion engine operates because the power is constrained and used to drive the piston, which drives the car. Were the energy not constrained and structured in a positive way, we wouldn't have transportation. Everything needs structure, just as your body needs bones. Boundaries are as wholesome as the skin on your body, which is itself a boundary.

Cancer, on the other hand, is an example of unstructured, pathogenic growth. Cancer is undisciplined. It just eats and grows and eats and grows, following the path of least resistance. It grows where it shouldn't and creates all kinds of problems in our physical organism. By the same token, when children are allowed to be selfish and are never trained to discipline themselves, they grow up to infect our society with disease, violence, and anger.

Ray Guarendi tells of a mother who had eighteen children. This experienced woman said that it took several years and a few kids before she and her husband understood the value of the word *no.* She said:

Our biggest failures as parents were when we were afraid to make our kids unhappy by saying no. When we saw that there was no way to ever make them completely happy with our decisions, we began to stick to our principles better. The younger kids turned out happier because we did.

▼

"The Lord disciplines those he loves, as a father the son he delights in."

A Form of Love

Whoever says, "If I just love my kids enough, I won't have to discipline them" is simply asking for trouble. We all know that approach won't work even with a dog. Now, you know I'm not comparing your child to a dog, but you also know that you can't love a dog into fetching your slippers, guarding your children, or taking care of sheep; and you can't love your child into being responsible and honorable—you must train your child also. No athlete could ever compete in the Olympics without disciplined training. No child will grow up to be what God wants him or her to be without disciplined training. James Dobson says that through persistent discipline

> you will establish yourself as a leader to whom the child owes obedience. At the same time, however, you must seek numerous and continual ways of telling this youngster how much you adore him. That formula of love and discipline has been tested and validated over many centuries of time, and it will work for you.[9]

Without discipline, love is incomplete; without love, discipline is irrelevant. Read that last sentence again. Discipline is an essential ingredient of love; and without love, discipline does not teach or train. The Bible explains the relationship between love and discipline this way:

My son, don't despise the Lord's discipline and do not resent his rebuke, because the Lord disciplines those he loves, as a father the son he delights in.[10]

Indeed, love and discipline *do* go together. "He who loves [his son] is careful to discipline him."[11]

When you feel your resolve to discipline and train slipping, remind yourself of this beautiful explanation:

No discipline seems pleasant at the time, but painful. Later on, however, it produces a harvest of righteousness and peace for those who have been trained by it.[12]

This is what you desire for your child—a "harvest of righteousness and peace."

Four Parenting Styles

There are four styles of parenting: permissive, trusting, authoritative, and authoritarian—as described in the following chart. Interestingly, none of the parents we interviewed used the styles on the outside edges, the *permissive* or the *authoritarian*. All the parents we interviewed practiced either the *trusting* or the *authoritative* styles of parenting.

	Permissive	Trusting	Authoritative	Authoritarian
Perceived Attention	None	Personal	Personal	Parental
Perceived Love	Little	Much	Much	Concern
Rules	None	Few	Many	Many/Harsh
Boundaries	None	Strong	Some	Few
Expectations	Few	High-Child	High-Child	High-Parental
This model is:	Worst	Best	Best	Bad

Extreme Styles

Authoritarian

The authoritarian parent takes what I call the "redneck" position: he or she demands unquestioning obedience and gives punitive discipline. Kevin Leman says that the authoritarian parent

> rules with an iron hand, his word is law, he is right even when he is wrong. He doesn't listen to the child's point of view. He doesn't think he needs to.[13]

One research article reports,

> Parents who use punitive discipline methods or disagree with their spouses about discipline are more likely to report that their children are aggressive, have control problems, and are disobedient.[14]

Children reared in authoritarian homes often perceive that they are not listened to and that attention is focused on the parent, who in essence says, "Pay attention to *me!* Listen to *me!*"

▼

Authoritarian parents are big on rules; and unfortunately, the rules are usually harsh and demanding.

Regarding perception of love, these children don't so much perceive love as much as they perceive *concern.* These parents are concerned about what their children do, but they are often more concerned about the public image of the family name, perhaps wanting to appear to be the perfect family. They are sometimes more concerned about being embarrassed by their child's behavior than about what is best for the child's training, self-esteem, and perception of love.

Authoritarian parents are big on rules; and unfortunately, the rules are usually harsh and demanding. These families do not operate within *boundaries.* Boundaries aren't needed because there are so many rules.

These parents have exceedingly high expectations for their children, but again, the expectations revolve around what the parents want for the children, not necessarily what is best for the individual child.

Permissive

On the other end of the spectrum are the parents who are too permissive. These parents allow their children to get by with anything and give them just about whatever they want. Confrontation is avoided at almost all cost. Some parents call this approach *love,* but real love provides loving boundaries. These parents actually tend to neglect their children. Two Utah State University professors found that,

> sexual permissiveness and intercourse experience was highest among adolescents who viewed their parents as not being strict at all or not having any rules.[15]

Author and psychologist, David Elkind, says, "We have been unplacing teenagers by progressively removing the markers that set the limits and boundaries of age-appropriate thought and action."[16]

▼

Permissive parents actually tend to neglect their children.

Children who are reared by permissive parents tend to perceive almost no attention, and they perceive little love. They have virtually no rules or boundaries, and their parents have few expectations for them.

As you look at these extremes, you realize that neither is good. Researchers have found that most delinquents and criminals come from homes in which discipline was either overstrict (authoritarian) or erratic (permissive).[17] Unfortunately, many religious homes are overly strict. These parents may think they are doing the will of God, but they are falling right in line with the Pharisees, by being too legalistic and too judgmental.

Of the two, the permissive model has been deemed to be the worst, because the children in permissive homes perceive their parents as simply not caring. And as bad as the authoritarian model is, it is deemed a little better than the permissive model, because the children, at least, feel that the parents are concerned.

Touching on all four styles, Brenda Hunter tell us that,

> Children flourish when parents are warm, communicative, and firm. Rigid, authoritarian parents produce children with low self-esteem. Permissive parents raise children who lack self esteem.[18]

Positive Styles

The parents we interviewed all parented either by the *authoritative* or the *trusting* style, and both of these styles are excellent models. (Notice that there is a big difference in the authori*tarian* style and the authori*tative* style.) The main difference in the trusting and authoritative styles is not in the perceived attention or love—children of both styles perceive that their parents love them and give them personal attention. Nor does the difference lie in the area of expectations—both styles have high child-focused expectations (as opposed to parent-focused expectations). The main difference lies in the emphasis on rules as against boundaries. Authoritative families had more rules and some boundaries, while the trusting families had very strong boundaries and only a few rules.

Trusting

The parents who used the trusting style defined a *boundary* in statements like, "Just do the right thing." From the parents we heard,

> We put limits on the children, boundaries, not so many rules. We tried to avoid rules. Then we didn't try to define the boundaries, they were just axiomatic.

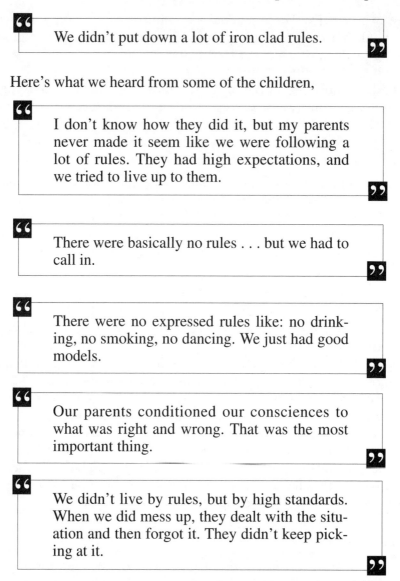

> " We didn't put down a lot of iron clad rules. "

Here's what we heard from some of the children,

> " I don't know how they did it, but my parents never made it seem like we were following a lot of rules. They had high expectations, and we tried to live up to them. "

> " There were basically no rules . . . but we had to call in. "

> " There were no expressed rules like: no drinking, no smoking, no dancing. We just had good models. "

> " Our parents conditioned our consciences to what was right and wrong. That was the most important thing. "

> " We didn't live by rules, but by high standards. When we did mess up, they dealt with the situation and then forgot it. They didn't keep picking at it. "

One question I asked was, "What would be the worst thing that would happen to you if you broke a rule?" And they would say things like,

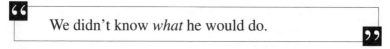

> " We didn't know *what* he would do. "

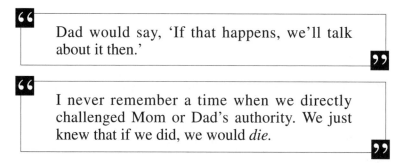

> Dad would say, 'If that happens, we'll talk about it then.'

> I never remember a time when we directly challenged Mom or Dad's authority. We just knew that if we did, we would *die.*

And this *not knowing* produced a healthy fear, because they didn't want to find out what would happen. Another child said, "Dad would ask the worst questions in the world, like: "What would you do if you were me?" and "What's it gonna take?" This is the Socratic method—putting the responsibility for learning back on the child. Another comment we heard was, "When we did break the rules, we felt bad because we felt so *guilty.*" There's something about being trusted that makes the conscience kick in.

When I was asked about their style of correction, I heard,

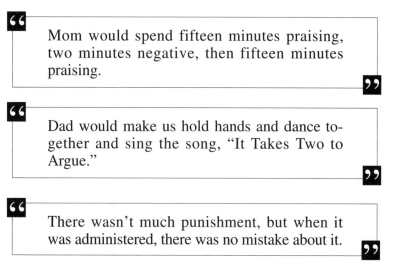

> Mom would spend fifteen minutes praising, two minutes negative, then fifteen minutes praising.

> Dad would make us hold hands and dance together and sing the song, "It Takes Two to Argue."

> There wasn't much punishment, but when it was administered, there was no mistake about it.

But even with the trusting style of parenting, there were *some* specific rules. A couple of examples are,

> Be in at a certain time, or I expect to hear the phone ringing.

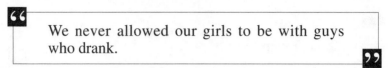

> We never allowed our girls to be with guys who drank.

Furthermore, when the situation required it, these families imposed tough rules, like when one daughter was dating her teacher and when one sixteen-year-old son was dating an eighteen-year-old girl with her own apartment. These parents had the wisdom to recognize that certain situations call for stricter methods. But rules were reserved for special circumstances, and the overall concept was trust and high expectations.

Authoritative

The second model we found in the families we interviewed was the *authoritative* model. These parents had more specific rules and fewer broad boundaries. But the rules were never harsh or over demanding. When I asked the children for examples of their rules growing up, they listed things like this:

> If you broke the rules you had TV and phone privileges revoked for six weeks.

> Our parents had to meet the person before you could date.

> We had lists for everybody to do, and everybody had to help clean the house—not just his room. It wasn't a short list either, it was a full page.

> You didn't get paid for work—work builds character.

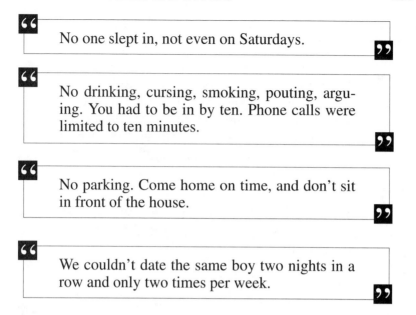

> No one slept in, not even on Saturdays.

> No drinking, cursing, smoking, pouting, arguing. You had to be in by ten. Phone calls were limited to ten minutes.

> No parking. Come home on time, and don't sit in front of the house.

> We couldn't date the same boy two nights in a row and only two times per week.

(That last one really disappointed the future sons-in-law.)

When I asked the children, "What would happen if you broke a rule?" I got answers like this:

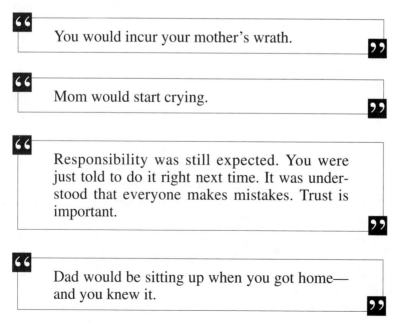

> You would incur your mother's wrath.

> Mom would start crying.

> Responsibility was still expected. You were just told to do it right next time. It was understood that everyone makes mistakes. Trust is important.

> Dad would be sitting up when you got home— and you knew it.

And when we asked them what kind of punishment they received from their parents, we got these kinds of responses.

> **"** If two kids argued, both were sent to their room to work it out, and then they had to report back with genuine smiles. If either one came back with a frown, *both* were sent back to their rooms till both could smile. **"**

> **"** We were told, 'You just can't squabble because you are going to be brothers and sisters the rest of your life, and you are going to decide early on that you are going to like one another. And we are not going to be a referee or a judge between you, so you must settle it yourselves.' **"**

> **"** If we argued with each other, we had to kiss on the lips and sit close to each other and smile. **"**

> **"** When Mom had to spank us, she made us go get our own switch. **"**

These parents were consistent and strict, but also creative and positive. Discipline was a teaching tool related to the specific misbehavior. Some disciplinary methods required a great deal of time—from both parent and child. One father told me that when his daughter did something wrong, he would make her look up the Scripture that dealt with what she had done. For example, if she lied, he would have her look up the Scriptures in the Bible related to lying, then she had to write two pages about how it applied to her. While the dad was telling this story, the brother, then a college student, broke in and said, "Yeah, and by now, she's completed a commentary!" And the whole family roared. Now I really find their attitude interesting, because it showed that even though they believed in strict discipline, they also believed in having a lot of fun. And even when looking back and describing a time of discipline, they were able to laugh.

One of the kids pointed out another important characteristic of these families:

> When our parents said we *couldn't* do something, they always provided some other alternative that we *could* do.

Finally, I think it's important to note that even the authoritative parents gradually eased up on the rules as the children got older, in order to allow them to become intrinsically, rather than extrinsically, disciplined. One child of authoritative parents said,

> When you were a high school senior, there were virtually no rules.

Allowing a child to make all, or virtually all, his or her own decisions while still under the protection and guidance of your home provides a safe time of learning and growing.

To summarize: Decide with your spouse what you want to accomplish in discipline. It is very important that the two of you agree on a style consistent with your value system and that you support each other in the discipline measures you use.

▼

"The welfare of the children rests more on parental unity than on any child-rearing expertise the parents may have."

17

10 KEYS TO EFFECTIVE DISCIPLINE

The ten keys outlined in this chapter are trademarks of intentional parenting. These keys are virtually unquestioned in the field of research and were confirmed in the lives of the families we interviewed. I believe that the amazing similarities in the wisdom we saw in these families regarding how best to discipline was directly related to their common dependence on the wisdom of a loving God.

These keys to effective discipline work, they *really* work. They will provide excellent guidelines for raising successful, godly children. But as you read through these keys, remember that each child is unique and that what works with one child may not work with another. And remember, too, that even the best parenting efforts sometimes fall short.

1. Parental Unity—Get It Together

John White, the famous Canadian psychiatrist and author, said,

> I cannot exaggerate the importance of parental harmony. The welfare of the children rests more on parental unity than on any child-rearing expertise the parents may have.[1]

Did you catch that? Mom and Dad must think and act as one. Shaping our children into responsible, unselfish adults is difficult even when both parents *are* working together, so if parents aren't one in purpose and philosophy, their chances for success begin to slip. The natural tendency of children (and of many adults, for that matter) is to look out for number one, to want to have things their own way. Our job as moms and dads is to love, nudge, and encourage them to walk a less selfish, wiser walk.

Mom and Dad have to stick together and work out disagreements—in advance and probably in private, because children are professionals at splitting parents. They'll try the "divide and conquer" technique if Mom and Dad don't present a consistent unified front and back each other up when one or the other is "backed up against a wall" by a child.

One family we dealt with had a simple solution to this problem:

> 66
>
> Whenever any child was caught leveraging one parent against the other, the immediate response was a negative.
>
> 99

Whatever the request, the answer would be *no*. It was just axiomatic.

The parents we interviewed would say,

> 66
>
> Our philosophy was alike. We agreed. We agreed on religion, children, beliefs, child rearing, the essence of life, the whole thing.
>
> 99

So this number one key is a must.

2. Turn Them Inside Out— From Extrinsic to Intrinsic Control

One of the overall goals of discipline is to help children shift from *extrinsic* discipline, or control, to *intrinsic* discipline. Extrinsic motivation and discipline come from outside the child—from parents, teachers, and other authority figures. But the best discipline—intrinsic, self-discipline—comes from the inside and moves outward.

The whole point of discipline is to help children learn to discipline themselves—to turn it inside out. I got into a pickup with one of my sons the other day, and as he buckled his own seat belt, he reminded me to buckle mine. I commented on his responsible attitude toward safety. (I'm not as careful as I should be.) He sheepishly admitted that two recent tickets for not wearing seat belts had helped him develop self-discipline. See? The *extrinsic* discipline of the policeman (if we listen and learn), eventually results in *intrinsic* self-discipline. That's what we're after!

▼

The whole point of discipline is to help children learn to discipline themselves—to turn it inside out.

Transferring ownership of values

At some point, our children must *own* the values—that is, they must believe in their own hearts that such things as lying, cheating, and stealing are wrong and that unselfishness, honesty, and honor are right. Hopefully they will transfer the major values of their parents to themselves, therefore disciplining themselves intrinsically.

As the inspired Book says, "God did not give us a spirit of timidity, but a spirit of power, of love and *self-discipline*."[2] In the book of Philemon, Paul says that he could have *ordered,* extrinsically, Philemon to treat Onesimus kindly.[3] But he didn't want to do that; instead, he appealed to him on the basis of love (intrinsic, or heartfelt, motivation).

Teaching postponement of pleasure

We live in a microwave world. Gratification is just a split-second away. But when it comes to the real issues of life, that's not how it works, is it? Our kids need to learn to discipline themselves to wait for things they want, and this discipline teaches our kids that lots of good things are worth waiting for—and working for.

One basic ingredient of intrinsic discipline is the ability to sacrifice immediate pleasure for long-term gain. It's not easy to set aside income now in order to meet the needs of a college education later; it's not easy to back away from food now so we can have better health later; it's not easy to say "no" to drugs and alcohol now in order to lengthen our life span and increase our long-term happiness. It's not easy to get out of bed early, say on Sunday mornings, but we do it because it brings long-term benefits—for ourselves and our children. It's not easy to say "no" to our children right now, but it makes things easier for the family and the children later on.

▼

Here I am, a six-foot-four man, and I got whipped by three Fritos.

I remember a battle I had with three Fritos—the kind I like the most—the *big* ones. They were lying out on the kitchen table, and each time I walked past the table, those Fritos got more enticing; in fact, they started talking to me as I walked past. I heard them say, "Eat me" (and then louder), "Wouldn't I taste good?" And finally, on about the fourth trip by, I grabbed those Fritos and gulped 'em down. I got to thinking later—here I am, a six-foot-four man, and I got whipped by three Fritos. It takes discipline to discipline. While we are teaching our children to be intrinsically disciplined and to postpone immediate pleasure, we are still working on ourselves.

▼

"You just have to decide whether you want the short-term pain for the long-term gain or long-term pain for the short-term gain."

One of the most convicting lessons comes from a CEO in a multi-billion dollar international corporation. This man was an extremely disciplined person, admired by many for his ability to follow through on his commitments. He made it look as if self-discipline came easily for him. When I asked him about his unusual ability to discipline himself, his answer was not what I expected. "I've been jogging four miles a day, four times a week, for the last twenty years; and I have hated every step of it." This really took me aback. Maybe I had been hoping he would say something like, "Certain people just have a gift for self-discipline; it comes easy for us. Those without the gift are not responsible." But that's not what he said at all. He went on to explain, "You just have to decide whether you want the short-term pain [such as jogging] for the long-term gain [energy and health], or long-term pain [such as not having the energy you need] for the short-term gain [staying in bed]."

So it's a conscious decision: if you want to live a long and healthy life, you go through the short-term pain in the morning for the long-term gain for the rest of your life. Too many of us choose the short-term gain of sleeping in or staying up late or eating the extra meal and dessert, and thus we choose to pay the rest of our lives with shortness of breath and overweight and a duller mind.

Inspiration puts it this way: "Like a city whose walls are broken down is a man who lacks self-control,"[4] and remember, the walls were the *last resort* of protection for a city.

Modeling intrinsic discipline

Helping our children make that shift from extrinsic to intrinsic discipline is extremely tough. The best method of teaching this is by example, by *model*. The F. I. Stanley family reared their children back in the 1920s, and they had seven boys who came up to be either full- or part-time preachers. Back in those farm days, people would keep their plates turned upside down on the table until they were ready to eat so the dust wouldn't collect on them. Well, old F. I. required that his boys recite a Scripture before they turned their plates over to eat. One of the sons, who was about seventy at the time I talked with him, was telling me this story. I said to him, "Well, I could do that, you know," and I quoted the shortest verse in the Bible, 'Jesus wept.' " And he said, "That'd be good, Paul . . . for *one* meal."

▼

Modeling does more to help our children catch intrinsic self-discipline than anything else.

So those boys were disciplined by their dad to memorize a different Scripture for *every* meal they ate. *But here's where the modeling came in.* The father told his sons, "Now, boys, for every Scripture you quote, I'll quote the one before it and the one after it." Can you imagine! I can just see those boys looking over in "third Hezekiah" for a Scripture their dad didn't know.

It's this modeling—the father's and the mother's willingness to commit to a higher level of living—that does more to help our children catch intrinsic self-discipline than anything else.

3. Emphasize Principles over Rules

Guidelines and principles point to the future and a purpose. Rules and punishment, on the other hand, look backward at past mistakes and forward only to the punishment that will come from failure to keep the rules.

Rules tend to make us want to break them

Rules have a tendency to make us angry, to make us want to break them. I think that's why the apostle Paul said, "Fathers, do not provoke your children to anger, but bring them up in the *discipline* and instruction [the nurture or admonition] of the Lord." [5] Note that Paul said *discipline,* not *rules,* and there's a big difference.

I remember when my mother told me, "Now, Paul, don't you put those hackberries in your ears." I had never thought about it, but when she gave me that rule, all of a sudden my ears were *craving* hackberries. Well, as you might guess, that afternoon Mama had to take me down to the doctor to take a hackberry out of my ear. Rules almost make us want to figure out some way we can break them without being caught.

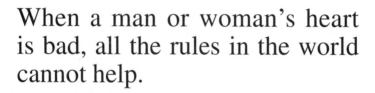

When a man or woman's heart is bad, all the rules in the world cannot help.

Perception of rules varies from person to person

Suppose a parent tells a child not to go in the front yard, and the child goes out on the porch. The angry parent says, "I thought I told you not to go outside!" The confused child says, "I thought you meant don't go off the porch." So perceptions vary, even when we give specific rules. Rules, like people, can be seen differently, depending on the angle we see them from.

Having lots of rules requires a good memory

Whoever is enforcing the rules, especially if there are a whole lot of them, has to have a real good memory. And most busy parents don't. So the child gets away with breaking rules because the parents can't remember all the rules they made. That's not good for the parents or the child.

Rules don't touch the heart

Another problem, and perhaps the greatest problem with rules, is they really don't get to the heart, and sometimes they don't even get to the head. This is because rules are often taken personally, *"You* do this, and *you* don't do that." When rules are broken, the child knows he is headed for a personal put down.

The goal of purposeful discipline is to set up a program of instruction and guidance that will touch the *heart* of a child. Rules rarely do that. Our government has all kinds of rules and laws, page after page after page, but they don't keep too many people out of prison. When a man or woman's heart is bad, all the rules in the world cannot help. We've got to touch their hearts. And the best way to touch a heart is with *another heart.*

What we need is not more, or even better, rules, but a higher and earlier system of instilling principles and ethics deep within our children's hearts.

▼

By the time your children hit puberty, you are wrestling not only with the will of your children, but with raging hormones.

---

4. Discipline Early

Many moms and dads just float along when their children are young and relatively easy to control. Then when children hit puberty and start talking back and acting out, the natural inclination of the parents is to *put a lid on it!* "We're going to put a stop to this right now!" "Nip it in the bud!" as Barney Fife would say.

But by the time your children hit puberty, it's usually too late. You are wrestling not only with the will of your children, but with raging hormones. The most effective time to train your children is from birth to sixth or seventh grade. Take advantage of this time. Dobson says that your child passes through a brief window of opportunity during late infancy and toddlerhood when respect and "awe" can be instilled. But that pliability will not last long. If his early reach for power is successful, he will not willingly give it up—ever.[6]

Even two-year-olds can learn to put away their toys or to give you their cups when they are finished drinking. Kay Kuzma, author of *Building Your Child's Character,* tells how her three-and-a-half-year-old daughter learned to resist the temptation to eat cookies, even though they were right beside her in the grocery sack in the back seat of the car.

One researcher put it this way:

> When begun early, discipline is at its most effective, its most durable, and, believe it or not, its easiest. Terrible two's is a relative term. Compared to a defiant ten-year-old, or a rebellious fifteen-year-old, a "terrible" two is a parenting dream.[7]

All the parents we talked with concentrated their discipline in the younger years, before the hormones got in the way.

5. Administer Punishment Sparingly and Carefully

Punishment is sometimes appropriate, even necessary. Here are some workable guidelines for the times you must punish.

When to spank

Spanking is sometimes necessary, but should be saved as a last resort—after you've tried every preventive and alternative possible (we'll talk about some alternatives in the next key principle). Ray Guarendi, in his study of exceptional families, found that about 70 percent of them spanked.[8]

Spanking is most effective when used in the early years. One family we interviewed began spanking their children when they were around nine months old. This is when they first noticed signs of obvious defiance. One example was when they told their child not to pull on the curtains, and the child headed straight for the curtains, steadily watching his parents to see just how far they would let him go, and how long they would let him pull on the curtains. But notice: these "spankings" were administered by tapping the child on the leg with one finger. A little later on, perhaps, with two fingers. And that was enough. In fact, that same family told me that by the time the children were eighteen months old, spankings were virtually unnecessary. And all seven of their children were beautifully disciplined. In the five hours we visited that family, there were no raised voices, there was no loud shouting. They all stayed in the room where we were visiting, and the ages ranged from eight months up to junior high school—seven children. I was impressed.

There are two situations when we almost *must* spank. The first one is when a child is attempting to do something dangerous, like running into streets or pulling at pans on the stove or hurting someone else. Children must receive a quick and powerful response to dangerous situations. The short, immediate pain of spanking is preferable to undisciplined children being permanently injured or injuring someone else because they haven't been trained by their parents.

A second thing we spank for is outright rebellion. Rebellion is when you tell a child not to do something, and that child looks straight at you and moves right toward that forbidden thing. James Dobson has this to say about spanking,

> The philosophy I am recommending is not born of harshness. It is conceived in love. Corporal punishment is reserved specifically for moments of willful, deliberate, on-purpose defiance by a child who is old enough to understand what he doing. These challenges to authority will begin at approximately fifteen months of age and should be met with loving firmness. A thump on the fingers or a single stinging slap on the upper legs will be sufficient to say, "You must listen when I tell you no." [9]

One of the parents we interviewed put it this way,

> 66
>
> Spanking does work, it's a crude way, but it works. If you're skilled enough, you don't have to use it much.
>
> 99

He went on to explain, "Spanking is good only for a short time. It is negative and it works, but only for a short time."

Focus on the act, not the child

To focus on the child makes the child feel you are angry at him or her. Focus on the act, instead. Let the child know that it is the *act* that is bad or harmful, not the child.

▼

The goal in punishment should be the child's training, not your peace and quiet.

Punishment must not be parent centered

For example, "If you disturb me one more time, I'm going to come in there and give you a good spanking." This kind of response is born of selfishness and focuses on what bothers the parent. The goal in punishment should be the child's training, not your peace and quiet.

Do not punish when you are angry

If you wait until you're angry, you will more than likely punish harshly. Some parents lose control and go to the point of abuse. Abusive parents rationalize that if the child did not misbehave, they would not have to resort to such methods; but in reality, they are lashing out with no thought to the child's well-being. When a punishment doesn't work, they increase the intensity (spank harder). The reasoning is: if a *little* didn't work, *more* will—sheer nonsense. Most child abuse is pure ignorance, but some is pure cruelty—whatever the cause, there is a lot going on in the United States.

Punishment must not be harsh

Good parents do sometimes punish their children, but the punishment is intentional, rational, and for the child's benefit. When punishment is *excessively* used, the child becomes either defiant or withdrawn—neither is good.

> Both overstrict [authoritarian] and firm [authoritative] parents punish their children, but the difference lies in the *severity* of punishment, the *fairness* with which it is administered, and the *extent* to which it is used in comparison with less aggressive ways of keeping the child in line.[10]

Never punish if you don't have all the facts

If we punish when we don't have enough information, we often make serious mistakes and end up doing far more harm than good. For example, when we spank a child for something he didn't do or spank a child for something some other child did, we damage both the trust and the relationship.

Occasionally, even the most conscientious parents will make a mistake in punishment. Haven't we all been spanked or treated unkindly for someone else's mistake? I remember confronting mother with a grievance because I was punished unjustly. She said, "Aw, go on with ya. Just count that as a spanking for one you *should* have gotten but *didn't.*" And she was right, and we both knew it.

Rewarm the atmosphere

And finally, when you punish be very sure that you rewarm the atmosphere *as soon as possible.* Deal out the punishment and then be done with it. Don't hold a grudge or put it in the memory bank to be called back up when the child acts out again. It's foolish and cruel to build up a bank of negative memories to be thrown up to the child again and again.

One daughter we interviewed spoke lovingly about the way her father handled spankings.

> **"** If Dad had to spank you, he would hold you in his arms afterwards and hug you until you stopped crying. **"**

Then, she told us that, he would ask them *why* they were spanked to make sure they understood. This dad understood the need to re-

warm the atmosphere and the relationship. These children understood that he punished them because he loved them enough not to
allow them to do something that wasn't in their best interest.

6. Alternatives to Punishment

Although punishment is sometimes necessary, there are many
instances where other alternatives are even more effective. And
that's what this section's about.

Natural and logical consequences

Often, the most effective discipline is to simply allow children
to experience the natural and logical consequences of their misbehavior. If children refuse to put their clothes in the hamper, then
their clothes will simply not be cleaned. It's just a natural consequence of not living up to their part of the bargain. When you call
your children to the dinner table, do it once. Make sure that they
hear you, but do it only once. If they don't come, then don't call
again. Simply sit down and eat the meal without them. It will not
hurt your child to go without a meal. The temporary hunger your
child feels is simply a natural and logical consequence of his or
her own choice.

▼

> Often, the most effective disci-
> pline is to simply allow children
> to experience the natural and
> logical consequences of their
> misbehavior.

One man I know was remodeling his house with the help of two
subcontractors. One afternoon, when his children came home from
school, he went outside to greet them, and he and his kids got to
playing, and they ended up rolling around in the grass—just having a ball together! The subcontractors were amazed at the won-

derful, fun relationship between this father and his children. One of them asked, "How is it that you have such a good time with your kids? Everything around *our* house is a hassle—especially mealtimes. Trying to get our kids to eat is h---." He continued, "I have to stand over them with a paint mixing board just to make them eat."

So the man explained how he and his wife handled mealtime. "When it's time to eat, we call our kids once. If they don't come, then they don't get to eat until the next morning."

The subcontractor was appalled, "Boy, it seems terrible to allow a child to go to bed hungry."

"It won't hurt, I promise. And furthermore, they'll be there for mealtime from then on, and you'll have less trouble getting them to eat."

The very next morning both of the subcontractors came back raving and shouting, "It works! It works!" And that afternoon both of their wives called the man to say "Hey, what else do we need to do?"

I like what Kevin Leman has to say about this tactic,

> Let the child experience hunger as a result of his choice. And then, do yourself a favor. Don't feel badly about the poor tyke having to go to bed with an empty stomach. It's a small price to pay for the valuable lesson he is learning.[11]

One of the little children in a family we interviewed was given a certain amount of money to cover all his expenses for one week. But he spent it all before the week was up and ended up having no money for lunch at the end of the week. When he asked his mother for more money, she told him she was sorry, but she couldn't give him any more. He would just have to budget his money better next time. But she did promise to have a big sandwich waiting for him when he got home and a great meal at dinner time. Well, the next week he came in with three jars. He said, "Mama, I'm not going to run out of lunch money this week. I am going to put my lunch money in one jar, my spending money in another jar, and my church money in another jar." That little guy not only managed money from that day until this, but he is now president of a large firm, thanks in part to Mom teaching him early on how to watch his pennies. This is the kind of discipline that really works and that pays off in the long run!

As a high school boy, I learned all about natural consequences from my ninth grade algebra teacher, Mrs. Shockley. Mrs. Shockley was very patriotic and believed that every American should know the national anthem. So she required that all of her students write all four verses of the "Star Spangled Banner" on her final exam. Of course, with my ninth-grade brilliance, I figured that she couldn't possibly face her fellow colleagues if she failed an algebra student for not knowing all four verses of the "Star Spangled Banner." When it came time for the final, I decided to turn in my paper—a reasonably good one, probably a B paper—*without* the "Star Spangled Banner." When I got my semester grades, I had a big F in algebra.

You would think that my mother would have gone to the teacher, the principal, and the school board and complained about this unfair treatment of her precious son. But Mother didn't do a thing. She was a teacher herself, and she knew that I was simply paying the natural and logical consequences for a not-so-smart stand.

▼

The key to allowing consequences to discipline our children is to *maximize actions* and *minimize words.*

I hate to tell you the rest of the story—because it will show you how really stubborn I was—but I must. Come next semester, I took the same teacher for the same course. I really liked Mrs. Shockley and honestly felt she couldn't fail me for not writing the "Star Spangled Banner" on my final if I made an A in her class. And I did make an A that semester—all except for the four verses of the Star Spangled Banner. So, you're reading about a boy who has *two* Fs on his junior high transcript for ninth grade algebra. And I'm not mad at Mrs. Shockley or the principal or the school board. I deserved the two Fs. It was a lesson well learned. And a lot more young people today need a Mrs. Shockley to teach them that choices do have consequences.

P.S. I knew algebra so well that my tenth grade teacher let me do some teaching, and I loved it! In fact, I believe that is why I ended up a university professor.

The key to allowing consequences to discipline our children is to *maximize actions* and *minimize words*—because actions speak louder than words. One of the moms we interviewed employed a natural consequence when her kids were fussin'. Her famous statement, according to the kids, was, "You two must really be tired to be fussin' like that; you just need to go up and take a nap." So they rarely fussed, because they knew Mama meant what she said.

Another family required that each fussing child give the other a big hug. And if they didn't do it quickly, then they had to give each other a hug *and* a kiss. As one of the little boys said, "Aw, mama, I'd rather kiss dirt." So it worked.

I've got to say something here about the dangers of "rescuing" your children from the consequences of their behavior. Of course, as Kevin Leman says,

> there are occasions when it is all right to bail your children out of a difficult situation, but if you do it again and again and again, you are definitely headed for trouble![12]

As dean of men at a Christian university for seven years, I often had to deal with discipline problems. One particular boy had been given several chances to do right and he just kept messing up. Finally, I dismissed him from school. So the boy and his father came to see me. The father was in a rage and informed me that I could *not* dismiss his son! I explained to him that not only could I, but for the sake of the boy and the school, I must.

"I'll not let it happen!" the father insisted. "I'll go to the president."

When I got up from my seat and told him I'd be happy to introduce him to the president, the man finally said, "Okay, let's stop right here and talk about this." He sent his son out of the room and told me his sad story.

"When that boy was four years old, I told him to do something and he refused. I spanked him, just a swat or two, and again told him to do it. But he just clamped his jaw shut and wouldn't cry or give in. After about two more tries, I stopped. Ever since that day, I have gotten that boy out of whatever problem he's gotten into. I have bought him off. But it looks like I can't get him out of this one."

The father had only prolonged the time that his son would finally have to face the consequences of his behavior. It's a shame that he waited until he had almost ruined the boy's life. It may have been easier to handle things that way for the short run, but it sure was harder in the long run. Allowing children to get what they want or "buying them off" when they get into trouble is the way to train sociopaths (people who abuse others with little or no conscience, believing that if they get into deep water, someone will rescue them).

Allowing natural consequences to take their course teaches children to take responsibility for their actions. It teaches accountability. If the action is good, then the consequences are good. If the action is bad, then the consequences are bad. Too many adults still blame others for all their problems, because when they were kids, Mom and Dad failed to teach accountability.

When using the natural consequences technique, let the consequences be

- swift
- reasonable
- related to the offense
- absolutely certain to occur
- not too severe

Choices

Another alternative to punishment is to avoid needing it in the first place. It we can come at potentially troublesome situations in a different way, many times we can short-circuit the need for punishment. You can often prevent problems by giving your child a choice.

This alternative is a must for all parents, because it works like a charm. It empowers children and boosts their self-esteem, and it prevents many a power play from developing. It goes like this: When you want your children to clean up their rooms, instead of saying "Go clean up your room," you give them a choice. "Would you rather clean up your room or help me with dinner?" Simply giving children a choice puts the power of choice in *their* hands.

▼

You can often prevent problems by giving your child a choice.

One of the parents we interviewed gave his son this choice after he had misbehaved: "You can take a spanking or you can memorize all the countries in the Near East and their capitals and learn how to spell them correctly." The young boy chose to memorize the countries, which also happened to be part of his schoolwork. So the child, by choosing, got a double payoff—he got his homework done and he got out of a spanking.

One of the children in Ray Guarendi's study said,

> As we grew older, we were given increasingly responsible roles in making choices for ourselves, but we were never abandoned to those choices. We could always go to my parents for help and advice. My parents taught me that making decisions was easy. It was the consequences that could be difficult to deal with.[13]

If you give your child an ultimatum or offer only one choice—especially if you have a bad tone to your voice—resistance is likely. It's not just the size of the decision that makes young people feel special, it's the fact that they have a say.

"If, then" scenarios

Here's how this one works: *if* a child does a certain thing, *then* he will get a certain serendipity, or reward, for doing his part. For example, "If you pick up your room, then we'll go to the zoo" or "If you help clean up the dishes, then I'll fix a special treat for you before you go to bed."

Positive questions

Questions like, "Would you like to go to bed?" "Would you like to take out the trash?" "Would you like to clean up your room?"

just *beg* to be answered with an emphatic, "No." Better questions would be, "Are you making a good choice?" or "Is this a responsible decision?" Such questions help children make their own decisions. It won't be long before they'll be asked to make momentous moral decisions about stealing, speeding, lying, cheating, and premarital sex, and they need to have a lot of experience. Wise parents will give their children plenty of opportunities to practice good judgment in making choices, while they're still young and still under the protection of your home.

▼

It won't be long before they'll be asked to make momentous moral decisions.

---

7. Teach Children How to Make Amends

Now when your children make bad decisions, and all children do at one time or another (usually, *many* times), show them how to turn it around and make things right.

Again, the best way I know to teach this is through modeling. If you make a mistake in judgment or you are too harsh in your discipline, go to your child and ask forgiveness. This teaches your children that we all make mistakes, and it models for them how to ask for forgiveness.

Another thing you can do is allow them to comment on your mistakes. If your son notices that you forgot to put the forks on the table, it's a simple thing for the parent to say, "I sure did. Thanks for reminding me."

Or if you run a stop sign and your daughter calls it to your attention, instead of rebuffing her, you could say, "I can't believe I did that! If a policeman had been there, I'd have gotten a ticket, and what's worse, I may have endangered someone's life. Thanks for helping me be a better driver."

Now I know this requires a bit of humility, and that's not always easy, especially in front of our children; but your example will pay off big time when *they* mess up—and they will!

8. Be Consistent

Consistency is what makes a good clock. You can count on it to have accurate time every time you look at it. The same thing is true of an automobile. If it's a good car, it will give you consistently good service for a long period of time. And of course the same thing is true with parents. Almost all the children we talked with indicated that if their parents said something, they meant it; and they were consistent, virtually every time.

The children would say things like,

> **66**
> If it is a rule today, it will be a rule tomorrow. **99**

And then they'd explain, "Bedtime meant bedtime."
Another child said,

> **66**
> When they told you to come in on time, they weren't saying you could come in late once or twice. They checked on it, and made sure you were in on time, everytime. **99**

Now we're not saying that consistency is rigidity or stubbornness. As Ray Guarendi says, "[Consistency] is not stubbornly clinging to some overkill consequence blurted out in a discipline frenzy."[14] Most kids can tell the difference, as can most parents, between a well thought out, reasonable policy and a knee-jerk response. So even though it's sometimes necessary to make exceptions, they need to be just that—*exceptions*.

In *Why Good Parents Have Bad Kids*, Kent Hayes said that when he evaluated the behavior of successful parents to identify their "secret ingredient," he "discovered that these are the people who follow through. They are consistent and do what they say they are going to do."[15]

Consistency is not so much a God-given talent as it is a learned behavior. It's something we as parents have to work on day in and day out. Kids know immediately when our level of consistency begins to break down, and they will take advantage of it, everytime. It's just natural. That's just the way kids think and operate. It's to their advantage to think that way. But parents who are consistent are rarely challenged because the child's past experience confirms that it doesn't work.

Most of us have experienced our small children putting our consistency on trial when we're on the telephone. They'll jump on the furniture, run through the house, raid the refrigerator, take little sister's toys, or scream at the top of their lungs—because from their past experience they know we won't put the phone down to correct them and be consistent.

▼

Most kids can tell the difference between a well thought out, reasonable policy and a knee-jerk response.

9. Don't Sweat the Small Stuff

In other words, don't equate cultural trends with core values. Cultural trends are things like long hair, strange haircuts, and weird clothes. Things like the age girls can wear makeup and whether or not to pierce ears are also largely cultural. Why, in some Hispanic cultures, it seems that little girls are *born* with pierced ears, while in other cultures parents object to pierced ears until the girls are sixteen years old. Some families have almost split up over the issue of long hair on boys. But what constitutes *long?* And is it worth the destruction of relationships?

One father who had made a big issue out of his son's long hair came to his senses and told the boy, "I'm not going to lose you over your hair. I don't like it, but I can live with it. Grow it to your toes if you want to." Two weeks later the son's coach said, "It's time for a haircut," and *zip,* off it came—no problem.

We need to be very careful about saying that certain cultural issues violate biblical principles, when in reality they don't. Sometimes they just violate our comfort zone. Or maybe a son with long hair or a daughter who dresses differently causes us embarrassment, and that becomes a major concern. But sooner or later our misplaced priorities catch up with us, because our children know that certain cultural issues are not equal to immorality.

I think we can better come at these issues by dealing with the heart and the intent. This raises the questions beyond the *do* or *don't* list to a level of intent and aspirations. I like the approach of Jesus, when he told his critics they were straining out a gnat while swallowing a camel. Yes, I believe the gnats are important to strain out, but Jesus was telling us to attack the bigger issues, the camels. We'll do better to attack not the *fruits* of the tree of evil, but the *roots* of the tree of evil. Get down to the heart of the matter.

▼

Let's not split families and break relationships over cultural trends.

Of course, there are some things that we absolutely cannot put up with. Sometimes, parents have to say to their children, "This far, and no farther." While we may be able to accept things like long hair or unusual dress or some music, we may have to draw the line on issues like coming home whenever they please or treating their parents disrespectfully or bringing home drugs, alcohol, and immoral peers. At some point in time, we may have to make some really tough decisions for the welfare of our child and the peace of our family.

But let's not draw any *unnecessary* lines in the sand. Let's not split families and break relationships over gnats, over cultural trends. Many of these issues require intense prayer and reliance on the help and counsel of others. Choose your battles wisely.

10. Make It Fun

I like the little story that Guarendi tells about what one of the fathers would do when his children were fussing with each other. He would "hold court."

> I'd put a dishrag on my head and say, "I'm the judge." I would then call court to order. We had witnesses, and no one could talk while another person was talking. Usually I knew how things would end up. There would be fault found on both sides. I would pass judgment and give suggestions about what the kids could do if a similar situation came up. Court bothered them because it took time and because one would have to shut up while the other talked. I think they got to the point where they dreaded court more than the discipline.[16]

One of the parents we talked to had asked her child to do something for her. "If you will, I'll give you a hug and a kiss." And he had said, "No, he didn't want to do it." So she said, "Well, I'll give you a hug and a kiss and a kick in the seat of the pants." And he said, "No, I don't think so." And so she went on, "I'll give you a hug and a kiss and a kick in the seat of the pants and nibble on your ear." And she just kept going till it got so funny that he finally did what she asked him to do. How could he resist?

We need to use humor whenever we can to lighten the load. Humor and laughter can put smiles on faces and break some of those stubborn streaks right down the middle.

Discipline is one of the major marks of intentional parenting. But interestingly, we learned from the families we interviewed that the parents who have the greatest will to discipline, actually end up doing less disciplining. It works this way because the children know that the parents *will* discipline if necessary, and that there will be no two ways about it. Ray Guarendi put it this way, "The stronger a parent's will to discipline is the weaker a child's desire to test that will."[17] He's exactly right. Because the will to discipline makes the act of discipline less necessary.

But the best quote I know ties discipline and compassion together. It comes straight from God, and it describes our loving, heavenly Father as *compassionate and gracious, . . . slow to anger, abounding in love and faithfulness, maintaining love to thousands, and forgiving wickedness, rebellion and sin. Yet he does not leave the guilty unpunished; he punishes the children and their children for the sin of the fathers to the third and fourth generation.*[18]

▼

"The stronger a parent's will to discipline, the weaker a child's desire to test that will."

I think God is saying, first of all, that he is gracious and loving and longsuffering, and secondly, that if we don't punish our children, if we leave our children unpunished, that three more generations of children down the line will pay the price. It is our responsibility to train *this* generation to be responsible Christians so the following generation won't have to pay the price for our rebellious children.

FAMILY TRADITIONS THAT LAST

SECTION FIVE

"Without our traditions, our lives would be as shaky . . . as shaky as a fiddler on the roof."

INTRODUCTION

Traditions have had a bad rap for a number of years—and with some reason. History has shown us that traditions sometimes lock us into repetitive behavior or styles of doing things that have lost their meaning and are no longer effective.

But, oh, there is another side to traditions! Traditions provide us with equilibruim in an otherwise shaky world. Traditions give us something to hold on to—something we can trust and count on. They provide connections, links with our past. Traditions provide predictable and reliable times for togetherness. They are a medium for time well spent.

18

THE VALUE OF TRADITIONS

We begin in *Anatevka*—a small village, deep in Russia—at the time of the Bolshevik Revolution. Our main character is Tevye, a tradition-bound Jewish father of five daughters. You know where we are. We are watching the opening of the beloved musical, *The Fiddler on the Roof.* You remember the tiny Jewish settlement and you remember Tevye and his milk cart. Tevye stands in the foreground with his milk cart, and behind him is the little village. The houses of his Jewish neighbors are scattered in the background, and strangely, on top of one of the houses is a fiddler, a violin player of all things.

And when the audience is stilled, Tevye opens the play something like this,

> A fiddler on the roof? Sounds crazy, no? But in our little vil-
> lage of Anatevka, you might say everyone of us is a fiddler on
> the roof, trying to scratch out a pleasant, simple tune without
> breaking his neck. It isn't easy, you know. You may ask, "Why

do you stay up there if it's so dangerous?" We stay because Anatevka is our home. And how do we keep our balance? That I can tell you in a word—tradition! Because of our traditions, we've kept our balance for many, many years. Because of our traditions, everyone knows who he is and what God expects him to do.

At that moment, the orchestra breaks into music, and Tevye sings the song *Tradition!* In this song he explains the different role expectations for the mama, the papa, the sons, the daughters, and for the people in the village, like the priest and the constable and the matchmaker . . . *matchmaker, matchmaker, make me a match . . .*

And then, as the music dies down, Tevye addresses the audience again, "Without our traditions, our lives would be as shaky . . . *as shaky as a fiddler on the roof."*

▼

"And how do we keep our balance? That I can tell you in a word—tradition!"

He is saying that traditions give us something to hold on to. We need to have some things passed down to us—things that hold us as families and people together, things that we don't have to think about or figure out. Traditions provide us relief from some of our decision making—with traditions, we don't have to decide every action and reaction anew.

As Alfred Klsedzin said,

> We enjoy things only when we can commit some part of our daily life to tradition, when we can act ceremonially, ritualistically, instead of having to decide in each case which act to perform, and how to go about it, and what you would actually get out of it.

Traditions, then, are a way of life passed down from generation to generation. Psychologist Paul Pearsall says that "ritual within the family is one of the most important aspects of sound human development, physically, mentally, emotionally, and spiritually."[1]

To show you just how powerful traditions can be, let me tell you about the Joe Shulam family. Joe comes from a family of Jews who were banished from Spain in 1492. His forefathers migrated to Bulgaria. But even in this distant land, they held to their family traditions, including the Spanish language. They eventually migrated to Israel, where they are today, and this family still lapses into the Spanish language some 500 years later, because of those consistent traditions that were handed down.

Traditions have five basic benefits: they give us a way to define ourselves; they provide stability; they enhance flexibility; they help us maintain high values; and they create a field of dialogue.

Traditions Give Us a Way to Define Ourselves

Remember what Tevye said? He said, "Because of our traditions, everyone knows who he is and what God expects him to do." Traditions provide individuals and families with a definition of who they are and their purpose in life. Traditions can help answer two of the great questions of life: *Who am I?* and *Why am I here?*

Traditions give us a link to the past, a connection that is revealed in stories and memories of events gone by. The Jews in Old Testament time (and even today) had a much better appreciation of the importance of this "connectedness" than we do. When the little Jewish children were eating the Passover meal with their families and they asked their fathers, "What does this mean?" the fathers would then recall the memories and retell the stories of the Lord delivering them out of Egypt with a mighty hand and bringing them out of slavery and into a land flowing with milk and honey. And the father could say, "Remember who you are and what God expects you to be."

When the Israelites crossed the Jordan River, God instructed them to set up a monument of stones. And he said, "In the future *when your children ask you,* 'What do these stones mean?' tell them. . . ." And then he went on to say, "These stones are to be a memorial to the people of Israel forever."[2] God knows how easily we forget: thus the importance of traditions, of passing on memories, of retelling the stories. So when the Jewish children saw the monument of stones they would ask their fathers, "What do these stones mean?" and the fathers could again tell them the story of God's marvelous care and his mighty miracles—how God stopped the waters from coming down from the north and how the water stood up like a wall and how God delivered their people. The history lesson connected them with their fathers and grandfathers and reminded them that God had been in their lives for many years. And the father could say, "Remember who you are and what God expects you to be."

The Jews have always had their phylacteries, worn on their foreheads or wrists, to remind them that whatever their minds think and whatever their hands do, they do it in the name of Yahweh, because their identity is found in him. Or they have the mezuzah, the little box on their front door containing the verse from Deuteronomy 6, to remind them that as they come and go from the house, they do so in the name of the Lord. With all these little things, little traditions as well as big, they were constantly reminded that Yahweh is their God.

Contrast the Jewish traditions with contemporary American traditions. In America, even in Christian homes, we have virtually no traditions. We have our evenings around the TV set, which remind us of our popular culture rather than our heritage. For our phylacteries, we have substituted business cards; for our mezuzahs and prayer shawls, we have substituted BMWs and portable computers to define ourselves as successful. They define us all right, but as followers of the *American* way, the American value system, not as followers of God.

Robert Bellah, author of *Habits of the Heart,* wrote,

> We cannot know who we are without some practical ritual and moral structure that orders our freedom and binds our choices into something like habits of the heart.[3]

Families who have had traditions passed down to them find it much easier to continue those traditions in their own families and then to pass them on to future generations. Families that are scattered or divorced have a more difficult time—but it can be done! These families just have to work harder, but it is worth the effort.

Traditions Provide Stability

"In orthodox Judaism . . . the center of the religious life is not the synagogue or school, but the *home*."[4] Even our religious traditions must be rooted in the home. We must not rely solely on our churches to provide them for us. My friend Allen Loy McGinnis says, "Rituals are the mortar that helps hold families together when crisis come."[5] Ray Guarendi talks about a sense of security that is engendered by rituals. He says,

> No matter what forces shake the family, no matter what its members endure, traditions are something around which wrap a sense of belonging. They can insulate from life's uncertainties. They are a constant.[6]

Barbara Fiese, a psychologist at Syracuse University, said that

> for children 5 to 7 years of age, rituals are particularly important as a stabilizing force in life. . . . Their families' rituals give children a sense of security and how their family works together, which is crucial to their own sense of identity.

▼

We all need some constants in our lives, some things we can count on—no matter what.

We all need some constants in our lives, some things we can count on—no matter what. It's just like Tevye said, without our traditions we'd be as shaky . . . as shaky as a fiddler on the roof.

Traditions Enhance Flexibility

This may sound strange, but there's really no contradiction between flexibility and stability. Tradition is like the vaulting box that anchors the vaulting pole. A man runs down a runway and plants his pole in the box, and it holds his pole; it will not let it shift to the left or the right. And because of the stability of one end of the pole, the vaulter can confidently launch himself with a very *flexible* pole, fifteen to twenty feet up into the air and over a cross-bar. And so it is with our families. A sturdy vaulting box, rich in family tradition and stability, is like a launching pad, enabling your children to venture out into the world in any variety of directions. They may not do the same kind of work we do or live the exact kind of lifestyle we live, but because of their sturdy underpinnings, they can still keep their balance.

Traditions, contrary to the perceptions of some, do not necessarily tie us down and restrict our flexibility; on the contrary, the right kind of family traditions actually provide leverage for the person on the pole. When hard times come, and they most definitely will, your children will have their poles secure in that box; they will be able to withstand all kinds of hardships, because they are grounded in the security of their family. Steven Wolin, a psychiatrist at Family Research Center at the George Washington University said, "if you grow up in a family with strong rituals, you're *more likely to be resilient as an adult."*[7]

▼

"If you grow up in a family with strong rituals, you're more likely to be resilient as an adult."

Traditions Help Us Maintain High Values

Family traditions play a big role in helping our children hold to a high moral value system. While of course some traditions outlive their usefulness and need to be discarded, other traditions are based on eternal principles like the one Paul speaks of in 2 Thessalonians,

> *Hold to the traditions which you were taught by us, either by word of mouth or by letter.*[8]

A wonderful illustration of how traditions can help us hold to our moral values comes from the Old Testament. The Recabite family was invited by one of God's holy men to the temple for a special dinner. When the holy man attempted to serve them wine, they refused. The family said,

> Neither we nor our wives nor our sons and daughters have ever drunk wine or built houses to live in or had vineyards, fields or crops. We have lived in tents and have fully obeyed everything our forefather Jonadab commanded us.[9]

The forefather, Jonadab, had so instilled these standards in his descendants that they had remained in that family for generations. So strongly did this family hold to their values that not even a man of God could jar them loose.

And today, says Janie Roberts, "People are returning to family rituals, because the world is losing a sense of what's important, offering instead shallow beliefs and sound-bite values."[10]

▼

Traditions open up avenues of communication—sometimes when nothing else can.

Traditions Create a Field of Dialogue

A final serendipity of traditions is that they open up avenues of communication, they get people talking—sometimes when nothing else can.

Stephen Glenn says that

> families who organized themselves with rituals, traditions, and activities in the midst of their busy lifestyle to increase the base of informal dialogue among family members by as little as 30 minutes average a week (4 minutes a day) enjoy a 32% lower rate of delinquency, a 27% lower rate of chemical dependency and a 21% lower rate of chronic truancy, absenteeism, and identified underachievement in their children than identical families on the same street, going to the same schools, but who were at or below the national average in activities that produce dialogue.[11]

It's amazing that just plain ol' conversation can bring so many benefits to our families. A scene in a movie several years back illustrates the importance of this informal field of dialogue. Several male characters were discussing their early years with their own fathers, and one of them mentioned his gratitude for baseball. When he and his father could not talk about anything else without some kind of sparks flying, they could always talk about baseball. It was their only "safe" subject for a number of years, and it gave them a place to connect with each other. This point of dialogue held them together through some difficult times.

The great families we interviewed all understood the value of traditions and had plenty of them.

Tevye still says it best,

> And how do we keep our balance? That I can tell you in a word—tradition! Because of our traditions, we've kept our balance for many, many years. Because of our traditions, everyone knows who he is and what God expects him to do.

▼

"Any excuse was good enough to make a family tradition."

19

CREATING TRADITIONS

Now that we've talked about the value of traditions, let's look at some of the fantastic traditions that intentional parents hold to. We'll be looking at three different kinds of traditions: announced, cultural, and family exclusives. And then I want to talk with you about creating a special tradition for your own family—the blessing.

Of course, you won't be able to incorporate *all* these traditions in your family—remember these are a collection from thirty families—but you can choose traditions that will be special to your own family.

Announced Traditions

Announced traditions are the kind we just simply do because that's who we are. These traditions are nonnegotiable. There were

303

two announced traditions that we found characteristic of the families we interviewed. The first one was church attendance. Church attendance wasn't a *rule,* they just always did it. One daughter said,

> There was never a question of what happens on Sunday or Wednesday, you always go to church and that makes it easy. If Dad ever forgot to give a contribution, Mom reminded him of it twenty times. Dad would even call us when we were in college and ask, 'Are you missing any church?'

One wife recalled how important church attendance had been growing up.

> Things got so bad my parents lost their car, but that just meant we walked to church.

They walked a mile there and a mile back, the whole family, three times each week. The girls and Mom walked a fourth time also, to attend ladies' Bible class on Tuesday mornings.

Regular, undisputed church attendance *shouts* two things: first, that we as parents think that Christian values are important; and second, that the church as *family* is important. And if our children don't learn one thing from what goes on at church, but they catch these two principles, then they will have learned two exceedingly valuable lessons. But of course, truth be known, our kids *will* get more from church attendance than just these two messages— there's a lot said and practiced there that will help establish the value system of our children.

The second announced tradition was family dinner. According to sociologist John Kelley, "Dinner together is one of the absolute, critical symbols in the cohesion of the family."[1]

Psychologist Michael Lewis, from the Robert Wood Johnson Medical School in New Brunswick, put it this way, "The bellwether indicator of ritual life is the family dinner." He went on to say that

Dinner is the single disaster as a family ritual, too rushed, too hassled, with parents using it as a time to discipline and socialize their kids.[2]

All the way through the Old Testament, the Jewish people feasted; they fasted occasionally too, but they feasted often. They had the Passover Feast and the Feast of the Pentecost and the Feast of Ingathering and the Feast of the Unleavened Bread and on and on. They were a feasting, joyous people. Jesus performed his first miracle at a wedding feast; he attended a feast at the home of Levi. Jesus himself fed literally thousands of people. The early disciples continued steadfastly in the fellowship and the breaking of bread. Even more significant is the Lord's Supper, which focuses our attention on much more than filling our stomachs.

▼

One family described the family history of their tables.

In fact, Stephen Glenn found in one study that the talk around the table raises the IQ of children age four to five by an average of eight points![3] The families we interviewed had a lot to say about what happened around the meal table. One family described the family history of their tables. The mother told us that when they first got married they had a card table; then they advanced to a table made out of a door with legs screwed on it. A little later, they improved the door-table by putting formica on it. Now they have a lovely dining table, but they fondly remembered each table and its dents and scratches and *stories*. The tables have all become conversation pieces for a family tied together by the evening meal ritual. And as they talked about the tables, their emphasis shifted to the people who gathered around those tables rather than on how inexpensive or fancy the tables were.

Others talked about waiting for Dad to come home for supper. Most families didn't eat till Dad got home. The wives "held them over" with peanut butter sandwiches or crackers and jam until Dad could come home and they could all have supper together. One policeman's wife said that when her husband's schedule required that he work till 10 P.M., she would plan dinner for shortly after 10. The kids were preschool age, so they stayed up to have dinner and play with Dad and then slept late the next morning. Some of the families mentioned that if Dad couldn't get home in time for dinner, he would always call and let them know, because he knew how important dinner was and that they would be waiting for him.

And these meals weren't quick ones; one of the boys said their meals would sometimes "last for hours." When Gladys and I were in China, we joined in the Chinese tradition of eating meals that had anywhere from eighteen to twenty-one courses. It wasn't the food that was important, it was the conversation—the joy, the laughter, the getting acquainted, the recalling of memories.

All kinds of discussions took place around the tables of the families we interviewed. The children of one family said,

> **"**
> It was the talk around the table that helped Mom and Dad find out everything there was to know about us.
> **"**

These parents made an effort to avoid questions that could be answered with a yes or a no, or a yep or a naw. Rather they'd ask open-ended questions like, "How do you feel about that?" "What are you interested in?" "What was good about today?" "What did you do?" "What would be a good decision here?" And these parents were not only good "question askers," these parents were great listeners. One of the children said,

> **"**
> They listened! *They really listened to us.* They really cared about our opinions.
> **"**

These families discussed everything—they talked about drugs, dating, school, politics, *anything!* They used mealtime to debate whatever subject the family was interested in. One of the children said,

> **"**
> We could think and openly discuss ideas at the table. Regimented ideas were not rammed down our throats.
> **"**

And of course they also had some conflicts around the dinner table; but learning how to resolve these conflicts, how to listen and be listened to, was part of the indispensable educational function of the common meal.

▼

Even the busiest of families can work their day so they spend time together at the evening meal.

I think a great summary of what we've been saying is found in Robert Bellah's book, *The Good Society*.

> Many of the most time-consuming family tasks have to do with meals: food shopping, preparing, and cleaning up. But the family meal . . . is the chief family celebration, even a family sacrament. . . . If everyone joins in the common tasks, husband as well as wife, and children, too, as much as they are able, then the family can enjoy at least several common meals a week, celebrate the pleasure they have in each other's presence and the good things they have mutually helped to prepare.
>
> Where else does a child interact with adults, learn the art of conversation—both speaking and listening—find out what is going on in the lives of other family members, and celebrate in big and little ways the events of family life? Birthdays, exams passed, first jobs, merit badges, and all the other experiences mean more when shared with the people closest to us. It is worth the effort.[4]

Many families have never consistently had family meals together. As a result, they lose out—not only on rituals and traditions, but on friendships and conversation skills and esteem-building encouragement as well. Even the busiest of families can work their day so they spend time together at the evening meal.

Cultural Traditions

The second group of traditions that these families practiced, we call *cultural*. They picked up things like Christmas and Thanksgiving and birthdays from the culture and adopted them as their own family traditions, and they usually celebrated these holidays in a really big way. Most of them embellished the usual traditions with special twists of their own. And the truth of the matter is, any excuse was good enough to make a family tradition, if they liked what it did for their family. One girl said,

> **"**
> We celebrate everything! You wouldn't believe how we have this place decorated up for the holidays.
> **"**

The key word was *special*. Let's start with the Christmas tradition. These families all honored and kept Christmas, and even though they all had *different* traditions, they nevertheless had traditions. For example, some opened all their presents on Christmas Eve, others opened only one present on Christmas Eve and all the rest on Christmas morning. One family hand made almost all of their Christmas gifts to each other. Another family bought a live Christmas tree every year and brought it into the house to decorate. After Christmas, they took it outside and planted it. What wonderful memories would be associated with each tree!

▼

They embellished the usual traditions with special twists.

Four of the families we interviewed had formed singing groups—family quartets, sextets, whatever worked. When one of the families moved to Germany, they serenaded their neighbors on Christmas day. They didn't know that the Germans had very elaborate Christmas dinners in formal attire, so they inadvertently interrupted their neighbors' dinners, but the neighbors enjoyed it so much and welcomed them so warmly that it became a traditional thing for them to do. Another family in East Texas went around the neighborhood caroling at Christmas time. Another actually went on the road and performed choruses during the Christmas season. And a fourth family formed a chorus that was so good that the workers of the computer company he managed insisted that they serenade the whole factory. So they rigged up a platform on wheels and had the family pulled all through the plant as they sang.

My own mother started a rather strange tradition in our family. It all began because my wife Gladys always puts fun, crazy things in everybody's stockings, and one Christmas she put peashooters in the socks. Everyone had pretty much overlooked them, until my ninety-year-old mother loaded her peashooter when no one was looking and began popping everyone in the room. Well, of course, everybody ran to their stockings and pulled out their peashooters, and we had the biggest time with our peashooter fight. Since that day, one of our Christmas traditions is that Gladys puts something in our stockings to shoot each other with. We've had popguns, ping-pong-ball shooters, and rubber guns. I don't know what will happen next Christmas, but I can't wait to find out.

▼

Tomato soup and crackers was the traditional Christmas meal for one family.

Christmas dinners came in all different forms. Tomato soup and crackers was the traditional meal for one family who liked to concentrate on visiting and playing with toys as opposed to cooking. Others had the big turkey dinner with all the trimmings and special desserts. Several families told us about special dishes or candies that were made only at Christmas time. Many invited family members to share the meal, and one or two invited their whole church family to join them Christmas afternoon.

Birthdays were another cause for big-time celebration. One family celebrated birthdays for a whole week, doing different things each day. In another family, everyone would share their dreams for the birthday person. Many of the kids loved birthdays even more than Christmas, because that was the one special day, as one daughter put it, "that was just for me." One of our own family traditions was that we took each of our daughters out for a special meal on her sixteenth birthday.

One family we interviewed had all girls, and they really went all out on their fifteenth birthdays. The mother would spend several weeks planning for that special day. She and the daughter would shop together for a special dress, purse, and shoes—the whole outfit. And then when her birthday came, she and her daddy would go out for a fancy meal together. When she got to the restaurant, she would find sweet notes and poems from her mother in her new purse. So both the mother and father got to spend some special time with the daughter as she "came of age."

In another family we interviewed, the birthday person would give little gifts to everyone else in the family. In another family everyone hid the gifts and made a "treasure hunt," with clues left around for the birthday person.

And then of course, there's the Hispanic quinceañera. On the fifteenth birthday of their children, they pull out all the stops and really have a blow-out. They invite their neighbors, their friends, and everybody else to participate in and help pay for a real extravaganza. Our family was invited to a quinceañera that was held in a rented section of a civic center. These children are made to feel *very* special.

My research assistant and her husband have had the tradition for years of reading the blessings and cursings from Deuteronomy 29 and 30 on the anniversary of their children's new-birth days (the date of their baptism). In this passage of Scripture, God addresses Israel with great blessings for doing right and severe curses for doing wrong. This family uses this passage to remind their whole family of the seriousness of God's calling.

Mother's Day was also celebrated as a special family tradition. I met with three families in 1991 on Mother's Day, who had come together to honor their mothers. They'd only been sharing their thoughts for a few minutes when I looked around and saw that everybody was in tears. They had been talking about how beautiful their mothers were and what they'd done for their families.

Easter was another day that was celebrated as a family tradition. One year, one family decided to meet on a pond for a sunrise service early Easter morning. It made such an impact on their children that they invited their friends and their friends' families the next year. The celebration eventually grew to include several families. This same family fasted during the Easter season. You remember the two girls we mentioned earlier who became rather rebellious during their adolescent years. And remember that when Easter came around, even though they were working at a concession stand around all that food, they continued their tradition of fasting because it was so embedded in them. And one year it was that fast that restored peace to the family.

New Year's Days were big days for some of these families. One family in middle Tennessee celebrated by renting and borrowing enough TVs so they could watch every game that was going on at the same time. They watched football and ate Mexican food all day long.

▼

One family always had a big rubber band gunfight every Thanksgiving.

The Fourth of July was also celebrated big by this middle Tennessee family. From noon till night, they would feast 250 people or so. They'd have barbecued pig and goat and roast beef. They decorated with flags and all kinds of Americana. And they always had a guest speaker—I mean someone really significant—like George Washington or Abe Lincoln or even the Lord Jesus. Actually, it was a local person dressed up like those folks, but it always made the day even more special. And at the end of the day, there were firecrackers and skyrockets and prayer.

Thanksgiving was another day these families celebrated. One family had a tradition of writing an unsigned note about what he or she was thankful for and placing it in a big pottery turkey. The turkey was then passed around the room and everybody would draw out one note. They would read it out loud and try to guess who the author was. Another family always had a big rubber band gunfight sometime in the afternoon. It seems that a couple of the boys started the fight when they were pretty young, and it was so much fun, they just kept doing it every year, even when the children got older.

And when graduation time came, almost all of these families made sure that everybody was there. They wouldn't miss it. They'd drive for miles to be back home when their brother or sister was graduating from high school or college. One family had a tradition that when a person graduated from high school or college, they would take that child on a long trip—anywhere in the United States they wanted to go.

Family Exclusives

Family exclusives were the traditions that the families made up on their own, traditions that were uniquely theirs. One family moved so much—all over Europe and across the United States—that they couldn't have traditions that were tied to certain houses or locations. So they had "portable traditions." They enjoyed baking or making special food. One was the best fudge maker, another was the best taffy puller, someone else specialized in making popcorn balls. They sang a lot, they wrote songs, they made video tapes and wrote poems—all kinds of traditions they could take with them—traditions that became very important to them.

▼

One family moved so much that they had "portable traditions."

Letters can be a form of tradition. Letters are so much more meaningful and lasting than phone calls. Phone calls are easily forgotten, especially when folks get older, and a phone call is just heard once. But a letter can be read again and again. And it's not so easily misunderstood. Let me encourage you to *write*.

You see, I'll never have a chance to pick out another Mother's Day or birthday card for my mother. I will never have another occasion to write a letter to my dad. They're both gone. If your parents are living, you've still got time. Please write. After my mother died, my sister did something for me that I'll never forget. She returned to me all the letters I'd written to my mother over the years. I actually had no idea that Mother had kept the letters; but there they were, dating as far back as my junior high school years. And I got reacquainted with a small junior-high kid, and maybe he wasn't as bad as I imagined him to be. But it was easy for me to see how early he got started on his atrocious spelling!

I would also encourage you to journal or keep a diary. I use my journal to talk to the Lord, to reflect on what I've read in his Word, and to meditate about what I want to be and become. And when I look back at what I wrote in my journal a year ago, I can see what my blessings and troubles were, how I have reevaluated since then, and how God has led me since then.

I also think those writings would be awfully good for your children and grandchildren to have after you've passed on. Before my father died, my brother gave him a list of questions and asked him to respond to them. My father wrote about eight or ten pages, in response to those questions, about his early rearing. I was impressed. I would give anything if he had written more. I wish I had known him a whole lot better, and I think I could have if he'd kept some kind of a journal.

▼

Letters are so much more meaningful and lasting than phone calls.

Another family exclusive we came across was a celebration of the first snow. When that first good snow came, this family would shut down the business and everybody would head for the "snow hills," and they always invited several from the community and the workers from their business. Granddad would get on the tractor and pull a line of inner tubes up to the top of the hill. Then everybody would slide down, and Granddaddy would pull everyone back up. And this would go on all day long. At the end of the day, one of the family members would say, "Let's play train; this is the last run." And everybody would jump on their inner tubes and lock themselves around the person in front of them. Then the instigator would say, "I'll be the caboose!" But he had a secret plan the newcomers didn't know about. He would run them down that hill and all the way into the knee-deep creek. Of course, they had plenty of blankets and a warm fire at the bottom of the hill.

Vacations can turn into all kinds of family exclusive traditions. Many of these families did lots of camping—they went to national parks and vacation Bible school camps. One family had what they called a half-day vacation week. At the time, this family was too poor to take a week-long, out-of-town vacation. So one week they worked hard from 6 A.M. till noon every morning, then every afternoon they went to the country club on a borrowed pass and swam. They ended each day by going to Dairy Queen and getting a banana split. The kids told me that that was one of the best vacation weeks they ever had. Money was not necessary to create a great tradition with great memories.

One of the families had a Day with Daddy. On this special day, the child would stay out of school and spend the whole day just with Daddy. The boy or girl would go to work with Daddy, go out to eat with Daddy, and see what Daddy did during his day. I asked what would happen if that day caused the child to lose a perfect attendance record at school, and the parents said, "We don't care so much about perfect attendance. Our children do well in school, and what they gain from this day with their father is more important than perfect attendance." This same family also had a Day with Mom. On this day the child would stay home, and the child and Mom would cook and bake, and Mom would just pamper that child the whole day long. Now if you are a school teacher, please don't fuss at me for encouraging this—I come from a long line of public school teachers, including my mother, both sisters, my brother, my wife (for a while), a daughter, a daughter-in-law coach, and myself.

▼

One family had what they called half-day vacations.

One of the neatest and most creative family exclusives we learned about was Cousins' Camp. This particular family has had Cousins' Camp for several years now. They want all the cousins to really get to *know* each other—not just be *acquainted* with each other. They all get a special Cousins' Camp T-shirt that they wear for the week. They ride horses, they go to the zoo, they swim, and they make their own special photo albums to take home. One time they put on a circus for the neighborhood; another time they picked peaches to sell in town, and they made thirty-one dollars apiece. During the week, the boys set the table and the girls cleaned up after meals. And they all got a milkshake every night before they went to bed. Then they had an award ceremony at the end of the session, and they were sure to find something in each child worth recognizing. They had an award for courage, for being creative, for being a good servant, you name it.

By the way, we started a Cousins' Camp of our own last year— what a buzz! Gladys is the best grandmother ever. She insisted that I look up and down all the back alleys in town until I found a *big* refrigerator box; and sure enough, it was the hit of the week. I had my fun helping each one make and paint a birdhouse. We have already started taking our vitamins for Cousins' Camp two!

And of course there were ever so many families that had family reunions. One family has been having family reunions since 1978. I had the privilege of attending one of their reunions—and there were seventy-three people there. They played tennis and put on plays and sang songs and performed skits and awarded trophies and broke a piñata. They too had a T-shirt for everybody, and the T-shirt said "The Family Affair." Some of the folks had driven halfway across the country to get there. In this family, it was a tradition not to miss the family reunions. One of the funniest stories came from another family reunion where one of their traditions was to have a cake contest. One of the fathers entered a beautifully decorated cake that he had done all by himself, and he won *first* prize. But he was disqualified when it was discovered that the "cake" was actually a go-cart wheel between two pieces of cardboard.

One other interesting, unique family tradition was a male spiritual retreat. In this family, the men would go off for a weekend and have a spiritual retreat. I did this with our two sons and our two sons-in-law. We played golf one afternoon and tennis the next. Over the weekend, we parceled out different parts of a special book, and each one made a presentation from his section. It was a powerful experience. Our wives joined us on Sunday afternoon, and we had a big feast. It is a great tradition, and I highly recommend it. I didn't do too good on the golf, though. I took twenty-four balls, and I think I came back with three, but who cares—it's just a game . . . isn't it?

The Blessing

I want to talk a bit about rites of passage. In the Jewish community, a boy becomes a man at his bar mitzvah. The bar mitzvah ceremony is a very special time for family and friends. In one ceremony, a son is presented with several candles by various special friends. One candle is called the candle of integrity, another the candle of character, etc. This event reminds the boy that not only is he loved, but that it's time for him to assume certain responsibilities; it's a time when a boy becomes a man.

But our American culture offers no clear rites of passage for our boys and girls. Ellen Goodman, a liberal, feminist columnist for the *Boston Globe,* notes that in America, "the rites of passage have been reduced to drinking, driving, and sex," and that's so sad.

We need to make every good turning point in our children's lives a celebration. When they are born, when they cut their teeth, when they take their first step, when they go to kindergarten, when they get their first haircut, and on and on. There are a jillion things to celebrate.

▼

In America, "the rites of passage have been reduced to drinking, driving, and sex."

Good businessmen know the principle well: loyalty to a company (or family) comes from encouragement, celebration, and support through good and bad times. Good employees do *not* work for money alone. I just counseled with a lady last week who left a good job for one which paid *less,* but the new firm encouraged and supported her. Companies that celebrate accomplishments go a long way in developing devoted employees.

You just can't have too many celebrations in life. Even babies love to celebrate—when they do something good, they clap for themselves. One family we interviewed made a big event out of the first day of school. They set the child in a special chair and presented him or her with school supplies to "help the mind." Then each family member offered words of encouragement to encourage the spirit.

One significant event that Christians should celebrate is the new birth that we learn about in the Bible. It's so easy to let this significant act pass by without a major celebration. The Christian new birth ought to be celebrated as significantly as any bar mitzvah.

And now I come to the blessing. If there was any one tradition that I would wish for every family, it is the tradition of the blessing. Concerning this tradition, this rite, Samuel Osherson said,

> Such rituals and rites . . . provide both parties with what they so desperately need: *a blessing* from the male community, *a welcome* from fathers to their sons, and *a thank-you* from the sons to the fathers.[5]

Although Osherson is concentrating on the male blessing, I am proposing a blessing for all children. I am talking about a special ceremony, at a special time, with family and friends, where certain blessings are passed on to our children. And my how we all need that affirmation, that blessing. Normally the formal blessing has at least these five components.

A meaningful touch

This means that you actually lay your hands on your child—on his or her shoulder or head. There's just something about *touching*. The Hebrew father would always place his hand on the child when he blessed him.

A spoken message of love

Here, you look the child in the eyes. Men may have more trouble with this than women, but it's a must. Too many children never experience their parents looking at them, eye to loving eye, with no embarrassment, telling them how much they love them. An unexpressed blessing is no blessing at all. And we tell them that we love them *just as they are*—not because they perform well, not because they do well, not because they're good looking or anything else; we love them just because they are.

An affirmation of value

Children value themselves to the degree that they are valued by others. If someone special loves me, then I must be someone special. That's why we sing that blessed little children's song—"Jesus Loves Me This I Know." Tell your child, "God knew you before you were ever born. Before you took your first breath, before you took your first step, God knew and loved you. Jesus was willing to die for you, that's how much he loved you. And nothing will ever separate you from the love of God. Nothing."

▼

Children value themselves to the degree that they are valued by others.

A special "prophecy"

When a Jewish father blessed a child, he would look into the future as if to foresee what God might have in store for him. And I think that we can convey a positive, self-fulfilling prophecy by sharing with our children what we wish for them (attainable goals of course). We might even say, "What can you become?—a teacher, a preacher, a president?" And then say, "It really makes little difference what you become in terms of your vocation. What I foresee in your future is that you will be a person of love and integrity and character, that you will care for others and cherish your spouse and children." These are goals that can be accomplished by almost every child. After all, isn't that what we would wish for them more that just earthly attainments?

Don't you love that special prayer of blessing that Tevye, in *The Fiddler on the Roof* sings to his daughters?

> May the Lord protect you and defend you.
> May he always shield you from shame.
> May you come to be in Israel a shining name.
> May you be like Ruth and like Esther.
> May you be deserving of praise.

A commitment to help fulfill these blessings

The parents must back up their blessings with time and money and actions and efforts and prayer and praise and dreams. That's what I believe the Bible is talking about when it says, "Train up a child in the way that he should go, and when he is old he will not depart from it."[6]

I need to share with you that my father never planned special blessing times for me. But he didn't know any better, and I really didn't know what I was missing. And regretfully, as my children were growing up, I didn't plan special blessing times for them either, because I didn't know any better. So I'm in the process of writing a personal blessing for all of our children and grandchildren. I want to make it special. But now we all know better. Begin making plans now. Plan a special blessing ceremony for your child. Invite family and maybe friends. Make it a day your child will never forget.

▼

Now he knows that *all he has* is *all he needs*.

Before we close the book, we return to Anatevka. Tevye is standing in front of his house with his wife, his two youngest daughters, and his cart. Just three days earlier, the constable had come and delivered the message that the Russians wanted them all to clear out, to sell everything they had, and go. As this Jewish community meets in front of their little village, every face flooded with tears, we find Tevye. He had just come from the house in which he reared all five of his precious girls. One of his girls had married a Gentile, of all things, another had married a Russian rebel, and another had married down the social ladder. By God's grace, they had managed to work through all those broken traditions. But how could they walk away from this tradition-laden village, in which they created all those precious traditions. Everything he owns is on his two-wheel cart. No milk cans now. They had been left behind in the barn with his lame mule and all his milk cows.

And as he turns his back on his beloved Anatevka, he sighs, because he knows he is leaving all of his traditions, all of his history, all of himself. *And then he thinks he hears a sound.* He listens more carefully. It sounds like a fiddler. He turns around, and sure enough, he sees the fiddler, following behind him, dancing as he comes; and suddenly Tevye knows that the *real* traditions, *lasting* traditions, are *portable!*

So he turns and grins, and as he nods his head toward God, he winks and smiles. Because now he knows that *all he has* is *all he needs.* Now he is ready to begin anew.

So it is with you, dear reader. All you have is all you need to raise the family that later will rise up and call you blessed.[7]

APPENDIX 1

Recommended Reading

General Parenting

Bennett, William J. *The Book of Virtues*. New York: Simon & Schuster, 1993.

Canter, Lee, and Marlene Canter. *Assertive Discipline for Parents*. New York: Harper & Row, 1988.

Clabby, John F. and Marice J. Elias. *Teach Your Child Decision Making*. Garden City, New York: Doubleday, 1987.

Clark, Lynn. *SOS: Help For Parents*. Bowling Green, KY: Parents Press, 1989.

Dinkmeyer, Don, and Gary D. McKay. *The Parent's Handbook*. Circle Pines, MN: American Guidance Service, 1989.

Dargatz, Jan. *52 Ways to Help Your Child Do Better in School*. Nashville: Thomas Nelson Publishers, 1993.

Dobson, James C. *Parenting Isn't For Cowards*. Waco: Word Books, 1987.

Farrar, Steve. *Better Homes and Jungles*. Portland, OR: Multnomah, 1991.

Gangel, Kenneth, and Elizabeth Gangel. *Building a Christian Family: A Guide for Parents*. Chicago: Moody Press, 1987.

Glenn, Stephen, and Jane Nelson. *Raising Self-Reliant Children in a Self-Indulgent World.* Provo, UT: Sunrise Press, 1987. (Formerly titled *Raising Children For Success.*)

Guarendi, Ray. *Back to the Family: Lessons from One Hundred of America's Happiest Families.* NY: Villard Books, 1990.

Hosier, Helen. *You Never Stop Being a Parent.* Old Tappan, NJ: Fleming H. Revell Company, 1986.

Ketterman, Grace. *Mothering: The Complete Guide for Mothers of All Ages.* Nashville: Thomas Nelson Publishers, 1991.

Kuzma, Kay. *Building Your Child's Character.* Elgin, IL: David C. Cook Publishing, 1988.

Leman, Kevin. *Getting the Best Out of Your Kids.* Eugene, OR: Harvest House, 1992

———. *Keeping Your Family Together When the World is Falling Apart.* New York: Delacorte Press, 1992.

———. *Making Children Mind Without Losing Yours.* New York: Dell Publishing, 1986.

Lewis, Paul. *Forty Ways to Teach Your Child Values.* Wheaton, IL: Tyndale House Publishing, 1987.

Nelsen, Jane, and Lynn Lott. *I'm On Your Side.* Rocklin, CA: Prima Publishers, 1990.

Rose, Ron. *7 Things Kids Never Forget.* Sisters, OR: Multnomah, 1993.

Rosemond, John K. *John Rosemond's Six-Point Plan for Raising Happy, Healthy Children.* Kansas City: Andrews and McMeel, 1989.

Stinnett, Nick, and John DeFrain. *Secrets of Strong Families.* New York: Berkeley Books, 1985.

Strommen, Marton B., and A. Irene Strommen. *Five Cries of Parents.* San Francisco: Harper & Row, 1985.

Weinhaus, Evonne, and Karen Friedman. *Stop Struggling with Your Child.* New York: Harper Collins, 1991.

Ziglar, Zig. *Raising Positive Kids in a Negative World.* New York: Ballantine Books, 1985.

Business and Time Management

Covey, Stephen. *Seven Habits of Highly Effective People.* New York: Simon and Schuster, 1989.

Eyre, Richard, and Linda Eyre. *LifeBalance*. New York: Ballantine Books, 1987.

Death

Stein, Sara Bonnett. *About Dying*. 1974.
Zolotow, Charlotte. *My Grandson Lew*. 1974

Developmental

Allen, Roger, and Ron Rose. *Common Sense Discipline*. Ft. Worth: Sweet Publishing, 1986.
Elkind, David. *The Hurried Child*. Reading, MA: Addison-Wesley, 1988.

Family Devotional

Wright, H. Norman. *Quiet Times for Couples (A Daily Devotional)* Eugene, OR: Harvest House Publishing, 1990.

Fathers

Bly, Stephen. *How to Be a Good Dad*. Chicago: Moody Press, 1986.
Farrar, Steve. *Point Man*. Portland, OR: Multnomah, 1990.
Simmons, Dave. *Dad, The Family Coach*. Wheaton, IL: Victor Books, 1991.
————. *Dad, The Family Counselor*. Wheaton, IL: Victor Books, 1991.
Webber, Stu. *Tender Warrior*. Sisters, OR: Multnomah, 1992.

Marriage

Clinebell, Howard J., and Charlotte H. Clinebell. *The Intimate Marriage*. New York: Harper & Row, 1970.
Crabb, Lawrence. *The Marriage Builder*. Grand Rapids, MI: Zondervan, 1982.
Harley, Willard. *His Needs, Her Needs*. Old Tappan, NJ: Fleming Revell Company, 1986.
————. *Love Busters*. Grand Rapids, MI: Fleming H. Revell, Company, 1992.

Hendrix, Harville. *Getting the Love You Want: A Guide for Couples.* New York: Harper Collins Publishers, 1988.

Smalley, Gary. *For Better or Best.* Grand Rapids, MI: Zondervan, 1979.

Mid-life and Aging

Bianchi, Eugene C. *Aging is a Spiritual Journey.* New York: The Crossroad Publishing Company, 1990.

Brewi, Janice, and Anne Brennan. *Mid-Life Psychological and Spiritual Perspectives.* New York: The Crossroad Publishing Company, 1989.

———. *Celebrate Mid-Life: Jungian Archetypes and Mid-Life Spirituality.* New York: 1990.

Conway, Jim. *Men in Mid-Life Crisis.* Elgin, IL: David C. Cook Publishing Company, 1978.

Olson, Richard P. *Mid-Life: A Time to Discover, A Time to Decide.* Valley Forge, PA: Judson Press, 1980.

White, Jerry, and Mary White. *The Christian in Mid-Life: Biblical Guideline and Inspiration for Men and Women Facing the Challenges of Mid-Life.* Colorado Springs, CO: NavPress, 1980.

Worthington, Lowell A. *Forty-Five and Satisfied.* Abilene, TX: Quality Publications, 1983.

Prosperity

Brooks, Andree Aelion. *Children of Fast-Track Parents.* New York: Viking, 1989.

Minear, Ralph, and William Proctor. *Kids Who Have Too Much.* Nashville, TN: Thomas Nelson Publishers, 1989.

Dying to Self/Spirituality

Boyer, Ernest. *A Way in the World: Family Life as a Spiritual Discipline.* San Francisco: Harper and Row, 1984.

Foster, Richard. *A Celebration of Discipline.*

Wright, Wendy. *Sacred Dwellings: Spirituality of Family Life.* New York: Crossroad, 1990.

Sex Education

Calderone, M. S., and J. W. Ramey. *Talking with Your Child About Sex: Questions and Answers for Children from Birth to Puberty.* 1982.

Gordon, Sol, and J. Gordon. *Did the Son Shine Before You Were Born?* 1977.

Koblinsky, Sally. "Sex Education with Young Children." *Young Children.* 36 (1980): 1.

Nilsson, Lennart. *A Child Is Born.* 1989.

Stein, Sara Bonnett. *Making Babies.* 1974.

———. *That New Baby.* 1974.

Theology

Anderson, Ray, and Dennis Guernsey. *On Being Family: A Social Theology of the Family.* Grand Rapids: Eerdmans, 1985.

Theory

Friedman, Edwin H. *Generation to Generation: Family Process in Church and Synagogue.* New York: Guilford Press, 1985.

APPENDIX 2

Suggested Classics

For Parents

Let's Make a Memory by Gloria Gaither and Shirley Dobson. Word Publishing, 1983.
The Read-Aloud Handbook by John Trelease.

For Young Children

Alexander and the Terrible, Horrible, No Good, Very Bad Day and *If I Were In Charge of the World and Other Worries* by Judith Viorst. Aladdin Books, Macmillan Publishing Company, 1972.
Curious George by H. A. Rey. Sandpiper Books, Houghton Mifflin, 1969.
The Giving Tree and *Where the Sidewalk Ends* by Shel Silverstein. Harper Collins, 1964.
Goodnight Moon and *Runaway Bunny* by Margaret Wise Brown. Harper & Row Publishers, 1947.
Hey Al by Arthur Yorinks. Farrar, 1986.
If You Give a Mouse a Cookie by Laura Numeroff. Harper, 1985.
Jump and Jump Again (The Adventures of Brer Rabbit) by Joel Chandler Harris. Harcourt Brace Jovanovich, 1986.
Love You Forever by Robert Munche. Firefly, 1986.

Mother Goose by Tomie DePaola. Putnam, 1985.
Two Bad Ants by Chris Van Allsburg. Houghton, 1988.
Where the Wild Things Are by Maurice Sendak. Harper, 1963.
All of the Carl Dog books.
All the Dr. Seuss books by Theodore S. Geisel.
All of the Mrs. Piggle-Wiggle books.

For Older Children

Charlotte's Web by E. B. White. Harper, 1952.
The Jungle Book by Rudyard Kipling. Puffin, 1988 (reprint).
White Fang by Jack London. Puffin, 1985.
The Wind in the Willows by Kenneth Grahame. Aladdin Books, MacMillan, 1981 edition.
The Anne of Green Gables Series by L. M. Montgomery.
The Janette Oke series.
The Little House Series by Laura Ingalls Wilder, Harper, 1971.
   By the Shores of Silver Lake
   Farmer Boy
   Little House in the Big Woods
   Little House on the Prairie
   Little Town on the Prairie
   The First Four Years
   The Long Winter
   On the Banks of Plum Creek
The Little Women Series by Louisa May Alcott. Scholastic.
   Jo's Boys
   Little Men
   Little Women
The Narnia Chronicles by C.S. Lewis. Collier Books, Macmillan. 1951.
   The Horse and His Boy
   The Last Battle
   The Lion, the Witch and the Wardrobe
   The Magician's Nephew
   Prince Caspian
   The Silver Chair
   The Voyage of the "Dawn Treader"

Magazines

Christian Parenting. (503) 549-8261.
For Dads Only. PO Box 340, Julian, CA 92036.
Partnership Magazine. 1-800-627-4942.

Programs

Active Parenting Today: For Parents of 2 to 12 Year Olds by
Michael Popkin. Available from Active Parenting Publishers,
810 B Franklin Court, Marietta, GA 30067 (1-800-825-0060).

Thanks to Drs. Ed and Jane Coates and Dr. and Mrs. Carl
Brecheen for their assistance in compiling this appendix.

APPENDIX 3

Experts Validate Our Thirty Families

One of the serendipities that we found in our study was the fact that the traits these exceptional families exhibited correlated so well with what experts in the field of family strengths have been telling us for years. *These families knew instinctively what worked,* and when we lined up the traits we saw in their families with the results of other studies, they all fit together. The only difference was in the language the experts used to describe what we saw. Sometimes it was couched in therapeutic terms, sometimes in sociological terms, sometimes in academic terms, but basically the meaning was similar or identical. What follows is a breakdown of the individual studies by the name of the author, referencing them in terms of our findings.

1. **Intentionality, Vision, Mission, Commitment, Persistence:** Walsh, Kantor and Lehr, Reiss, Becvar and Becvar, Textor, Lewis, Stinnett, Krysan et al, Curran, Otto, Sanders, Rampey, Thomas, Turner, Satir, Allen, Rosemond, Guarendi, Glenn

2. **Religious Faith:** Walsh, Stinnet and DeFrain, Krysan et al, Curran, Otto, Gabler and Otto, Sanders, Brigman, Turner, Hill, Allen, Guarendi

3. **Love, Affection, Intimacy, Support:** Olson, Beavers, Becvar and Becvar, Barnhill, Lewis, Stinnett, Krysan et al, Curran, Otto, Sanders, Thomas, Turner, Satir, Allen, Rosemond, Guarendi

4. **Servant Leaders:** Beavers, Becvar and Becvar, Lewis, Curran, Gabler and Otto, Thomas, Guarendi

5. **Humor and Fun:** Olson, Beavers, Textor, Lewis, Stinnett, Curran, Otto, Sanders, Thomas, Allen, Rosemond, Guarendi

6. **Transparent, Open:** Walsh, Olson, Beavers, Lewis, Stinnett, Krysan et al, Curan, Gabler and Otto, Thomas, Satir

7. **Networked and Autonomous**: Walsh, Kantor and Lehr, Olson, Beavers, Textor, Barnhill, Lewis, Reiss, Krysan et al, Curran, Gabler and Otto, Sanders, Hill, Satir, Whitaker, Allen

8. **Able to Relabel Tragedy and Difficulty, Oversomers:** Walsh, Reiss, Becvar and Becvar, Textor, Barnhill, Lewis, Stinnett, Krysan et al, Curran, Gabler and Otto, Thomas, Whitaker, Guarendi, Glenn

NOTES

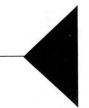

INTRODUCTION.

1. Tom Peters and Nancy Austin, *A Passion for Excellence* (New York: Random House), 419.

2. Frank S. Pittman, "Children of the Rich," *Family Process* (1985).

3. Prov. 30:8-9.

CHAPTER 1. Parent on Purpose—Intentionally

1. Phil. 2:3b.

2. "100 Companies," *Fortune 500.*

3. *Topics in Family Psychology and Counseling,* Jan., 92.

4. James 1:2-3.

5. 2 Tim. 4:7.

CHAPTER 2. Values—The Foundation of the Family

1. William J. Bennett, *The De-Valuing of America: The Fight for Our Culture and Our Children* (New York: Summit Books, 1992), 35.

2. Karl Menninger, *Whatever Became of Sin?* (New York: Hawthorne Books, 1973).

3. Matt. 6:19-20.

4. Ray Guarendi, *Back to the Family: Lessons from One Hundred of America's Happiest Familes* (New York: Villard Books, 1990), 102 (hereafter cited as *Family*).

5. Philip Yancy, "Health and the God Factor," *Christianity Today,* 88.

6. *Abilene Reporter-News,* Jan. 19, 1993.

CHAPTER 3. Love Them—Adore Them

1. Urie Bronfenbrenner, "Discovering What Families Do," *Rebuilding the Nest,* ed. David Blankenhorn, Steven Bayme, and Jean Bethke Elshtain (Milwaukee, WI: Family Service America, 1990).

2. Luke 15:20.

3. Ps. 139:4, 13.

4. Matt. 10:30.

5. From the findings of Carol Franz, Daved C. Mclelland, and Joel Weinberg in *Journal of Personality and Social Psychology,* quoted in *USA Today,* Apr. 19, 1991, 2.

6. Rom. 12:10; Rom. 15:7; Gal. 5:13; Eph. 4:2; 1 Thess. 5:11.

7. J. Allan Petersen, *Happiness is Homemade.*

8. John Gottman, *Why Marriages Succeed or Fail* (New York: Simon and Schuster, 1994), 57.

9. Ibid., 29.

10. Luke 15:11-32.

CHAPTER 4. Be a Servant—Lead From the Foot of the Table

1. Willard Gaylin, *Our Changing American Values,* quoted by Bill Moyers, 120.

CHAPTER 5. Give the Gift of Laughter

1. Ralph E. Minear and William Proctor, *Kids Who Have Too Much* (Nashville: Thomas Nelson, 1989), 63.

CHAPTER 7. Hold Them Tight, Then Turn Them Loose

1. Hodding Carter, *Where Main Street Meets the River* (New York: Rinehart, 1953).

2. Brenda Hunter, *What Every Mother Needs to Know* (Sisters, OR: Questar, 1993).

3. Robert Beavers and Robert Hampson, *Successful Families: Assessment and Intervention* (New York: Norton, 1990).

CHAPTER 8. Learn to Cope Positively with Tragedy and Failure

1. Guarendi, *Family,* 44.
2. 1 Pet. 1:6.
3. Rom. 12:3.
4. Alexander Solzhenitsyn, *The Gulag Archipelago* (New York: Harper & Row, 1976).
5. Luke 9:22.
6. 2 Cor. 12:7-10.
7. Frankl Viktor, *Man's Search for Meaning,* revised and updated (New York: Washington Square Press, Div. of Simon & Schuster, 1984).

CHAPTER 9. The Power of Parenting

1. Michael Novak, "The Family Out of Favor," *Harper's,* Apr. 1976, 38.
2. *USA Today,* Mar. 19, 1991.
3. Novak, "The Family Out of Favor," *Harper's,* Apr. 1976, 38.
4. "The Fractured Family," *Christianity Today,* May 25, 1979, 2.
5. Carley Dodd and David Lewis, "The Many Faces of Christ" (Survey presented at the 8th Annual Conference on Youth & Family Ministry: A Trilogy on Adolescent Spirituality, Phase II, Feb. 27-28, 1992. Report of the conference, 81a, 109).
6. J. Allan Petersen, "Family Happiness is Homemade," *Family Concern,* 10 (Sept. 1986).
7. 2 Kings 17:41.

CHAPTER 10. The Intentional Mother

1. Study via Search Institute of Minn., underwritten by Eli Lilly.
2. Robert S. Weiss, "It's Lonely at the Top—But Let's Not Discuss It," *Staying the Course: The Emotional and Social Lives of Men Who Do Well at Work,* a book review, from *Newsweek.*
3. Christine Gorman, *Time,* Jan. 20, 1992, 46.
4. *Making Right Decisions in a Complex World,* 96.
5. Sally Helgesen, *Megatrends for Women,* 94.
6. Ibid.

7. Carol Gilligan, *In a Different Voice,* 159-160.

8. Judith Viorst, *Necessary Losses* (New York: Simon & Schuster, 1986), 222.

9. Prov. 31:28–RSV.

10. Barbara Bush, Wellseley College Commencement, 1990, quoted in *Newsweek,* June 11, 1990, 26.

CHAPTER 11. The Intentional Father

1. Christopher N. Bacorn, "Dear Dads: Save Your Sons," *Newsweek,* Dec. 7, 1992.

2. David Blankenhorn of the Institute for American Values, New York, NY, via *Breakpoint.*

3. Bacorn, *Newsweek,* Dec. 7, 1992.

4. *Dallas Morning News,* June 21, 1992, sec. 7J.

5. Urie Bronfenbrenner.

6. Judith S. Wallerstein and Sandra Blakeslee, *Second Chances: Men, Women, and Children a Decade after Divorce* (New York: Ticknor & Fields, 1990), 244.

7. Mal. 4:5-6.

8. David Blankenhorn, *The Good Family Man: Fatherhood and the Pursuit of Happiness in America,* of the Institute for American Values, New York, NY, WP 12, 1991.

9. T. McNab (Doctoral dissertation, University of California at Berkeley).

10. James Q. Wilson (paper presented to the Brookings Institute Seminar on Values and Public Policy, Nov. 5, 1991).

11. Gilmore, *Manhood in the Making* (New Haven: Yale University Press, 1990), 224.

12. Num. 11:11-15.

13. 1 Tim. 5:8.

14. Mario Cuomo, *The New Yorker,* Apr. 9, 1984, 51.

15. Ps. 78:5-6.

16. Chaim Waxman, "The Jewish Father: Past and Present," *A Mensch Among Men: Explorations in Jewish Masculinity,* ed. Harry Brod (Freedom, CA: Crossing Printers, 1988), 60-61.

17. John Demos, *Past, Present, and Personal: The Family and The Life Course in American History* (New York: Oxford University Press, 1986).

18. Robert McCall, "The Importance of Fathers," *Parents,* July 1985.

19. Judith Viorst, *Necessary Losses,* 71.

20. Paul Henry Mussen, *Handbook of Research Methods in Child Development* (New York: Wiley, 1960).

21. 1 Cor. 16:13–KJV.

22. Gilmore via *The Good Family Man,* ed. David Blankenhorn of the Institute for American Values, Nov. 1991, 26-29.

23. Samuel Osherson, *Finding Our Fathers,* 6.

24. "Field of Fathers," *Networker,* Sept. 1989, 85.

25. E. Kent Hayes, *Why Good Parents Have Bad Kids* (New York: Doubleday, 1989), 204.

26. James Carroll (notes in a review of *Good Morning, Merry Sunshine,* by B. Greene), *New York Times* Book Review, June 10, 1984.

27. *Fit to Be Tied* (Grand Rapids: Zondervan, 1991), 178.

28. Lewis Smedes, *Choices* (San Francisco: Harper & Row, 1986).

CHAPTER 12. Dual-Career Families

1. Dr. Sirgay Sanger and John Kelley, *The Woman Who Works, The Parent Who Cares* (Boston • Toronto: Little, Brown and Company, 1987), 34.

2. Ibid., 34.

3. Ibid., 33.

4. Ibid., 87.

5. Ibid., 43.

6. Ibid., 115.

7. Richard Louv, *Childhood's Future* (Boston: Houghton Mifflin, 1990).

8. Sanger and Kelley, *The Woman Who Works, The Parent Who Cares,* 37.

CHAPTER 13. Strategies of the Heart

1. Marjorie Thompson, *Family: The Forming Center* (Nashville: Upper Room Books, 1989).

2. *U.S. News and World Report,* Apr. 4, 1994.

3. Deut. 6:6-7.

4. Lamar Alexander, *Six Months Off* (New York: William Morris & Co., Inc., 1988), 28.

5. Luke 6:38.

6. Minear, *Kids Who Have Too Much,* 120.

7. Prov. 11:4.

8. Gary Bauer, "The Family Time Famine," *Family Policy,* 3 vols. (1990), 1.

9. Richard Louv, *Childhood's Future,* 23.

10. Gerald Kushel, ed., *Bottom Line,* Institute for Effective Thinkers.

11. Hunter, *What Every Mother Needs to Know.*

12. *Rebuilding the Nest,* ed. David Blankenhorn, Steven Bayme, and Jean Bethke Elshtain.

13. Alida S. Westman, "Do People's Presence More Than Their Presents Make Children Happy?" *Perceptual and Motor Skills* 71 (1990): 674.

14. Paul Faulkner.

CHAPTER 14. Strategies for Living

1. Gen. 27:46.

2. *Parents,* Nov. 1991.

3 *Readers Digest,* Jan. 1986, 95.

4. Robert Coles, *Priviledged Ones: The Well-Off and the Rich* (Boston: Little, Brown, 1977).

5. Andree Aelion Brooks, *Children of Fast-Track Parents* (New York: Viking, 1989).

6. Kay Kuzma, *Building Your Child's Character* (Elgin, IL: David C. Cook Publishing, 1988).

7. *Marriage Partnership,* Winter 1991, 84.

8. Jane Healy, *Endangered Minds* (New York: Simon & Schuster, 1990).

9. Minear, *Kids Who Have Too Much,* 117.

10. *Journal of Home Economics,* Summer 1993.

11. Robert Bellah, *Habits of the Heart* (Harper & Row, 1986), 117.

12. David Elkind, *The Hurried Child and MisEducation: Preschoolers at Risk* (Reading, MA: Addison-Wesley, 1988).

13. *Megatrends for Women,* 58.

14. Guarendi, *Family,* 165.

15. James A. Cavanaugh, *Basics: A Program Designed to Help You Recognize and Enhance Your Child's Abilities* (Carol Publishing Group, 600 Madison Ave., N.Y.U. 10022).

CHAPTER 15. Motivation—Prevention Discipline

1. Ps. 51:17.
2. Albert Schweitzer quoted in Malcom MacGregor, *Training Your Children* (Minn: Bethany Fellowship, 1980), 111.
3. John 12:32.
4. John 3:16–KJV.
5. H. Stephen Glenn and Jane Nelsen, *Raising Children for Success* (Fair Oaks, CA: Sunrise Press, 1987), 177.
6. Guarendi, *Family,* 165.
7. Ibid., 161 (emphasis added).
8. *The Individual Psychology of Alfred Adler* (New York: Basic Book, 1956).
9. 1 Thess. 2:11-12.
10. Research Institute on Addictions.
11."Parental Support and Control as Predictors of Adolescent Drinking, Delinquency, and Related Problem Behavior," *Journal of Marriage and Family,* Nov. 1992, 763-776.
12. Alexander, *Six Month Off,* 33.

CHAPTER 16. Discipline: Principles and Styles

1. Hayes, *Why Good Parents Have Bad Kids.*
2. Minear, *Kids Who Have Too Much,* 45.
3. Wallerstein and Blakeslee, *Second Chances.*
4. Mark Mellman, Edward Lazarus, and Allen Rivlin, "Family Time, Family Values," *Rebuilding the Nest,* 73.
5. *Dallas Morning News.*
6. Minear, *Kids Who Have Too Much,* 48.
7. John Rosemond, *Six-Point Plan for Raising Happy, Healthy Children* (Kansas City: Andrews and McMeel, 1989), 189.
8. Ps. 23:4–KJV.
9. James C. Dobson, *Parenting Isn't for Cowards* (Waco, TX: Word Publishing, 1987), 93.
10. Prov. 3:11-12.
11. Prov. 13:24.

12. Heb. 12:11.

13. Kevin Leman, *Getting the Best Out of Your Kids* (Eugene, OR: Harvest House, 1992).

14. Denise Kandel, "Parenting Styles, Drug Use, and Children's Adjustment in Families of Young Adults," *Journal of Marriage and the Family* 52 (Feb. 1990): 183.

15. *Journal of Marriage and the Family*, Aug. 1986, 503.

16. Elkind, *The Hurried Child*, xi.

17. Glueck, Sheldon, and Eleanor, *Family Envirnoment and Delinquency* (Boston: Houghton Mifflin, 1962).

18. Hunter, *What Every Mother Needs to Know.*

CHAPTER 17. 10 Keys to Effective Discipline

1. John White, *Parents in Pain* (Grand Rapids: InterVarsity, 1979), 106.

2. 2 Tim. 1:7 (emphasis added).

3. Philem. 8.

4. Prov. 25:28.

5. Eph. 6:4–RSV (emphasis added).

6. Dobson, *Parenting Isn't for Cowards,* 93.

7. Guarendi, *Family,* 187.

8. Ibid., 216.

9. Dobson, *Parenting Isn't for Cowards,* 92.

10. Bonnidell Clouse, *Moral Development* (Grand Rapids: Baker, 1985), 78.

11. Leman, *Getting the Best Out of Your Kids,* 116.

12. Ibid., 28.

13. Guarendi, *Family.*

14. Ibid., 203.

15. Hayes, *Why Good Parents Have Bad Kids,* 96.

16. Guarendi, *Family,* 231.

17. Ibid., 180.

18. Exod. 34:6-7.

Chapter 18. The Value of Tradition

1. Paul Pearsall, *The Family in America*, Rockford Institute, Aug. 1993.

2. Josh. 4:6-7 (emphasis added).

3. Bellah, *Habits of the Heart,* 137.

4. Dr. Edward Hoffman, "Thriving Families in Urban America: The Lubavitcher Hasidm," *The Family in America* 4 (Oct. 1990): 5.

5. Alan Loy McGinnis, *The Power of Optimism* (San Francisco: Harper & Row, 1990), 52.

6. Guarendi, *Family,* 1237.

7. Steve Wolin, *The Resilient Child* (1993).

8. 2 Thess. 2:15–RSV (emphasis added).

9. Jer. 35:8b-10.

10. Harper Collins, "Rituals for Our Time." *NY Times* news service, ed. Daniel Goleman.

11. Glenn, *Raising Children for Success,* 102.

CHAPTER 19. Creating Traditions

1. John R. Kelley, *Megatrends for Women,* (University of Illinois, Champaign-Urbana), 226.

2. Michael Lewis, "Family Rituals May Promote Better Emotional Adjustment," *New York Times,* quoted by Daniel Goleman.

3. Glenn, *Raising Children for Success,* 139.

4. Robert Bellah, *The Good Society,* 265.

5. Samuel Osherson, *Finding Our Fathers* (New York: Free Press, 1986), 46.

6. Prov. 22:6–RSV.

7. Prov. 31:28.

BIBLIOGRAPHY

Alexander, Lamar. *Six Months Off*. New York: William Morrow and Co., Inc., 1988.

Bennett, William J. *The Book of Virtues*. New York: Simon & Schuster, 1993.

———. *The De-Valuing of America*. New York: Summit Books, 1992.

Brooks, Andree Aelion. *Children of Fast-Track Parents*. New York: Viking, 1989.

Coles, Robert. *Privileged Ones: The Well-Off and the Rich*. Boston: Little, Brown, 1977.

Curran, Dolores. *Traits of a Healthy Family*. San Franciso: Harper & Row, 1983.

Glenn, H. Stephen and Jane Nelson. *Raising Children For Success*. Fair Oaks, CA: Sunrise Press, 1987.

Guarendi, Ray. *Back to the Family: Lessons from One Hundred of America's Happiest Families*. New York: Villard Books, 1990.

Hemfelt, Robert and Paul Warren. *Kids Who Carry Our Pain*. Nashville: Thomas Nelson, 1990.

Ketterman, Grace H. *The Complete Book of Baby and Child Care for Christian Parents*. Old Tappan, NJ: F. H. Revell, 1982.

———. *The Complete Guide for Mothers of All Ages*. Nashville: Thomas Nelson, 1991.

Kuzma, Kay. *Building Your Child's Character*. Elgin, IL: David C. Cook Publishing, 1988.

Leman, Kevin. *Getting the Best Out of Your Kids*. Eugene, OR: Harvest House, 1992.

Louv, Richard. *Childhood's Future*. Boston: Houghton Mifflin, 1990.

Menninger, Karl. *Whatever Became of Sin?* New York: Hawthorn Books, 1973.

Minear, Ralph E. and William Proctor. *Kids Who Have Too Much*. Nashville: Thomas Nelson, 1989.

343

Rosemond, John. *Six-Point Plan For Raising Happy, Healthy Children.* Kansas City: Andrews and McMeel, 1989.

Satir, Virginia. *Helping Families to Change.* New York: J. Aronson, 1975.

———. *Peoplemaking.* Palo Alto, CA: Science and Behavior Books, 1972.

Secunda, Victoria. *Women and Their Fathers.* New York: Delacorte Press, 1992.

Smedes, Lewis. *Choices.* San Francisco: Harper & Row, 1986.

———. *Forgive and Forget.* San Francisco: Harper & Row, 1984.

———. *Love Within Limits.* Grand Rapids: Eerdmans, 1982.

Solzhenitsyn, Alexander. *The Gulag Archipelago.* New York: Harper & Row, 1976.

Stinnett, Nick and John DeFrain. *Secrets of Strong Families.* New York: Berkeley Books, 1985.

Viorst, Judith. *Necessary Losses.* New York: Simon & Schuster, 1986.

Wallerstein, Judith S. and Sandra Blakeslee. *Second Chances.* New York: Ticknor & Fields, 1989.

White, John. *Parents In Pain.* Grand Rapids: InterVarsity, 1979.

Ziglar, Zig. *Raising Positive Kids in a Negative World.* New York: Ballantine Books, 1989.